JNU

Praise for the Book

'This important book comes at an inflection point in Indian democracy when identity politics are no longer just about social justice, but have come into conflict with the Republic itself, even with the Constitution, and with the idea of nationhood. JNU has long been a vaunted institution of higher education but with each passing year has become an avenue for ever-greater politico-ideological rifts, and with an ever-widening chasm with the bulk of public opinion. I am glad Professor Paranjape has taken up the challenge to share an insider's perspective of the tumult within the campus of this once hallowed institution. He brings immense erudition to this gripping account of nationalism and Indianness in these most turbulent of years.'

—**Baijayant 'Jay' Panda**, national vice president and national spokesperson, BJP

'In 2016, when "Urban Naxal" students ran a sinister campaign to break India and all media, intelligentsia and academics stood silent and watched meekly, one man raised his voice against it. He fought them alone with courage and conviction. And above all, with his commitment to the integrity of India. One of the university's senior-most professors, Makarand R. Paranjape, presents an unbiased account of the goings-on in JNU, as well as some creative vision on how to fix the problem.'

—**Vivek Ranjan Agnihotri**, filmmaker and author

'JNU is known for creating concocted history and anti-India student groups, in addition to false and negative archaeology which prevented a resolution of the Ayodhya problem for two decades. It is a mouthpiece of communist parties with Indian taxpayers' money. But the insider, Professor Makarand R. Paranjape, known for his courage and objectivity, has offered a balanced picture based on personal experiences.'

—**Dr S.L. Bhyrappa**, internationally renowned Kannada novelist

'There is an ongoing battle for the soul of India—a legitimate political encounter marred by competitive intolerance. Through this study of the unrest in one of India's premier universities, Makarand R. Paranjape demonstrates how political fashion and a warped sense of correctness have crippled the intellectual climate in India. It is a must-read for those who dare to love India and swim against the tide of coercive rootlessness.'

—**Dr Swapan Dasgupta**, author and Member of Parliament

'Makarand R. Paranjape's insightful and eminently readable analysis offers the possibility of looking at JNU beyond the binaries of Left and Right, noting instead the bigger issues of a systematic decline in academic excellence and the acceptance of mediocre populism as the dominant discourse. The best part of this seminal book is that it offers a blueprint for the resurrection of the university, which if followed can restore JNU to its numero uno position.'
—**Dr Sanjeev Chopra**, vice president, JNUSU 1982–83 and former Director, LBS National Academy of Administration, Mussoorie

'Makarand writes with honesty and nuance. The skill to deep dive and present a point of view which neither gets addled in the floodlight of popular sentiment nor hubristic in the shade of moribund academia is rare. His first-hand experience and reflection in this book would be truly interesting to explore.'
—**Prasoon Joshi**, writer, poet and internationally acclaimed communication specialist

'Professor Makarand R. Paranjape provides a stark narrative of what a shut shop JNU has become, full of extremist ideologies and far from the lofty principles and objectives on which it was founded. Professor Paranjape weaves many of his own experiences on campus to give us an account of the tensions and radicalism at JNU over the last four years. He also provides a comprehensive blueprint for reforming JNU, steering it away from ideological fights and restoring it to the original vision of Jawaharlal Nehru. India needs JNU to lead in liberal thoughts and not languish as a victim of failed ideologies.'
—**T.V. Mohandas Pai**, chairman, Manipal Global Education and Aarin Capital

'A commanding look at the trials and tribulations of an academic in JNU, at once illuminating and masterfully crafted; not so much a cry in the wilderness as it is a cry out for change. This book is a must-read.'
—**Anand Ranganathan**, professor at Special Centre for Molecular Medicine, Jawaharlal Nehru University, author and commentator

'I don't always agree with Makarand R. Paranjape but I have enormous respect for his scholarship and his intellect. This is an insider's account from the heart of JNU and is essential reading for anyone who wants to develop a balanced perspective of the truth behind the headlines.'
—**Vir Sanghvi**, media personality, author, editor and food critic

'Makarand R. Paranjape's deeply thoughtful book on JNU is essential reading for anyone wishing to understand the root causes of the recent ideological clashes

the university has seen, and the pivotal role a culturally rooted yet dialogic nationalism must play in building India's future.'
—**Pavan Varma**, author, and vice president, Trinamool Congress

'This is an insider's account of JNU's infamous "tukde-tukde" inspired troubles in February 2016 and its aftermath. The author, one of JNU's most senior and respected professors, Makarand R. Paranjape, tells us the causes of the academic degeneration of this once distinguished institution. Unlike others, he also offers positive prescriptions on how to cure and reform an ailing university instead of killing it.'
—**Prabhu Chawla**, senior journalist and editorial director, New Indian Express Group

'Universities everywhere around the world should be laboratories to engage and energize the minds of young people. They should offer an atmosphere that encourages lifelong curiosity and a thirst for learning. Makarand R. Paranjape, as an educator, writer and thinker who has intimately known one of India's foremost universities, reveals many aspects of Jawaharlal Nehru University. In a very timely manner, he seeks to right the wrongs of over-politicization and biases that have crept in to dissuade true inquiry, honest dissent and the desperate need for intellectual activity to be truly objective. He does this with the passion and the literary flair of a person who really cares, not just about education but about what nationalism and the transformation of India should mean to us all.'
—**Jaya Jaitly**, former president, Samata Party, activist, author and Indian handicrafts curator

'Makarand R. Paranjape, a leading intellectual in the country, has written a thought-provoking and, for some, controversial book on what is happening in one of India's premier educational institutions, Jawaharlal Nehru University... Makarand is clear that student politics in JNU should be dialogical rather than confrontational. He insists that he is not for substituting Left primacy with Right primacy. Rather, he insists, it is important to "heal, join and unite".'
—**Siddhartha**, writer, social activist and founder of the Inter-Religious Centre, Fireflies Ashram, Bengaluru

'Makarand R. Paranjape's book on JNU could not have been better timed. In much of the democratic world, an intolerant creed has emerged, threatening decades and centuries of human and civilizational progress through context-free and reason-free arguments, claims and counter claims. Makarand's book offers yet another opportunity for the sensible among us—regardless of ideological or political affiliations—to reflect on what truly constitutes liberal values and

behaviour. Writing with verve, passion and humour, Makarand combines the racy pace of a journalist with the depth of a philosopher. For politicians and educational administrators—both in and out of office—the book is a "must-read".'
>   —**Dr Venkataraman Anantha Nageswaran**, author, economist, and chief economic advisor, Government of India

'Makarand R. Paranjape's book is a new and refreshing take on a premier educational institution's slide to near anarchy. Unlike many earlier authors, while describing the changing, standing and workings of the university, he also documents the growth of "nationalism" in India, and its rather partisan, and of late, violent denouement in JNU.

A book well worth reading, not only for its fresh perspective, but because Paranjape offers solutions to re-energize the university, and reclaim the lost excellence and bandwidth of JNU. Instead of merely delving into the past, an achievable, brighter future is mapped out, in keeping with the optimism and confidence of a resurgent New India.'
>   —**Lalitha Kumaramangalam**, director, India Foundation, former chairperson, National Commission for Women and national secretary, BJP

'After a long time, I enjoyed a book about nationalism and the Left that was so gripping that I almost finished it in two sittings!

Paranjape's sharp intellect can make even a dry subject like nationalism so engrossing. Behind that genteel self-effacing, almost Gandhian, persona lies a steely determination that doesn't shy away from confrontation. I never suspected the good professor of having such a great sense of humour and surgical sarcasm. He is an academician who sticks by his principles…'
>   —**Ratan Sharda**, writer, columnist and television commentator

'What made heroes has always been a swim against the tide. If "पुराणमित्येव न साधु सर्वम्…" made Kalidasa a hero in the antiquity-worshipping times, guts to say "नवीनमित्येव न साधु सर्वम्…" makes one a hero in these novelty-alone selling times. Professor Makarand R. Paranjape emerged as a hero by fighting a lone fight on behalf of nationalism in a "Left-Liberal-Fascist" space. The beauty of the work lies in pleading for freedom of thought, speech and debate in academic spaces in the true tradition of a nation that lived as a torchbearer of that freedom while reminiscing his experience of facing intolerance, in the name of "azadi", to the freedom of speaking for the same nation and its true traditions.'
>   —**Dr Nagaraj Paturi**, director, Inter-Gurukula University Centre, Indic Academy

JNU

NATIONALISM AND INDIA'S UNCIVIL WAR

MAKARAND R. PARANJAPE

RUPA

First published by
Rupa Publications India Pvt. Ltd 2022
7/16, Ansari Road, Daryaganj
New Delhi 110002

Sales Centres:
Allahabad Bengaluru Chennai
Hyderabad Jaipur Kathmandu
Kolkata Mumbai

Copyright © Makarand R. Paranjape 2022

The views and opinions expressed in this book are the author's own and the facts are as reported by him which have been verified to the extent possible, and the publishers are not in any way liable for the same.

All rights reserved.
No part of this publication may be reproduced, transmitted, or stored in a retrieval system, in any form or by any means, electronic, mechanical, photocopying, recording or otherwise, without the prior permission of the publisher.

ISBN: 978-93-5520-321-2

Second impression 2022

10 9 8 7 6 5 4 3 2

The moral right of the author has been asserted.

Printed in India.

This book is sold subject to the condition that it shall not, by way of trade or otherwise, be lent, resold, hired out, or otherwise circulated, without the publisher's prior consent, in any form of binding or cover other than that in which it is published.

To
Gayatri, my wife, who walked into my home in JNU one afternoon on the Ides of March—and never left

CONTENTS

Prologue		*xi*
1.	JNU: The Clash of Narratives	1
2.	The Odd Man Out: Why I Joined JNU	21
3	The JNU Row: How I Got Involved	41
4.	Tagore, Gandhi, JNU... and What's 'Left' of the Nation	58
5.	Five Contrarian Epistles	114
6.	JNU and the State of Strife	170
7.	*JNU Ki Azadi: Ek-Do Saal Baad*	190
8.	A Nation United, a University Divided	214
9.	How Not to Destroy JNU	235
Epilogue		269
Index		275

PROLOGUE

This is the book that I almost did not write. And after it was written in the most unexpected fashion, I was almost prevented from publishing it.

It would not be an exaggeration to say that its contents were unforeseen. I had never planned to join Jawaharlal Nehru University (JNU), let alone write a book on its tumult and transformation.

How both came to pass is recounted in these pages.

The book, however, is not merely a collection of anecdotes or personal experiences. Nor is it an exercise in institutional historiography or hagiography.[1] Instead, it is an informed insider's account of the cataclysmic changes in one of India's premier institutions of higher education during a five year period, 2016–2021.

But more than that, I would like to believe that this book is also a history of our times, of India's ongoing transformation. It is the story of the changing self-apprehension of a people, of the multiple meanings of nationalism. It is about being Indian itself.

JNU, as I shall show, is at the centre of discussions and debates on topics of national importance. It always has been. So that is

---

[1] See Rakesh Batabyal's *JNU: The Making of a University* (New Delhi: HarperCollins, 2015), which comes close to such an endeavour. On the other hand, *JNU Stories: The First 50 Years* edited by Neeladri Bhattacharya, Kunal Chakrabarti, S. Gunasekaran, Janaki Nair and Joy L.K. Pachuau (New Delhi: Aleph, 2021) is a collection of essays and reminiscences of those who were a part of the JNU story from the earliest times.

not what makes these times special. What is different now is that the university, which went through an unprecedented crisis, was the location and theatre of this larger change.

As this book goes to press, JNU's future as a coveted destination for students from all over India, as also from abroad, is in question. The image of the university has taken a severe beating in the last five years. Given so much negative publicity, many parents do not wish to send their children to study there.

What, then, will happen to this once-prized, premier university? Will it weather this crisis? Will it actually emerge stronger and more stable? Or will it go under, overwhelmed by the pressures that it faces? Will its reputation and character be destroyed forever? Will it be downgraded into just another failed institution of higher learning such as dot the intellectual landscape of our country?

In its larger context, this book tries to find answers to such questions too.

It also provides a corrective to the excessive condemnation and denigration of JNU. It is a plea to save the university, to safeguard its culture of democracy and dissent, as also to restore academics, rather than politics, to the pole position. As such, the book critiques the dominant, mostly Leftist student and faculty politics at the university.

But while it deplores the ideological hegemony and intolerance of the Left in JNU, arguing that it has brought the university to such a sorry pass, this book also makes a case for not simply substituting the dogmatic Left with the doctrinaire Right. Or using the sledgehammer approach to crush and pulverize all opposition to the current regime, which the present JNU administration is supposed to represent.

The book pleads for the restoration of civil disagreement in place of bitter opposition, dialogue rather than irreconcilable conflict. It proposes remedial strategies of dealing with differences, along with intermedial hermeneutics to negotiate extreme positions and bipolar oppositions. In a later chapter, I explain at greater length what such intermediality would entail.

Right at the outset, I can confirm that intermedial hermeneutics demands a humane, non-reductive way of understanding texts and traditions, individuals and society, as well as the conflicts such as in JNU. It thus implies and enables a new approach to conflict resolution. More specifically, when applied to JNU, it shows the way to create a new JNU in which academics rather than politics constitute the primary purpose of the university.

As to the specific circumstances of this book's genesis, much of it emerged out of my continuous public engagement with the happenings in JNU since February 2016. Not so much written from scratch or from some vantage point in the present, it is, rather, a record of my own ongoing involvement in my university. My point of view is not that of an administrator or activist, but as a concerned member of the faculty and taxpaying citizen. Also as a social, political and intellectual stakeholder and influencer in what is now a much larger argument about our changing republic.

The book begins with the outline of the wider context. The national, even worldwide, debates on liberalism and nationalism, thus, form the core of Chapter One. Particularly, how a certain brand of the latter has come to substitute the Nehruvian version of the former as the driving ideology of India.

In Chapter Two, I narrate how I joined JNU under somewhat unusual circumstances. I recount my culture shock at confronting its time-warped Leftist politics, which I considered a combination of delusion and opportunism.

Chapter Three is about the events that led to those fateful days in February 2016. Starting on 9 February, the university entered a phase of turbulence when a rally was taken out against the so-called 'judicial murder' of two convicted criminals, Afzal Guru and Maqbool Bhat. The chapter goes on to recount the slogans that were shouted on campus, the clash between two student groups, and how JNU came, for all the wrong reasons, into national and international limelight. That is how I myself got involved, somewhat unwittingly, in the university's troubles.

Then, in Chapter Four, I come directly to the heart of the book, the lecture on nationalism that I delivered at the 'Teach-in' on 3 March 2016. In this most comprehensive and augmented version of my talk, I record how I confronted the then JNU Students' Union (JNUSU) president, Kanhaiya Kumar. That, however, is only a small part of the chapter. Actually, it is an extended reflection on the meaning of Indian nationalism. The chapter tries to deepen our understanding of the changing contours of nationalism in India. I reread two great makers of modern India, Rabindranath Tagore and M.K. Gandhi, before offering my analysis of what ails JNU and its skewed support of 'anti-nationalism'.

Chapter Five, 'Five Contrarian Epistles', may be read as my own humble attempt to document the times. In Hindi, it would be called 'JNU dastavez'. It contains some uniquely context-specific interventions in the ongoing clash of narratives in JNU. I respond to five 'open letters' published against me in various forums. These letters were attempts to discredit, defame and, possibly, silence me. Because I had to refute them, I became, one might say, a public intellectual.[2] These animadversions consumed a lot of my time and energy, but I am glad I did not succumb to the temptation of vacating the verbal battlefield or running away from the word war.

The three chapters that follow are all about events that erupted after the February 2016 JNU roils. Chapter Six recounts the story of two students who disappeared or died, Najeeb and Rajini, respectively. I report and reflect on not just the sad loss of two precious lives, but how agitating students tried to politicize and take advantage of such misfortunes.

---

[2] All these texts are presented in slightly revised and enhanced versions, so that the arguments presented are not merely topical, but acquire a wider relevance and resonance. Their earlier, published versions, are also cited.

Chapter Seven is about an anniversary of the protests which was marked by—what else—more protests. Students displaying pellet mark-like make-up to show how protesters in Kashmir were fired upon with plastic bullets by the security agencies. But, more dramatically for me, how I was stopped from going into my own office building by agitators who had blockaded it. But I did manage to get inside by pushing them aside and burrowing through.

Gheraos, lockdowns, and even violence form the bulk of Chapter Eight. The continuous infighting in JNU, the clash between students and the administration, culminating in the terrible violence of 5 January, when masked hoodlums went on a rampage on campus, beating up students and destroying property inside the campus. For the first and, in JNU's history of 55 years, I hope the last time.

Finally, in Chapter Nine, I once again go beyond the immediate context of JNU to the crisis of higher education in India. What can be done, both vis-à-vis JNU and the rest of the country, to improve standards and the quality of higher education? Can we remain in the present state of apathy and inaction, while university after university declines and goes under? Or will we do what we must to make 'excellence' and 'competence' the watchwords in India's education landscape once again?

The primacy of teaching and learning must be restored in India. We are never tired of reminding the world that we were once a knowledge society or that we aspire to become a knowledge superpower again. For future generations, especially if we have any intentions of competing with other countries and contributing to a better future for all of humanity, we will have to reform the education sector root and branch. Far afield is the prospect or promise of being a *visvaguru* (world teacher). First, we must set our own house in order.

Before concluding this Prologue, I have a pleasant task to perform. I have incurred many debts in writing this book. Here, I acknowledge them most gladly. First of all, to the editors and the periodicals, where some portions of the book appeared in earlier versions as op-ed articles or columns. Of these, I am especially grateful to *Mail Today* and *Daily News* and *Analysis*, both of which have now closed down. *ThePrint, Open* and *Swarajya* have supported my work over the last four or five years. I offer my continuing gratitude to their editors for publishing the earlier versions of some of the contents of this book. My views on JNU during the fateful months in 2016 were also carried in other forums such as *FirstPost, Scroll* and News 18. My thanks to them too for giving me an opportunity to put across my side of the JNU story.

A small band of JNU students showed exceptional loyalty and courage in standing by me when I took contrary and unpopular positions. They not only registered for my classes when others boycotted them, but also spoke up and wrote in my support. One even fasted in atonement for what some of my detractors had done, which was to try and block me from entering my office. A few faculty colleagues remained my friends throughout my ordeal. I am thankful to them all.

Paradoxically, while the 'official' Right Wing in JNU did little to help me or endorse what I stood for, I had overwhelming encouragement and sustenance from well-meaning Indians not just in India, but also abroad. I am not a member of any political party or outfit. That is why I am thankful for the unselfish affinity and fellowship of those who have defended and protected me.

When it comes to this book, it is to Kapish Mehra of Rupa Publications, to whom I owe much. When he heard that I had a book on JNU, he said he wanted it. And that he would not take no for an answer. Rupa Publications are my old publishers. My first book of poems, *The Serene Flame*, was published in their poetry series in 1991. Since then, I have done six other books with them. I am, therefore, happy to return to them after a gap. At Rupa, I am also grateful to Yamini, Oorja, Sandhya, and the other members of the team for all their editorial inputs as I am to Rachita for the cover design.

Dr Sanjeev Chopra, himself an alum, JNUSU vice president, and former director, Lal Bahadur Shastri National Academy of Administration, read the entire manuscript, offering helpful suggestions and comments. I am also grateful to my friend, Hari Kiran Vadlamani, the founder of Indic Academy and Indic Book Club. He has supported my intellectual and creative endeavours these last several years.

My colleagues at JNU's Centre for English Studies continued to offer encouragement even when I was away on deputation as the director of the Indian Institute of Advanced Study (IIAS), Shimla. At IIAS, my colleagues, staff, fellows and associates deserve praise, though they didn't know I was writing this book. But working with them, despite its challenges, has been inspiring.

My special thanks to the distinguished writers, leaders and luminaries who were kind enough to endorse or encourage this book.

My mother has been a source of continuing encouragement to me. As one of my faithful readers, she, I hope, is pleased with this book.

Above all, I thank my wife and life partner, Gayatri. She not only read and commented on early drafts but created the time and space in which I could complete the manuscript.

1

JNU: THE CLASH OF NARRATIVES

JNU and the State of the Nation

This book is about Jawaharlal Nehru University (JNU), where I have been professor of English since 1999. It is also, to some extent, about me—why I joined JNU, what got me embroiled in its charged and fractious politics and how I countered what had come to be accepted as JNU's dominant Leftist ideology. Intertwining two biographies—one institutional and the other personal—this is my story as much as it is JNU's.

The nucleus of this narrative is the decisive series of events of February 2016—a highly fraught and contentious time in JNU's history. There were student clashes, azadi rallies, daily demonstrations, arrests, campus-wide protests and the indefinite shutdown of the university. We might call it the *tukde tukde* phase after the slogans which were shouted.[1]

During this period, the JNU Teachers' Association (JNUTA) organized a 'Teach-in', with evening lectures on 'What the Nation Really Needs to Know'. I too was invited to deliver a lecture in this series. In that lecture, which forms an independent chapter of the book, I challenged the overwhelmingly anti-government, one might also say anti-national, stance of the JNU Students Union

---

[1] '*Bharat tere tukde honge, Inshallah, Inshallah!* [India you will break into pieces, Allah-willing, Allah-willing!]'. More on this in Chapter 3.

(JNUSU). In doing so, I also publicly confronted its president, Kanhaiya Kumar.

Perhaps no one had stood up to him in that fashion inside JNU or elsewhere—especially because, Kumar, just out on bail, was somewhat of a national icon, immensely popular not only on campus but also outside. He was also propped up by the media and opposition parties. Some even went to the extent of hailing him as a challenger to Narendra Modi.[2] But my face-off with Kumar had a surprising fallout. In the months to come, I received overwhelming support and commendation from all over India and abroad.

My stand, if timely, was also principled rather than premeditated. It was not informed by short- or long-term calculations. At that point, what did I, or anyone for that matter, know how things would turn out? The media and popular opinion were very much in favour of Kumar and his band of dissenters. It was as if I was in a minority of one on my own campus.

What I presented was my considered position, consistent with my views articulated over the years. On a number of issues of national importance, of which JNU was just one, albeit latest. That the videos of my talk would go viral, circulated and recirculated on social media was, therefore, quite unexpected. I could never have imagined the extent or degree of anger that common people felt over the goings-on in JNU.

On the home front, however—on my own campus particularly, but also among friends and students—I was singled out for blame. After that lecture, I became the target of a barrage of attacks and open letters. I also was forced to turn, somewhat by accident, into a 'public intellectual'.

---

[2]Born in 1987, Kumar comes from a Begusarai (Bihar) family that has traditionally supported the Communist Party of India (CPI). On 28 September 2021, he joined the Congress after losing from the Begusarai constituency as a CPI candidate in the 2019 Lok Sabha elections.

How this happened is a story in its own right. But the reason, paradoxically, was that I had very little backing. I was alone, with no one to defend me. In that situation, I could have retreated or ducked, turned tail or fled. Instead, I decided to stick it out, to fight back. Mainly because I felt responsible to rebut the campaign against me, I began to write for national newspapers and web portals. It is not that I had never done so before, but earlier, my writings were mostly literary, rather than political. Increasingly, I began to speak out in public forums too.

Yes, I would be the first to admit that my stance arose primarily from a moral conviction. Not, indeed, entirely from my anger over being cornered or curtailed. In fact, the urge to hit back was also largely absent. If I entered the lists, it was partly because of the nature of the duel. It was mostly an intellectual and ideological battle, with words being the main weapons. Even though it was also a psychological warfare, its medium was largely verbal. I discovered that that was to my advantage. I saw no reason to back down.

People who were hell-bent upon attacking me usually did not have the requisite intellectual resources, skills or stamina. When I refuted or rebutted them, they had little to offer by way of a comeback. Their argumentative skills were also not of the highest order either. The Left, in this respect, I discovered, though way ahead of the Right, was still not up to the mark. It was simply not smart enough to take on a really well-trained or determined adversary.

Eventually, it could be said that I won most of these contests. Even those who disliked me would have to admit that. I certainly did not lose. I was neither silenced nor pushed back or forced to admit defeat in any of these arguments. Instead, the point of view I represented, call it Centre-Right, suddenly came into much demand. It made me a speaker, invited to many national and international events.

Mainly because I dissented with the overriding Left-Liberal

(LeLi) ideology of most Indian academics and intellectuals, I fitted a slot that had few takers. At least at that time, the Hindu Right, by and large, lacked bench strength, especially when it came to the English-educated and foreign-returned. Now things are different, but it is still not a level playing field. That is because of what one might term the prevailing anti-intellectualism on both sides. Politics trumps everything else. Who cares for ideas? Since I cared, it became incumbent upon me to express myself.

I felt that it was imperative not just to trot out opinions expected of me, but to articulate my views in detail, with evidence and corroboration. I owed this not so much to my hosts or admirers but also to myself and any responsibility I had to posterity. The opportunities to speak and write, thus, enabled, and even compelled, me to give voice to what was a larger, unconscious longing. The time had suddenly come for alternatives to the minoritarian coalition made up of motley, and often contradictory, actors. It was time for the silent and silenced majority to speak up. Not in a reactive, insecure or aggressive manner, but in a measured, sensible and steady tone.

To refresh and communicate the knowledge thus produced is, therefore, as much a reason for writing this book as for documenting what happened in and to JNU. In the ultimate analysis, this book is not just about JNU or debates between those on the Left, Right and Centre of our political and intellectual spectrum. This book is really about India. The idea of India and what it means to be Indian in our times. It is about the nation and what it signifies in contemporary times.

Travails and Tyrannies of Liberalism

When we go back to 2016, it is clear that whatever happened in JNU had a wider context, both national and international. We might call it the crisis of liberalism and the resurgence of conservative nationalism. To start with the former, not just in

India, but all over the world, liberalism seemed to be in tatters. What is more, the calamity of global liberalism was mostly of its own making.

What caused the drastic decline, degeneration, and even death, of liberalism?

If 'liberalism' means the pursuit and promotion of individual freedoms, rule of law and constitutional government, most liberals have utterly miscarried their attempts to defend it. The sad truth is that it is liberals themselves who have failed liberalism. In his 2011 book, *The Twilight of Liberalism,* Robin Phillips characterizes the rise of a new intolerance the world over as 'Illiberal Liberalism':

> While liberal totalitarianism's dogmatic intolerance of dissent has put public debate in a state of paralysis, it has come to us in the package of 'tolerance', 'equality', 'human rights', and even—heaven help us—'freedom'.[3]

In the name of such grand values, liberals not only call out white supremacy, racism, sexism and economic equality, but also pillory Right-wing nationalists the world over. But why is it that these same liberals seldom castigate Islamist jihad, terrorism, violence or genocide in substantial, even if not equal, measure?

This is the question that Lee Harris asked in *The Suicide of Reason* way back in 2008, when the world had still not fully come to grips with the fallout of 9/11. Harris argued that the 'fanaticism of reason' of the liberal West was preventing it from clearly seeing the greatest threat to its way of life, which was 'the fanaticism of Islam'. Both liberals and conservatives failed to understand each other or the latter. According to the liberals, 'you couldn't really blame the terrorists, since they were merely the victims of an evil system—for Chomsky, American imperialism, for Wolfowitz, the corrupt and despotic regimes of the Middle East.'[4]

---

[3]Phillips, Robin. *The Twilight of Liberalism,* London: Lulu Press, 2011, p. 5.
[4]Harris, Lee. *The Suicide of Reason,* Basic Books, 2008, p. 41.

We are living with this dilemma not only in the US or Canada, but also in Europe, South America and other parts of the world including India. While there are real dangers in the Right-wing upsurge in our societies, it is equally true that the excessive preoccupation of the Left-Liberal intellectual establishment with this resurgence has made it blind to other forms of intolerance and totalitarianism, including Liberal and Islamic fanaticism.[5]

Not surprisingly, the phenomenon of 'Illiberal Liberalism' is as rampant in India as elsewhere in the free world. The same sort of blindness or duplicity, evidently, prevails here. LeLi journalist-intellectuals and the periodicals they patronize, often train their polemical guns on the Hindu Right, but seldom on Muslim and other forms of 'minoritarian' intolerance.

They soft-pedal the latter as if it poses no real threat to Indian liberalism. If the Sharia-like conditions are imposed on reluctant Muslims in Muslim-dominated areas, or even on non-Muslims, they are silent. If entire neighbourhoods become minority ghettos and no-go zones for sari-clad women or clean-shaven men, they do not protest. Even more harmful to national unity and integrity, if Kashmiri separatists actually peddle Islamic theocracy in the guise of azadi, they look the other way.

If predatory conversion, 'love jihad' or illegal immigration destabilize demographic and electoral scales in certain regions of the country, our LeLis do not cavil or worry. If Hindus are abducted, raped, killed or converted in Pakistan or Bangladesh, they do not raise any alarm or stage a demonstration. Instead, Marxist-Dalit-anti-Brahminical-minority-feminist-'anti-Hindu' alliances are applauded and promoted.

In intellectual circles across the world, these LeLis shut out not just dissenting voices but any 'contaminating contact' with the Bharatiya Janata Party (BJP)/Rashtriya Swayamsevak Sangh

---

[5]The works of David Horowitz, Robert Spencer, Tarek Fatah, Ben Shapiro, Jordan B. Peterson and Ayaan Hirsi Ali, to name a few, are ample testimony.

(RSS) or the Hindu Right. For decades, they have practised such prejudice, tantamount to a new form of untouchability, in the name of liberalism and political correctness. Their selective outrages force us to question not just their intentions, but also their competence and ethics. Rather than being in denial, LeLis must set their own house in order before trying to set the world right.

In India, today, no side or shade in our political continuum, in a strict sense, is truly liberal. Most political parties, regardless of their beliefs, are statist, if not status-quoist. All of them push for greater bureaucratic and political control of our lives.

Our sorrow, in fact, is that instead of being increasingly independent and self-reliant economically, socially and culturally, Indian citizens are getting more and more politicized and politics-oriented. The political parties which lead us, in turn, are more statist than swarajist.

No wonder today the state is everywhere. Politics, moreover, has become the art of capturing the state for private, community or party gains. Only secondarily, if at all, for serving the people. Despite whatever claims or counterclaims leading parties make, we notice the instrumentalization of the state as the primary engine of growth, progress and change. Also of control of the populace and settling scores against opponents.

When it comes to liberalism, admittedly, traditional fault lines in its framework and discourse become evident. There is often a clash between classical liberalism and social liberalism—the former stands for economic, cultural and social freedom, while the latter has tended to be more interventionist and regulatory, focussing on justice and equality, rather than liberty. But the real reason for the failure of liberalism is not its inability to reconcile rights with duties or freedom with justice.

Liberalism the world over has failed because of one deadly disease—hypocrisy—which is just a polite form of falsehood.

Liberals seem to despise those who disagree with them. Instead of free and fair debate, they are more interested in rigging or slanting outcomes and decisions. Liberals, it would seem, no longer want the best ideas to compete for public attention. Instead, they wish to dominate by exercising unearned privileges. Hegemony, instead of discussion, seems to be their way. When they are thwarted, they become extremely upset, even bullying and violent.

The defeat of pseudo-liberals is the first step towards restoring true liberalism to its rightful place as the guardian of a way of life that most of us hold dear. Lest we forget, in the heyday of communism, many western liberals colluded, even spied, for the Soviet Union. How could they justify such a betrayal?

The answer is simple—a combination of ideology and expediency. Today's liberals are similarly seen supporting or countenancing radical Islam, which though in a different manner and register, is also terribly intolerant. Just as Soviet-style socialism used to be. Even if countries like Saudi Arabia themselves are pushing through radical reforms, any criticism of Islamic intolerance is immediately branded as 'Islamophobia' and targeted for cancellation. Similarly, other 'woke' causes, some of them perfectly worthy in their own right, are imposed in a coercive and illiberal manner.

Many liberals lack the integrity to admit that they are compromised in supporting illiberal causes, such as the burqa or triple talaq, which for most is obviously a patriarchal-theological imposition rather than a matter of choice. I see similar patterns of hypocrisy, chicanery, expediency and, ultimately, rage, being played out in India when the older entrenched and entitled liberals are shunted out by the new regime.

Not that all liberals are totally anti-dharmic in the sense of not being ethical. However, they hardly have any knowledge or understanding of Dharma, that is, of Indic civilization. On a little sliver of derived and borrowed knowledge, they have lorded it over the 'unwashed masses' for decades.

Liberalism is in a sad state today, precisely because liberals themselves have betrayed it.

Liberalism vs Bharatiyata

On 29 March 2017, Pratap Bhanu Mehta wrote an op-ed for *The Indian Express* with a provocative title, 'Yes, Bring on Bharatiyata'.[6] One of India's leading liberals, Mehta taught at JNU for a short time. It is widely believed that his distaste for the intolerant and dogmatic JNU Left hastened his departure. I wrote a response, which was published in *Mail Today* and *DailyO*.[7]

In his article, while making a plea for 'genuine indigenization', Mehta's actual target is the RSS. But first let's look at what Mehta means by 'bharatiyata'. To him, it entails restoring 'autonomy to higher education', ending 'destructive nationalism in learning', confronting the 'guilt at our own social cruelty' and facing 'our own intellectual ossification'.

He rounds off with a rousing conclusion: 'A deep exposure to Indian culture might actually cure the custodians of Indian culture of prudishness, machismo and homophobia.' No surprise that the last exhortation also became the headline of his essay, published in bold just beneath the title.

Mehta's clarity of mind, lucidity of style and attitude of moral conviction are amply displayed in the article. In addition, there is an important strategic, if not rhetorical, twist that might be appreciated. Rather than deriding bharatiyata, he actually wants more of it.

In defining genuine bharatiyata, he foregrounds the virtues of autonomy, openness, pluralism and, above all, 'self-awareness'.

---

[6]Mehta, Pratap Bhanu. 'Yes, Bring on Bharatiyata', *The Indian Express*, 29 March 2017, https://indianexpress.com/article/opinion/columns/mohan-bhagwat-rss-workshop-at-delhi-university-yes-bring-on-bharatiyata-4590003/. Accessed on 27 August 2021. Quotations from Mehta that follow are from this article.
[7]Paranjape, Makarand R. 'My Response to Pratap Bhanu Mehta's "Bharatiyata" Article', *DailyO*, 5 April 2021, https://www.dailyo.in/politics/left-liberals-pratp-bhanu-mehta-babri-masjid-rm-temple-rss/story/1/16523.html. Accessed on 27 August 2021.

Indeed, our ability to interrogate, critique and correct ourselves is the hallmark of our intellectual traditions. Mehta is also right in urging us not to resort either to blame or ressentiment, but take responsibility for our failures and shortcomings.

On the contentious issue of the historicity of Shri Rama, Mehta argues that we 'stop seeking validation of Ram by the methodologies of alien knowledge like positivist history and archaeology. Surely, Ram's reality is different.'

Indeed. But it is here that Mehta most exposes his own inadequacies. What he fails to mention is that the ruse of history was used by a cabal of Leftist 'scholars' against the belief system of a people for whom the reality of Rama is self-evident.

It was they who denied that there was ever a Hindu place of worship beneath the mosque that Babar's deputy built on the ruins of a razed temple. To say, 'what stone the next dig throws up' doesn't matter, therefore, smacks of bad faith. If our secular LeLi establishment had respected the sentiments of Hindus who championed the cause of the Ram Mandir, the Babri Masjid may never have been destroyed.

Mehta, likewise, does not acknowledge that it was common practice of Muslim conquerors not just to destroy temples, but also to use the materials thus obtained to build mosques. The very first mosque in India, itself in ruins today, the Quwwat-ul-Islam (might of Islam) Masjid next to the Qutub Minar, as the Archaeological Survey of India (ASI) itself declares, was built on the demolished remains of 27 Hindu and Jain temple.[8] The Qutub Minar too is a victory tower, in the best (or for the subjugated, worst) traditions of Islamic conquest.

If 'confronting the self as much as confronting the other' is the highlight of bharatiyata, why doesn't Mehta confront

---

[8] Paranjape, Makarand R. 'We Can't Dwell in the Past, But Can We Afford to Ignore It?' *The New Indian Express*, 4 January 2021, https://www.newindianexpress.com/opinions/2021/jan/04/we-cant-dwell-in-the-past-but-can-we-afford-to-ignore-it-2245042.html. Accessed on 27 August 2021

himself and other Left-Liberals? Why aren't their failures, distortions, elisions and inadequacies acknowledged, discussed or questioned? Why don't the Left-Liberals come in for scrutiny in his work?

Isn't Mehta, in other words, one-sided, if not prejudiced? He chooses to depict the Right in the worst possible light, doubting both its intentions and competence. He disparages their nationalism as 'destructive', quoting 'Guruji' Golwalkar selectively and out of context to 'prove' that non-Hindus will be downgraded to second-class citizens. He conveniently fails to analyse what Golwalkar meant by 'Hindu', whether the term was used in a religio-theological or geo-cultural sense.

He calls 'the custodians of Indian culture' prudish, macho and homophobic. But on what basis? Where is his evidence? His diatribe appears like a parade of foregone conclusions. The trouble with Mehta and his ilk is their arrogance combined with ignorance. So sure are they of their own superiority that they do not apply the same standards of proof to their own declamations as they demand of their opponents.

I doubt whether Mehta has seriously read or engaged with V.D. Savarkar, M.S. Golwalkar, Deen Dayal Upadhyaya, Shyama Prasad Mukherjee or other important Right-wing thinkers or ideologues. If so, how can he make a virtue out of his unfamiliarity with this material? Perhaps what makes Mehta so sure that he is competent to hector those whom he calls 'custodians of Indian culture' is the belief that he—and a select few like him—are the super-custodians of Indian culture.

It is he and his ilk who will adjudicate what is authentic or inauthentic when it comes to bharatiyata. Surely, such tout court dismissals show neither the openness of the best of western-style liberalism nor of Indian *anekantavada*, from the Jain tradition to which Mehta belongs. And to think of it, Mehta is among the most distinguished and courageous Indian liberals.

Of course, all LeLis must not be lumped into one heap

and abused for their past prejudices and misdeeds. Most were sponsored by earlier Congress regimes, but failed to admit that their privileges were not natural or God-given, but largely unearned outcomes of patronage. That is why the question 'How does the mind get hold of its own operations?' probably applies as much to them—especially in the present context—as to the RSS and its ideological allies.

With lesser pride and not so much prejudice, LeLi critiques or commentaries may actually be more useful. But so used are they to preaching the lessons of intellectual integrity, fair-mindedness, evidence-based thinking and openness to opposing points of view that they have forgotten to practise these virtues themselves.

Should we not gently remind them of the old dictum—*cura te ipsum*—physician heal thyself?

The Clash of Lit Fests: 'Do Liberals Stifle Debate?'

'Do liberals stifle debate?' This question was actually the topic of the closing debate at the Jaipur Literature Festival (JLF) 2019. Itself largely a LeLi operation, it nevertheless used to be the greatest literature fest in the world. With over 500 speakers and footfall of half a million, it was indeed the *sahitya ka mahakumbh*.[9] In a post-COVID-19 world, with the future of such events in doubt, it remains to be seen how JLF will reinvent itself.

In 2019, the Zee JLF 2019 was, once again, a grand success, especially the closing debate, which attracted the widest audience

---

[9] Despite being on the other side, so to speak, I have myself stoutly defended JLF against unfair allegations and attacks. See Paranjape, Makarand R. 'Sahitya ka Mahakumbh, JLF Calling', *Sunday Guardian*, 25 January 2020, https://www.sundayguardianlive.com/news/sahitya-ka-mahakumbh-jlf-calling. Accessed on 27 August 2021; Paranjape, Makarand R. 'Arnab Goswami, Stop Attacking JLF. It's Not Just a Political Platform for Lost Lutyens Souls', *The Print*, 26 January 2020, https:// theprint.in/opinion/being-indian/arnab-goswami-stop-attacking-jlf-its-not-just-a-political-platform-for-lost-lutyens-souls/354560/. Accessed on 27 August 2021.

participation and maximum interest. As curator Namita Gokhale put it, 'Everyone who listens ends up feeling empowered. They know their voices and views matter.'

I was the opening speaker in a panel that was as daunting as distinguished. On the 'Left' were former Union ministers, Kapil Sibal and Salman Khurshid, both top-notch politician-advocates, as well as author Sagarika Ghose, whose book, *Why I Am a Liberal*, had just come out, and journalist-commentator, Mihir Sharma.

On the 'Right', were eminent former IFS officer and now minister of Housing and Urban Affairs and Minister of Petroleum and Natural Gas, Hardeep Singh Puri; cultural icon and Member of Parliament, Padma Vibhushan Sonal Mansingh; historian and curator, Vikram Sampath and me.

The debate was ably, wittily, sometimes provocatively, but always pleasantly moderated by Sreenivasan Jain of NDTV. Ironically, I was seated on the far left, having been the first one on the stage. I made a joke of it saying I was, after all, from JNU. But the issue at hand was far more serious. Do liberals stifle debate?

The answer was neither a simple 'yes' nor a straightforward 'no'. Ordinarily, liberals do not stifle debate, 'illiberals' or bigots do. But now the situation seems to have been reversed. Unfortunately, many liberals today are 'mostly' if not 'the most' illiberal of us. This is why we are going through the crisis, if not the end, of liberalism.

The world over, debate, discussion and dissent are stifled in the name of liberalism. Even Richard Dawkins was famously prevented from speaking at Berkeley. Was the illiberalism of Liberals one reason—someone from the US in the audience asked—that made Donald Trump win?

Nor is this intolerance of Liberals new. As mentioned earlier, liberals not only looked away from facing up to Stalinist atrocities, but actually collaborated with the Soviet Union, even going to the extent of spying for the USSR against their own country.

The extra-national and extraterritorial loyalties of some of our own Indian liberals are well known, whether they be champagne socialists holding the Chinese 'Fatherland' dearer than Mother India, or those, who while crying against the ills of economic liberalism, profiteer and cheat their own country, parking their ill-gotten gains in secret offshore accounts.

But what about us on the stage? We were all liberals ourselves, weren't we? Then whom were we debating? Or were we talking only to ourselves in yet another echo chamber of the privileged?

Liberal, conservative, Left, Right and so on—all such terms show up the poverty of our thought and are symptomatic of our colonization, which still continues. Like borrowed plumes, we also appropriate terminology, defining ourselves by parameters and frameworks that do not fit our social, cultural, historical or political reality.

Shouldn't we ask, instead, whether we are dharmic or adharmic, rather than liberal or illiberal? Or to shift to a Persianized idiom, are we imandaar or be-imaan? Our problem, then, is not lack of ideology but of integrity. Our failing is not (ill)liberalism but hypocrisy.

My personal experience with Indian liberals has only confirmed their intolerance, I said in my concluding remarks at the JLF debate.

As the founder and co-curator of another literature festival, The Pondy Lit Fest (PLF), I had experienced the virulence of the intolerants first hand just a few months before. When its inaugural edition was scheduled to kick off from 17 August 2018 in Puducherry, PLF was subjected to relentless attacks. Some called it a festival of 'BJP bootlickers', others complained of the 'saffronization' of literary festivals.

As if one side has a monopoly to hold them!

Five Dravidian and Left political parties came together to call for its closure or, failing that, boycott it. They even threatened to pelt the festival location visitors with stones. The venue partner,

Alliance Française, pulled out at the very last minute, a day before the start of the festival.[10]

We were abused in Left-leaning web portals and articles. This was despite my effort to invite writers and intellectuals professing alternate viewpoints. Of course, none condescended to come to Puducherry. Such intolerance was not new. Some time back, Sampath had been eased out of the Bangalore Literature Festival, which he co-founded. As noted author Manu Pillai said, 'It is regrettable that Mr Sampath should have had to resign on account of his personal views.'[11]

Personally, I do not subscribe to the Left versus Right bipolarity, nor support the uncivil war that is dividing our public sphere. Opinions of all colours and stripes should engage and vie for attention and acceptance. That is the great Indian way, which I call intermedial hermeneutics. But what is the cure or counter to entitlement combined with intolerance?

This book, in its understanding of our present crisis, is inspired by Sri Aurobindo, whom we ought to reread and return to on his 150th birth anniversary. He exhorted the national mind in 'The Renaissance in India', to 'turn new eyes on past culture, reawaken to its sense and import, and see it in relation to modern knowledge and ideas' so that 'out of this awakening vision and impulse the Indian renaissance may arise'.[12]

To this end, in the coming chapters, I advocate the reform,

---

[10]'Pondy Lit Fest: Left Leaders Oppose Free Speech, Alliance Française Distances Itself', 16 August 2018, *The Wire*, https://thewire.in/culture/pondy-lit-fest-left-leaders-oppose-free-speech-alliance-francaise-distances-itself. Accessed 22 September 2021.

[11]Pillai, Manu. 'Nothing Democratic about It', *The Hindu*, 1 December 2015, https://www.thehindu.com/opinion/op-ed/nothing-democratic-about-it/article7933847.ece. Accessed on 17 September 2021.

[12]Sri Aurobindo, *The Renaissance in India and Other Essays on Indian Culture*, Sri Aurobindo Ashram, 1997.

not destruction of JNU.[13] Similarly, Indian liberalism need not be obliterated. Even if it definitely needs to become more dharmic.

'NaMo' Nationalism

To return to the JNU scrapes of 2016, it is amply clear that they were directly related to the election of Narendra Modi as the prime minister of India in 2014. This single event strikes me as the most important when it comes to shaking the foundations of what has been termed the Nehruvian consensus informing India's ruling ideology.

As I show later, JNU and other universities in India were deliberately sought to be turned into flashpoints of anti-Modi and anti-BJP government protests. What was not as clearly understood then was that the anti-Modi agitation would hinge on divergent meanings of nationalism.

At the heart of the conflict was the idea of India. That is because an unexpected fallout of Prime Minister Modi's two years in office was the centre-staging of nationalism after such a long duration where it suddenly became the fulcrum of both policy and discourse.

The resurgence of nationalism was, however, a worldwide rather than uniquely Indian phenomenon. The revival of nationalism came as a surprise to most experts. For decades, nationalism was not only considered passé, but almost became a bad word. Social and political theory confidently advanced 'post-nationalist' models of the global order.

But its critics had underestimated the resilience of nationalism.

---

[13]JNU has produced over 22,000 PhD, MPhil and MTech theses since its inception. Its students are now teaching all over the world, besides making remarkable contributions to other professions and occupations. Such a university cannot just be closed down or downgraded as many advocate.

The largest free association of states in the post-World War era, the European Union, today appears rather breakable, if not quite endangered. Not only has one of its largest members, Britain, exited but several other member states also no longer seem sure of its future. Moreover, the influx of somewhat not-too-welcome refugees has only led to the strengthening of national identities. For instance, former US President Donald Trump wore his nationalism on his sleeve. In one of his announcements, he even threatened to stop immigration, which forms the very foundation of the US as a nation.[14]

Nationalism, thus, has struck back with a vengeance. Indian nationalism under Modi is, arguably, not quite as negative or defensive. It is a positive, even assertive upsurge. Its central theme, tone and tenor is the expectation that India should be great again. More than anyone else, it is Modi who has made Indians feel this way. He has restored the confidence of an entire civilization in its sense of manifest destiny. He has made India and Indians proud once more.

A renewed belief in India has also resulted in the reinvigoration of the country's civilizational mission, which lay dormant, if not moribund, since Independence. The millennial sense of special purpose and promise that fuelled the freedom movement had been totally missing from the post-Independence national imagination.

A hundred years ago, that is what gave Indians a sense of moral as well as spiritual ascendancy over their colonizers. However, this sense of India's special calling lay trampled and obscured for long. But what *is* India's civilizational mission? This is a question that few pause to consider or ponder over.

If we go by Sri Aurobindo's stirring avowal, then India rises

---

[14]Narea, Nicola. 'Trump's Executive Order to Stop Issuing Green Cards Temporarily, Explained', *Vox*, 23 April 2020, https://www.vox.com/policy-and-politics/2020/4/21/21229286/trump-immigration-ban-executive-order-coronavirus. Accessed on 27 August 2021.

for Dharma, not for its own selfish interests. To spell out the contents of such 'dharmic' nationalism, we might argue that India's special gifts include non-dualism in the realm of metaphysics, swaraj or non-aggressive autonomy in the realm of politics and non-exclusionism in the realm of culture.

Modi's two-pronged strategy to offer a corruption-free, efficient government within the country and to improve India's image overseas, contribute considerably to such a dharmic nationalism. Robust economic growth and a more muscular foreign policy add to this sense of India's strength. Indians are tired of weak, wishy-washy and indecisive leaders. Modi, in contrast, has demonstrated strength and commitment.

At his best, Modi can be inspiring and visionary. This was clearly borne out by his re-election in 2019 with even more seats in the Lok Sabha. During the Congress-led United Progressive Alliance (UPA) government, scam after brazen scam made us hang our heads in shame. The apathy and indifference of the government—not only of selfish netas, but also of callous babus—made us feel alienated from the state.

During all this, the ultra-rich found new ways of making even more money in India and stashing it away abroad. Rich or poor, no one felt a sense of belonging and ownership. There was an almost insurmountable trust deficit between the rulers and the ruled. In the face of severe odds, Modi has rehabilitated our idealism. Indians en masse have now become enthused with the possibility of our country rising to new heights. Now the government means business. For the first time, both ministers and bureaucrats seem to be accountable not just to their superiors but also to the people whom they are supposed to serve.

Modi has led from the front by calling himself India's *'pradhan sevak'* or servant-in-chief. Also, for the first time in decades, the government did not seem to represent or favour a particular section of society. NaMo nationalism, thus, is the chant of the mantra of unity, not division.

Modi has also spoken out, even though infrequently, against excesses of Hindutvavadis[15], including self-proclaimed cow vigilantes. He thus also shows the much-needed corrective to hyper-nationalism. A charge may be levelled that the whole thrust of this national upswing is Hindu.

This must be acknowledged; it is Hindus at large, who are fired by the zeal to unite and reassert themselves in the world. Like Indian, 'Hindu' too is no longer a term of shame or abuse. Today, those who poke fun at Hindu symbols, Hindu ideas and Hindu identity find themselves not only on the back foot, but outflanked by vast numbers of detractors and critics the world over.

The self-hating Hindu has gone out of fashion. In the process, some of his admirers have gone to the extent of calling Modi the *yuga purush*, the epochal man. Modi may well be the yuga purush—or he may not. But in his second term, he is certainly changing India in lasting and significant ways. This is the most important thing to bear in mind when trying to understand the phenomenon that is Modi.

Herein lies the sense and salience of 'NaMo' nationalism. It signifies not just the re-sacralization of the nation, but Modi's own special contribution to both the discourse and practise of nationalism. In addition to changing the course of the nation, Modi also wants to stamp his own lasting imprint as the shaper of India's destiny. He is doing so by separating, for most part, the political from the developmental, at times mixing them up astutely. A master political strategist, he is also a determined, driven, even, visionary leader with a cadre of politicians, bureaucrats and helpers fiercely loyal to him.

JNU, as this book shows, could not remain unaffected by this Modi wave that was engulfing the country. It became the very epicentre of the earthquake that shook India to its very

---

[15]Supporters of Hindutva.

foundation. Unfortunately for Modi haters and detractors, it was NaMo nationalism which came out stronger from the rubble.

2
THE ODD MAN OUT: WHY I JOINED JNU

Signs Taken for Wonders

The year was 1999. I almost did not join JNU. For one, I never applied for a job there.

I was an associate professor in the Department of Humanities and Social Sciences (HSS) at the Indian Institute of Technology, Delhi (IIT-D). In early February, I got a call on my direct office landline. It was the then chairperson of Centre for Linguistics and English (CLE) at JNU. I knew him a bit from our earlier meetings at conferences and committees.

He came to the point straightaway: 'Makarand, I was just going through the applications for our professorship in English and I find that you are not an applicant.'

I was a bit taken aback.

'Oh…' I said.

'Yes, you did not apply. Does that mean you're not interested?' There was the slightest note of annoyance tinged with belligerence.

I firmed up too, 'Actually, I was not aware of your advertisement.'

'Oh…' it was his turn to be somewhat taken aback. He recovered quickly, 'You might have missed the ad. It was in the major papers. We put it out in January.' When I said nothing, he added, 'In *Employment News* as well.'

As if anyone read the latter, I thought, but held my peace.

'Well? Are you interested?' he persisted. He couldn't help adding, 'JNU is a great place. You'll have all the freedom in the world.'

I said, 'To be perfectly honest, I am quite happy at IIT. I have a nice house, quite close to the main gate. The students are good—really smart. My colleagues are fine too… We actually have a nice group of like-minded faculty across departments and disciplines interested in alternate models of culture and development…'

He cut in, not too interested, but eager to press his own point. His voice rose a decibel, 'Let me tell you, Makarand, if you stick around in IIT, you'll be making a big mistake. Is there a single famous English professor at an IIT?'

When I said nothing, he repeated, 'Name one! But in JNU, haven't you heard of Meenakshi Mukherjee? Or H.S. Gill? Or, earlier, the Daswanis, both professors?' Actually, I had heard of some of these notables. But at IIT-Delhi, too, we had well-known names in English studies. But I didn't want to get into an argument.

He said, his voice softening, 'Are there any other considerations?'

I paused a bit and said, 'Actually, I've come up for a professorship here too.'

'In that case, why don't we do one thing? You keep an open mind. You don't have to apply. But if we call you for an interview, just drop by.'

I thought that was fair.

'You mean you'll invite me?'

'Yes, we have a provision for that. You just have to send us your CV.'

'That sounds fine,' I said.

'Deal? You drop by one of these days. You can meet our dean too. Come with some of your latest publications. We'll take it from there.'

There was no harm, I thought, in acting on what was such a generous, one might even say flattering, invitation. A few days later, I was at the home of the chairperson. Carrying not only my CV, but a satchel full of my publications. The chairperson looked over my CV smilingly and said, 'Oh you don't have to open that big bag. We know all about you already.'

'You've published so much at such a young age,' he said.

I felt disarmed. 'Thank you,' I mumbled.

Then, the dean, looking at me with a straight face, said, 'But there's just one problem.'

I was quiet.

'Won't you ask what it is?' he now smiled.

'Yes, tell me.'

'Well, you don't drink...' We all started laughing.

'I don't trust people who don't,' he added for good measure.

The fact is that I had politely turned down the proffered glass of whisky. I was a teetotaller. In fact, those days I didn't even drink tea or coffee.

'But we'll make an exception in your case,' said the chairperson, with a smirk on his face.

I practically forgot about this incident. After submitting my CV, it was not for me to follow up. Was the offer serious or one of those somewhat unreliable gestures that we encounter so often? I thought I shouldn't dwell on it. I shouldn't try to make it my business. I had no idea when they would hold the interviews, or if they would really call me to appear before the Selection Committee.

In the meanwhile, I got shortlisted, along with five other colleagues for a professorship at IIT. I felt pretty chuffed. Across the road, in JNU, the interviews were scheduled in March, much earlier than expected. What is more, I was sent a call letter.

I showed up at the vice chancellor's (VC) office at 9.30 a.m. as instructed.

There wasn't a soul in sight. Even the peons, who had just arrived, looked at me somewhat nonplussed. I showed them my call letter and said, 'I thought interviews for the professorship in

English are scheduled for today.'

'Yes, yes,' the VC's secretary stepped in, looking a bit apologetic, 'Please do take a seat, Sir.'

I was ushered into a largish and empty antechamber. Though I was the first one there, I wasn't miffed. I had plenty to do. I had a pile of papers to grade, what with IIT undergrad classes already touching 150 in those days. A huge increase in numbers after the notification of Other Backward Class (OBC) reservations.

While I was correcting papers, another colleague walked in. She was much senior to me and had actually taught for a day or two at my alma mater, St Stephen's, before moving to Hindu College across the road. I smiled at her. She barely acknowledged me. For some reason, she seemed upset.

Already an associate professor at the JNU Linguistics and English Centre, she was what you'd call an internal candidate. I thought I had no chance. Her publications and academic contributions were considerable. But before I could get up to greet her, she started berating the peon and the VC's secretary!

'You call us so early to waste our time? Why isn't the VC here? You haven't asked me to sit down or offered a cup of tea. This is atrocious. Deplorable!'

'Madam, Madam,' the VC's secretary tried to mollify her, 'The VC is on his way. We will begin soon…'

'Don't lie. Where are the experts? Where's the dean or the Centre chair? There's no one here.'

I continued with my grading, not looking up.

'Listen to me,' she said, her voice rising another couple of notches. She had really lost it. She was almost screaming, 'Show me the interview list. Tell me when you've scheduled my interview. I don't want to waste my time, twiddling my thumbs all day…'

She practically grabbed the piece of paper from the hands of the VC's secretary.

'Ah!' she snorted, 'I'm number eight. Give me a ring when you want me. I'll be in my office.'

The VC's secretary said, almost quaking, 'Madam, please come after lunch. No problem.' Then he added, desperately. 'Come whenever you like. I'm sure VC sahab will interview you at your convenience.'

'Hmmph!' she sniffed, putting up her nose in the air, and dashed out of the room.

Perhaps, I am exaggerating a bit. But, to be honest, this is how I seem to remember it. The other candidates, most of them older than me and quite distinguished, also gradually streamed in. There was some whispering among them too. One, whom I knew from Hyderabad, told the VC's secretary that he had no interest in appearing for the interview, but only wanted to collect his TA/DA (travelling and daily allowance). He exited after filling out some forms.

I was the third to be called in. My interview went well. I was grilled for over an hour. I recognized some of the members of the committee. The visitor's nominee was from Osmania University. He knew me from my days at the University of Hyderabad.

Another member had kindly invited me a couple of years back to a lecture at his university on Indian aesthetics. He had read my previous work and had been well-disposed towards me for long.

The VC, too, asked me a couple of questions. He was a biotechnologist. He asked me where's I'd done my PhD. When I mentioned the University of Illinois at Urbana-Champaign, he was suitably impressed.

'A very good school,' he said. He asked me if I knew a famous life scientist of Indian origin there. I mentioned the name and said I did. He was satisfied. After a while, he left, perhaps for lunch, showing up only towards the end of the interview. By then, I was reasonably content too. I thought I had acquitted myself well.

A couple of months later, I received a positive response from the JNU. To be honest, I wasn't entirely surprised. It was a proper appointment letter for the post of professor of English. It was the same position that a former colleague of mine at the University of Hyderabad, Meenakshi Mukherjee, had occupied. I felt very gratified. It was as if the hand of destiny was beckoning to me.

Many years ago, Professor Mukherjee, then a faculty member at Lady Shri Ram College, had happened to grade the Delhi University BA (Hons.) first-year fiction paper. She was so impressed with the answer of one student, to whom she gave record-breaking marks, that she made an effort to track him down.

I happened to be him. It was also a pleasant coincidence that both her daughters were studying in St Stephen's College, the elder one being my batchmate, though in another discipline. Several years later, when I joined the University of Hyderabad after my PhD, I found myself in the same department as Professor Mukherjee. She soon moved to JNU as a professor for the last stint of her career, retiring from there.

It was a great honour for me to be offered the position that she had vacated. But there was much talk about my appointment offer. It had created a sensation all over India in English Studies circles. I had been selected over the internal candidate. In addition, several others had also been, allegedly, bypassed.

Later, I gathered that the internal candidate wasn't on the best of terms with the then chair of the Centre even though both were avowed Leftists. In fact, the former's husband, a college senior, had also been a candidate. He wasn't selected either, though he had applied from the US.

The chairperson, apparently, didn't want a wife and husband combo at the Centre. It was another matter that his wife was already in the same Centre. I would learn later, the hard way, how much the Indian higher education system was led not so much by movers and shakers but run by fixers and manipulators and, in the worse cases, prey to those who resembled outright thugs.

The dean, a Right-wing professor, the one who had said my only disqualification was that I did not drink, was of the same view as the chairperson when it came to the most suitable candidate.

The internal politics of the Centre was something I had no idea of at that time. I only knew that I had given a really good interview and had been appointed.

Later, piecing together the evidence, it seemed that the most remarkable set of circumstances had conspired to bring me to JNU. A Left-Right punch, well-coordinated between the chairperson of the Centre and the dean of the school had, it would seem, swung things in my favour. The VC had put his stamp on what had been so well planned, ably executed and finally presented to him on a platter.

There was a lot of heartburn in the opposing camp. Naturally. I was not just the youngest of the candidates, but also somewhat of an overnight 'star'. One thing that my jealous detractors failed to mention was that I was also the best-published of all the applicants. Also puzzling to them was the fact that I had not joined JNU as soon as I got my appointment letter.

The two gentlemen who had worked so hard to bring me to JNU were actually apprehensive. What if I turned down the appointment? It would be even more astonishing than being offered it. Also, it would mean a great loss of prestige to them that could turn into a political setback. They were very keen that I join.

IIT-Delhi: A Reluctant Exit

When I got the much sought-after offer, however, I mulled over it for a good six months. One reason was that the IIT professorship was still under process. My inclination was to continue in IIT if I was made a professor. JNU was an unknown, not entirely appealing, prospect.

Suddenly, matters took an unexpected turn. Out of the five associate professors shortlisted for the professorship, three were 'un-shortlisted'. This was done perfunctorily, not by colleagues in the HSS Department, but by a new committee headed by a Chemistry professor. I was one of the 'un-shortlisted'. In the

IIT system, despite its several strengths, such authoritarian or arbitrary moves are not impossible even if not frequent—especially when it came to HSS, which was often perceived as a service department. An IIT director might have hesitated to do this with an engineering faculty selection.

I sought an appointment with the deputy director of Faculty Affairs. He looked over my obviously impressive CV. Then he mumbled something about my not having externally funded projects.

'But who in the discipline of English Studies, or for that matter in HSS, has projects?'

Neither of the two shortlisted colleagues had significant projects to speak of. The whole shortlisting process had been somewhat clumsily manipulated, it seemed, because the director only wanted to promote two people, the ones they had already shortlisted. Senior colleagues asked me not to be disheartened. My turn would come, they had said, in a couple of years. That was the IIT way.

In the meanwhile, I had a job I had not even applied for—professor of English at JNU, India's best university. But there was one other thing. I had a nice duplex flat at IIT, but no housing was offered at JNU.

I met the dean at JNU, the one who had encouraged me to apply. He was non-committal when it came to housing. I can't promise anything, he said frankly. We have transit accommodation but it may not suit you.

I checked it out. It was a small studio apartment. I didn't mind it. We were a small, three-member family. My wife said, 'Nothing doing. It's like going back to graduate school.' I was in a fix. After the shortlisting and un-shortlisting fiasco, I had felt unappreciated at IIT-D. Here at JNU, there was a full professorship on offer, but no accommodation.

Then, there came another twist in the tale. My guru, to whom I had conveyed all the developments, said in his own inimitable style, 'My Father says there is no need for Makarand Paranjape to leave IIT.'

Now my dilemma magnified manifold. I had to obey my guru! Do whatever he asked of me. On the other hand, would that be right? Shouldn't I use my own reason, however flawed, to come to a decision that I felt was best under the circumstances?

What was I to do?

Of course, I had to obey my guru. But, in the end, I did not.

It was not as if I had all the information or knowledge needed to make the right decision. I accepted my limited capacities, acknowledged my fallibility, weighed my options and thought that going to JNU was the better option of the two.

Having come to such a conclusion, I had the choice to take responsibility or go with what my guru had advised me. My faith wasn't strong enough to jump when the guru said so or stay put as per his command. At the same time, I knew that faking such faith, when I didn't actually have it, would be being false to myself and to my guru.

I felt alone. I had no help from anyone. My wife didn't want to get into the issue fully. She left it to me to take a call. In fact, she advised me to complain to the chairman of the IIT-D board against the 'un-shortlisting'. That was a bad idea because the institute issued me a memo for doing so. Complaining in the Indian system rarely gets one far; it only serves as nuisance value.

It seemed as if a bigger force was driving me towards JNU. I decided to be true to my own imperfections, to accept rather than evade responsibility. I took the plunge. In a sense, the un-shortlisting and what had followed had also pushed me to it.

Though no disciplinary action was taken against me, I felt cornered at IIT-D. They did not let me keep my house during the period that I was on lien with JNU. My bridges were burnt. There was no turning back.

After a year on probation, I was confirmed at JNU, my services transferred from IIT.

For years afterwards, I felt guilty for not obeying my guru. The whole issue still troubles me when I think of it. Newer insights and implications emerge when I reconsider what had transpired. But one thing is clear. A wrong turn does not mean the end of one's material or spiritual progress. It is, rather, an even more challenging learning opportunity. The universe operates on the principle of endless possibilities, not lost chances and punishments.

When I moved to JNU, I found that I wasn't being treated very well. It was as if after the appointment, I was left to my own devices. I wasn't even given a decent office, one befitting a professor. What was shown to me was windowless and tiny. Even half of my books wouldn't fit in.

The chairperson had also changed, no longer the person who had invited me to JNU. When I appealed to the new chair for a better office, he showed me his own room. 'Sit here till I am chairperson. I don't need two offices.' Though that was a considerate, even considerable, gesture on his part, I obviously declined.

The former dean was now the rector or pro-VC. He said, 'What does it matter where you sit? When we started teaching, we had no offices.' He was, of course, right in his own way. At the 'Golden Threshold', originally Sarojini Naidu's home, I too had begun practically office-less as a young lecturer at the University of Hyderabad.

But now times were different. Not just because I was a full professor, but because I had no university accommodation. We had moved to my in-laws' two-bedroom flat in Saket. There was no place there for a proper study. I needed a decent office space at JNU to do my work and store hundreds of my books.

It was almost as if there was no place for me at JNU. I had to give up at the very outset or strive to make my own place. I decided on the latter course of action.

Almost in desperation, I asked our office attendant,

Karamchand ji, if there was no other room in the entire building. He was not only the oldest employee of the Centre, but a never-say-die optimist. Truly, a one-of-a-kind character. He smiled at me and said, '*Kyon nahin, Sir. Kuch na kuch to ho hi jayega* [Why not, sir. Something or the other will surely be done].'

I explored the whole School of Languages building with him. All the good rooms were occupied. Finally, on the second floor, we came across a strangely shaped, triangular, corner space, with protrusion added to a normal room. It doubled as the switch room-cum-furniture dump. There were pictures of pin-up girls on the walls. The karamcharis smoked beedis there, over tea and gossip.

I was told that it could not be used as a faculty office because of the fire hazard that the huge array of electrical switches posed. Literally half of the building's current passed through that room. Fat, black cables snaked up the side wall, through a gaping hole in the floor, up to the ceiling, on to the floors above through another rough-hewn opening.

Somehow, I got the dean, a professor of Russian, to permit me to occupy it. 'I will be very careful, Sir. In fact, my being in that room will be the best protection against any risk to the rest of the building.' Another room right below, technically with my Centre, was allotted to the staff as their lunchtime lounge.

I removed the posters. Along with them, the plaster came off too. Rodents shimmied up the bulky power lines, sometimes poking their heads uncertainly through the opening in the floor, and then swiftly scampering up.

I asked the maintenance department to seal the holes and paint my room. They were very reluctant. It was winter time. The contract labourers had gone home. I had no furniture once the broken pieces of 'condemned' chairs and tables were removed. That turned out to be a bit of a blessing because we had lots of stuff from our IIT duplex flat that I could now shift here.

Then another mini miracle ensued. The commandant of

a large army brigade in Meerut wanted me to lecture to his regiment on Sri Aurobindo. I declined. I said I was in the midst of moving from IIT to JNU. One of his juniors, a dynamic major, got onto my case: 'Sir, we don't take "no" for an answer in the Indian Army.'

I had nothing to say. I threw up my hands. I told him it was not a good time. I was moving from IIT to JNU and had to shift all my stuff on my own.

He said, 'But you are not helpless, Sir. The army is with you.'

On a foggy December morning, when I couldn't even see 10 paces ahead, I found myself following a small army truck in my dinky Maruti. The vehicle ahead was full of my stuff—books, furniture, rugs, even a fridge. I furnished my office myself.

JNU had nothing to give me when I joined. Everyone was tardy or uncooperative. But I had four jawans on my side. They shifted my stuff in no time. What is more, they even got my room cleaned and whitewashed. The transition was both swift and painless. There were very few people around because of the winter break. But the karamcharis who were present were suitably impressed. They thought I was a very well-connected, very important person. In India, that is what matters.

Come summer, I put in my own air conditioner in the large window behind my desk. I got it as a gift for helping a wealthy techie write a book. I installed it with the dean's permission, of course. Now many more have air conditioners in my building. Then only the Dean and I had one.

When I moved in, I found that all the phone connections went through another box in my office. It felt ridiculously funny to have so much 'power'—to be able to switch off the phones and electricity of half my colleagues in the building.

A few years later, after some struggle and good luck, I managed to have the huge electrical switch boxes shifted out. But the phone connections still remain—even if my own landline phone fails to work ever so often.

JNU had embraced me. I realized it was a space full of possibilities. Even if you were in a minority of one.

I loved my office. It is one of the best and oddest faculty rooms on campus.

The Strange Politics of Planet JNU

Joining JNU was just crossing the road, literally. But it proved to be so much more, as time would reveal.

The back gate of IIT opens on the Vedanta Desika Mandir Marg, just after Ber Sarai. This same street, after the traffic light, becomes Aruna Asaf Ali Marg. Almost a symbolic transformation from the Right to the Left? That's where the JNU East or 'VC' gate is.

It is easy to drift from one campus to the other. But hardly anyone does. They seem to be two different worlds.

I did wander across once, in the company of a friend from the English Department in Chandigarh.

Sitting on a rock by Ganga Dhaba, he said, 'Makarand, you'd do well here in JNU, instead of teaching uninterested, would-be engineers at IIT. Here you'll be appreciated. You'll have a following.'

I wasn't so sure. I looked at the surroundings—shabby and ill-kept in comparison to the neat and trim IIT campus. Cleanliness is a bourgeois value, a JNU-ite snorted contemptuously.

I never thought that I would actually make the move from IIT to JNU. I have already narrated how that happened.

Then, rather unexpectedly, JNU offered me the much-coveted professorship in English.

The Leftists were shocked, dismayed. They had to do something. So, as usual, they protested.

Hiranmay Karlekar, a well-known journalist, then a member of the JNU Court, actually tried to stymie the appointment. The JNU Court is the highest body of the university. In its annual meeting, after I had joined, he asked how I had been appointed over so many other worthy (presumably Leftist) applicants.

Then VC, Asis Datta, shut him up by saying that the Selection Committee had unanimously recommended my appointment. The EC had ratified the selection, along with others. I had already joined. The appointment was both legal and incontrovertible. There was nothing more to be done.

That was my first taste of Leftist 'intolerance'.

I was in for more surprises. JNU was dominated by a futile and deluded, not to mention negative and destructive, Leftist student politics, shielded and protected by powerful faculty lobbies. The world may have changed, but JNU was caught in a time warp.

Students stayed on for decades, teachers took on more PhD students than they could handle. Some of them had over 20 enrolled under them. The joke was that one of these unfortunates was unable to meet his supervisor for two years, so he began stalking the professor, waiting outside his door or in the corridors.

Finally, one day the professor asked, 'Yes? What do you want?' The student, crestfallen, said, 'Sir… I am one of your PhD students.' The teacher, taken by surprise, apologized and gave the student the much-desired appointment. Apparently, the teacher had so many research scholars that he didn't even remember their names, let alone recognize them.

I don't know what happened to this particular student. Presumably, he was taken care of and graduated. Others, such as Rajini, whom I talk about later, were not so fortunate.

JNU tuition fee, I was astounded to learn, was then something like ₹20 a month. The hostel charges even less. Yearly tuition and room rent less than a thousand rupees. Some years ago, a well-known and well-off comrade was known to brag that he got through JNU on less than the cost of a packet of Dunhill's.

Bang next to us was Vasant Vihar, one of the poshest Delhi colonies. In fact, right opposite, in the haphazard and unauthorized Munirka shanties, a room in one of the precarious, slanting towers was ₹7,000 per month. Seven times what it cost to live in JNU for a whole year.

But what did the practically zero fees or hostel rents matter? If the students studied and learned to be the best in India, if not the world, it would all be worth it. I would even support free education to all those who made it through our selection process. Yet, instead of a culture of excellence and competence, the prevailing ethic appeared to be partisanship and parasitism.

Our indoctrinated students hated the bourgeois state. They made a virtue of freeloading off it. For them, it was a prelude, if not to revolution, at least to cushy civil service jobs. Exploit the State and use its resources to fight it. Then become a part of it yourself. Or of some other state-supported sector such a customs, excise, banking, teaching and so on.

Everything was political. Or politicized. Anti-government activists thriving at the government's expense. This was what JNU socialism seemed to boil down to. I was reminded of W.B. Yeats's words, 'The best lack all conviction, while the worst/ Are full of passionate intensity.'

Everywhere, on every bare wall, a poster war. With slogans frozen in time, reminiscent of the 1960s and 1970s. Supporting lost causes and failed hopes. Every now and then, there would be a protest march. This meant gathering near the Ganga or Sabarmati hostel lawns and then marching to the 'Pink Palace,' shouting slogans. Pink Palace was the derisive appellation for the administration building.

Was this all that revolution boiled down to? Campus marches from hostels to the administration building, shouting anti-this-or-that slogans? Endless hostel socials? Living cheaply, sharing rooms with any number of 'guests'? And, of course, bunking classes? Attendance being purely optional.

If the rhetoric needed to be ratcheted up, malcontents would gather at 11.00 a.m. for more action. Most having stayed up nights, anything earlier was anathema. Then they would go about disrupting classes and blockading buildings. If you had a lecture at 9.00 a.m., you might escape this outrage. But at that early hour, you wouldn't have more than three or four students, often day scholars. The hostel-dwellers couldn't be bothered.

There was also, I discovered, a season and schedule for such disruptions. It occurred at least twice a year, in the middle of each semester, strategically around Holi or Durga Puja. The Bengalis (Bongs) went home during the latter, the Biharis during the former. Half the semester was invariably wiped out in holidays and demonstrations.

The Biharis and the Bengalis were easily the largest regional groups. Most of the latter were Leftist, a good number of the former, Right-wing. It was all about class. The well-heeled, English-speaking bourgeoisie were usually Left-leaning. The aspiring lower-middle-class, Hindi-speakers formed the support base of the Akhil Bharatiya Vidyarthi Parishad (ABVP), a youth group of the RSS.

Ever since its inception in 1971, Leftist students had totally dominated the JNUSU. Some 22 JNUSU presidents have come from the Students' Federation of India (SFI), an affiliate of the Communist Party of India-Marxist (CPI[M]). For a while, the JNU SFI broke away from its parent organization, which, in turn, expelled the members of the breakaway unit. That included a former union president whom I had taught.

The All India Students' Association (AISA) candidates have won the JNUSU presidency 11 times. The AISA is the student wing of the Communist Party of India (Marxist-Leninist) Liberation or CPIML. This is the 1973 faction of the Communist Party of India (Marxist-Leninist). The latter was formed in 1969 by the All India Coordination Committee of Communist Revolutionaries (AICCCR), led by Kanu Sanyal and considered by many to be the forerunners of the Naxalite movement.[16]

---

[16] Roy, Saugata. 'Top Naxal Leader Kanu Sanyal Found Dead in His House', *The Times of India*, 23 March 2010, https://timesofindia.indiatimes.com/india/top-naxal-leader-kanu-sanyal-found-dead-in-his-house/articleshow/5715411.cms. Accessed on 8 December 2021.

Kanhaiya Kumar, JNUSU president in the critical year of 2016, belonged to yet another Leftist group, the All India Students' Federation (AISF). This is the student wing of the oldest of our Left parties, the Communist Party of India (CPI), founded way back in 1925, during the last decades of the Raj.

Other groups like the Democratic Students' Federation (DSF), an SFI splinter, were even more radical.

The National Students' Union of India (NSUI), promoted with the blessings of Prime Minister Indira Gandhi in 1971, was affiliated to the Congress. No NSUI candidate has become a JNUSU president. Its arch-rival, the ABVP, has fared scarcely better. Sandeep Mahapatra, who became president the year after I joined JNU, is the sole exception. He had a clean image, was personable and well-spoken. Not like other cadres who are derisively dismissed by the Leftists as 'lumpen'. He is a Supreme Court lawyer today, with a low political profile.

What, then, of the romance of Leftist politics? Doesn't it still haunt our intelligentsia, besides garnering international sympathy and support for JNU Leftists? Captured so tellingly in director Sudhir Mishra's *Hazaaron Khwaishein Aisi* (2005), wasn't there indeed something idealistic and attractive about those who wanted to work for social change?

However, in JNU there was little of that romance when I joined. Old timers may boast of the days of D.P. Tripathi, Sitaram Yechury or Jairus Banaji. Of freethinkers like Nirmala Sitharaman or politically engaged toppers like S. Jaishankar and Abhijit Banerjee. All that is now but faded glory. Except for the sly eroticism of ill-dressed comrades at late-night meetings, marches, slogan-shouting and poster-pasting, there is nothing remotely romantic in the JNU Left.

Why this decline? Why the prevalent cynicism and stupidity instead of meaningful and engaged political activism? The reason is simple—a decline in thinking, studying or taking issues seriously.

Many JNU Leftists haven't even read Marx, let alone Engels, Lenin, Trotsky or Mao. If you mention Bukharin or Plekhanov, they blink as if they have been caught on the wrong foot. As to critics of communism, from Koestler to Solzhenitsyn, Polanyi to Dikötter, these names have never been heard of. In all my years at JNU I never once found a Leftist student read or discuss, let alone bother to engage with a classic exposé such as *The Black Book of Communism—Crimes, Terror, Repression*.[17] There was absolutely no talk of the atrocities and enormities of this ideology. Even on a campus where students were supposed to be actively engaged in reading and studying.

I realized with a shock that no one believed in Marxism. It was mostly posturing, if not pure hogwash. The Left, then, was mostly confusion or careerism masquerading as the politics of demand-making and disruption. Skipping classes, occupying buildings, 'gheraoing' officials, sometimes even teachers, bringing the university to a standstill—these were their stock-in-trade. Later, most of the Leftist leaders become lecturers in Delhi University (DU) colleges.

Matters came to a head in 2016, after the rally in support of Afzal Guru. Masked outsiders made their first appearance on campus.[18] 'Tukde tukde' and 'azadi' slogans were chanted. Mattresses were spread across 'Freedom Square', as the administration building

---

[17]Edited by Stéphane Courtois and authored by Karel Bartošek, Joachim Gauck, Jean-Louis Margolin, Ehrhart Neubert, Andrzej Paczkowski, Jean-Louis Panné and Nicolas Werth, it was originally published in French as *Le Livre Noir du Communisme: Crimes, Terreur, Répression* in 1997. The English translation was published by Harvard University Press in 1999. The book provides an extensive documentation of repression, genocide, extrajudicial execution, deportation and killings in labour camps, artificially created famines and so on. Some of these practices, as also severe human rights violations, continue in the few remaining communist states in the world.

[18]Who these 'outsiders' were, is still not definite. The ones that I saw with my own eyes certainly did not look like JNU-ites.

came to be rechristened. Students shacked up around the Pink Palace. The intent was plain and simple—to create a nationwide student movement against the Modi sarkar.

Even in those days, I was clear about one thing. Left, Right or Centre, we all had to come together on one cause. That was academics. No university in the world could allow students to sabotage studies, prevent peers from taking exams or registering for courses. Why should JNU be an exception?

On 'demands' as flimsy as new water coolers in the school buildings, washing machines in hostels or cheaper cups of tea, agitationists could bring the university to a standstill. Then boast of their achievements if their demands were met. The culture of confrontation and protest made students claim false credit for what were essentially unearned hand-outs from the government. Students of a fully government-funded university were feigning that it was revolutionary to agitate for even more perks and gratuities.

But JNU was already so well-subsidized.

Both tea and coffee, quite terrible to taste, cost lower than anywhere else. Food was cheap and plentiful. Any number of 'guests' could find accommodation on campus. Some even had jobs outside, but lived inexpensively inside JNU. Whatever was not free, ranging from haircuts to ironing clothes, was available at prices half the ordinary. JNU was a world unto itself. Once in, why would anyone want to leave?

Yet, treating the administration as some sort of oppressor, landlord or representative of an illegitimate state, the students' pretence of being in the same class position as the struggling proletariat or peasantry was nothing short of fantastic or ridiculous.

JNU politics, however, was no laughing matter. It was harming thousands, to the point of ruining their futures. Professional mischief-makers learnt very little except politicking. Most were pretty bad, if not hopeless, in their studies. They had no real skills that could fetch them a decent livelihood.

All their lives, they might feed off others, using ideology as their excuse. Were we creating generations of malcontents and whingers? Or worse, parasites?

I realized at once that the media had made a huge mistake in glamourizing the JNU brand of politics. However sympathetic we may be to students' democratic right to express themselves or protest, to turn JNU agitators into heroes was a bad idea. Instead of becoming full-time political activists, students needed to return to their classes. Also, stop preventing others from studying.

It was clear to me that the only way forward during the current stand-off was to keep classes and labs open. The university had to be restored to its primary purpose—which was academics, not politics. But this is not what happened. Instead, JNU was rendered non-functional for months on end. And then, in 2020, the COVID-19 pandemic struck.

But going back to my early days in JNU, soon after I became a member of the faculty, I had figured out what was going on in JNU. I have never had reason to change them. On the contrary, my worst fears about the ill effects of student politics and agitations were proven true in the years to come.

As we shall see in the following chapters.

3
THE JNU ROW: HOW I GOT INVOLVED

India's Intolerance Wars

Way back in 1918–1919, Sri Aurobindo wrote on the 'inevitability of a war of cultures' in his periodical, *Arya*.

The immediate aggravation was the wholesale condemnation of Indian culture by the English drama critic, William Archer. In his book *India and the Future* (1917), Archer called India 'the most forward of the barbarous or the most backward of the civilized nations', arguing that India's barbarism was neither 'desirable nor permanently possible in the modern world.'[19]

Sri Aurobindo wrote a rebuttal in a series of essays, the first of which was provocatively titled 'Is India Civilized?' The title harked back to a book by the same title published by Sir John Woodroffe a few years earlier.[20]

The context, obviously, was India's bid for swaraj or political independence from British rule. The imperialists, on the other hand, wanted to tell the world that we were not yet ready, not 'civilized' enough for self-rule. A hundred years later, we are going through similar skirmishes, though we have been independent

---

[19] Archer, William. *India and the Future*, Alfred A. Knopf, 1917.
[20] Later collected and published as *The Renaissance in India and Other Essays on Indian Culture* (Pondicherry: Sri Aurobindo Ashram, 1997). The phrase referred to above occurs on p. 55.

for nearly 75 years now.

Our culture wars today are not political, but civilizational. Intellectual and cultural swaraj or self-rule is at stake. We have moved on from the fight between the colonizers and colonized, or even the terribly bloody and improvident communal war between Hindus and Muslims that resulted in Partition, to a new kind of civil war largely between Hindus themselves.

What we face today is internal civil strife in our nation and society over what it means to be Indian, or more specifically, Hindu. I have consistently argued that the conflict we are in the midst of has been erroneously characterized as one between intolerance and tolerance. Instead, it is actually between two kinds of intolerance.

Just because Left-wing intolerance has ruled the roost for so long in Indian academic and intellectual circles, it would be a grave mistake to substitute it with Right-wing intolerance. Pushing against one kind of intolerance, should we put in place, or succumb to, another?

The only kind of intolerance that we should accept is the intolerance of intolerance.

That, as Karl Popper reminded us, is the sine qua non of free societies. It has been characterized in the literature as the paradox of tolerance. Popper framed it as an imperative in his famous book, *The Open Society and Its Enemies*: 'We should therefore claim, in the name of tolerance, the right not to tolerate the intolerant.'[21]

Intolerance, whether of the Left, Right or Centre, must be resisted—except the intolerance of intolerance. That, indeed, is what I tried to do when I took a stand against what came subsequently to be labelled as JNU's tukde tukde gang.

---

[21] Popper, Karl. *The Open Society and Its Enemies*, Routledge, 2011.

JNU's Tukde Tukde Gang

On 9 February 2016, a protest was staged in JNU against the capital punishment meted out to Mohammad Afzal Guru.

Guru had received a death sentence after having been convicted of conspiring to attack the Indian parliament in 2001. After all appeals, including a mercy petition to the President of India, had been rejected, he was hanged to death on 9 February 2013. His death anniversary was sought to be commemorated by Kashmiri separatist students and their supporters in various campuses of Indian universities, JNU being at the forefront.

The JNU protest march was led by Umar Khalid and Anirban Bhattacharya, who belonged to a breakaway faction of the ultra-Left, Maoist Democratic Students Union (DSU).[22] Other members of the student community of JNU, chiefly the ABVP, affiliated to the ruling BJP, opposed the protest.

The following day, 10 February, there were more protests and counter-protests, during which several anti-India slogans were raised, some of which were recorded by the national media.

Among these, perhaps the most viciously dangerous and damaging was '*Bharat tere tukde honge, Inshallah, Inshallah* [India you will break into pieces, by the will of Allah, by the will of Allah]'. The president of JNUSU, Kanhaiya Kumar, along with other office-bearers, also got involved, chiefly in support of those protesting against Guru's execution.[23]

On 12 February, Kanhaiya Kumar was arrested by the Delhi

---

[22]'JNU Case: Delhi Police Has Evidence to Nail Umar Khalid, Anirban Bhattacharya, 7 Others', *Zee News*, 1 March 2016, https://zeenews.india.com/delhi/jnu-case-delhi-police-has-evidence-to-nail-umar-khalid-anirban-bhattacharya-7-others_1982316.html. Accessed on 27 August 2021.

[23]'"Bharat Tere Tukde Honge Is Now Their Official Slogan": BJP on Kanhaiya Kumar Joining Congress', *Zee News*, 29 September 2021, https://zeenews.india.com/india/bharat-tere-tukde-honge-is-now-their-official-slogan-bjp-on-kanhaiya-kumar-joining-congress-2398058.html. Accessed on 8 December 2021.

Police on charges of sedition. After 11 days, on 23 February, Umar Khalid and Anirban Bhattacharya, who had gone into hiding, also surrendered to the police. Kumar was released on bail on 2 March 2016 and the other two a couple of weeks after. The case, however, is still not closed.

Following Kumar's release and triumphant return to JNU, the university was turned into a battleground between opposing ideologies, with daily speeches, rallies, protests, gheraos and the picketing of administration buildings and classrooms.

Academic activities came to a total standstill. The JNUTA started a series of lectures in Freedom Square, just outside the picketed administration building, on 'What the Nation Needs to Know'. I was invited to speak on 3 March 2019 in this ongoing series of 'Teach-ins'. My lecture, 'India's Uncivil Wars: Tagore, Gandhi, JNU... and What's "Left" of the Nation', was subsequently revised and published in a widely circulated, 'bestselling' collection, *What the Nation Really Needs to Know: The JNU Nationalism Lectures*. The original lecture, which attracted several thousand views, is still available online.[24]

Freedom of Expression or Treason?

Although I was very much on campus during the eventful days of 9–12 February 2016, as mentioned above, my own involvement in the unfolding fracas was almost accidental and certainly not immediate.

A few days after the fracas and slogan-shouting, I was invited

---

[24]Prof. Makarand Paranjape's Nationalism Lecture at JNU Alternative Classroom, YouTube, https://www.youtube.com/watch?v=tBAuVr36b1A. Accessed on 27 August 2021; Its transcripts are also available online on various portals, including Scroll. '"Did You Check Your Facts?": Makarand Paranjape Has Some Questions for Kanhaiya, Leftists and JNU', *Scroll.in*, 8 March 2018, https://*scroll*.in/article/804802/did-you-check-your-facts-makarand-paranjape-has-some-questions-for-kanhaiya-leftists-and-jnu. Accessed on 27 August 2021.

as a speaker to the Sahitya Akademi's annual festival of letters on 'Gandhi, Nehru, Ambedkar: Continuities and Discontinuities'. I was to be in the morning panel of 19 February 2016 with one of India's leading writers—Kannada novelist, S.L. Bhyrappa. The third panellist was a noted Hindi critic and academic, Sudhish Pachauri. Our topic was 'Freedom of Expression' or *'Abhivyakti ki Svatantrata'*. Pachauri spoke of *Jantantra Mein Lekhak aur Lekhak ka Jantantra* (the writer in a democracy and the democracy of the writer). He said that while there are various levels and kinds of freedom, each writer needed to find a way to be free of the shackles of state or society.

My presentation was titled 'India's Intolerance Wars'. I began by asking, 'Is tolerance the opposite of intolerance or is it only a mask of intolerance?' If you don't like what someone is saying, you can call them intolerant to shame them or shut them up. In today's India, it would seem that only one kind of tolerance is tolerated; everything other than that is branded as bigotry. But who is the real bigot? The one who believes that only one side is correct? Or the one who wants many views to have a freedom of expression? Yet, it is the latter, the pluralist, who is being policed by what we might term the 'single-view tolerants'. We are right, they insist; everyone else is intolerant. It would seem that those who speak in the name of tolerance are today the most intolerant.

Bhyrappa himself was targeted for daring to express a point of view that was different from that of the literary and critical establishment. He was also the victim of horrible intolerance in Karnataka. Instead of shouting slogans or being part of a political agitation, however, he chose to write the novel, *Aavarana*, to document how fake histories and ideologically driven cultural controllers were hoodwinking society.[25] Bhyrappa has shown us how writers should fight intolerance, with the weapons they know

---

[25] S.L. Bhyrappa and Sandeep Balakrishna. *Aavarana: The Veil*, Rupa Publications; 1st edition, 2014.

best and have at their command. Their own words, which they can deploy creatively in literary and critical works.

In my talk, I now turned to JNU, which was very much in the news. I mentioned how its 'uncivil war' was being reported in a one-sided manner, with an important fact not highlighted. The form requesting permission to hold the programme on 9 February 2016 did not mention that it was to commemorate Mohammad Afzal Guru and Maqbool Bhat.

Thus, approval was sought and obtained on false pretexts.

The posters also advertised it as a 'cultural evening' though the small print gave away its true intentions. The event's title, 'A Country without a Post Office', was taken from the poem of the Late Agha Shahid Ali, a poet of Kashmiri origin, who had moved to the US. I knew Shahid and was thus sad at the distortion of his work. As Souradeep Roy observes in his sensitive reflection on the issue:

> [T]he trouble with turning a poet into a spokesperson for any cause is that it is bound to be restrictive in its very attempt. The assertion of his Kashmiri identity is a negation, or at least a muted silencing of other identities. It is true that Agha Shahid Ali is a Kashmiri poet, but there are several other Agha Shahid Alis.[26]

I felt similarly. What had his poetry to do with the absurdly illogical and casteist label, 'Brahmanical "Collective Conscience"' against which the organizers had called for a struggle? The fissiparous appeal of the poster was, however, absolutely clear in its call for solidarity with the 'struggle of the Kashmiri people for their democratic right to self-determination'. Predictably, there was no mention of how the Kashmiri Hindus, mostly Brahmins, were driven out of the state. Weren't they Kashmiris too?

---

[26] Roy, Souradeep. 'Agha Shahid Ali: The Mastermind behind the Country without a Post Office ', *Wande Magazine*, 20 February 2018, http://www.wandemag.com/agha-shahid-ali-mastermind-post-office/. Accessed on 22 September 2021.

When the small print betrayed the intentions of the organizers, including the protest against the 'judicial killings' of Guru and Bhat, permission was denied by the authorities. Carrying out the real purpose of the so-called cultural programme, Umar Khalid and his associates took out their rally in any case.[27]

As opposed to this deliberately flagrant provocation, I said that we needed a new politics. A politics of harmony and unity, not of divisiveness and antagonism. But for that, the one-sided 'tolerants', who were really the 'intolerants', had to be defeated. That was the work of sahitya, in its truest sense, that which benefited and uplifted all. That was the work of literature, aesthetics and spiritual renewal—jodna, not todna.

---

[27] PTI. 'Afzal Guru Event: Anti-India Slogans at JNU Campus; "Disciplinary" Enquiry Ordered', *The Indian Express*, 10 February 2016, https://indianexpress.com/article/india/india-news-india/afzal-guru-event-anti-india-slogan-at-jnu-campus-disciplinary-enquiry-ordered/. Accessed on 22 September 2021.

Partition had been India's bloodiest civil war in recent times. Now we had civil strife over who or what was a Hindu. JNU's turf war was also a part of India's 'uncivil' war. We were not up in arms or at each other's throats, but the public space had been decisively divided into two camps. What we needed, definitely in JNU, was the poetics of de-politicization.

We had two options in our 'uncivil' war—one, to heal, join and unite—or the other, to fight to the finish. Wasn't the former way better than the latter? Contests among fellow citizens of one nation needed to be resolved through dialogue and debate, not a war of words or shouting match. Poems were better than slogans when it came to resolving differences. That is why we needed hermeneutics of generosity, not of suspicion. But politics is 'easy', while academics and art are difficult. That is why it is as if we are battling phantoms. Who would stand and speak for truth in these troubled times? Nothing short of a new satyagraha[28] is demanded of us.

On the one hand, real people were dying: Narendra Achyut Dabholkar, Govind Pansare, Malleshappa Madivalappa Kalburgi and Gauri Lankesh, as well as RSS workers like P.V. Sujith (in Kerala). Why wasn't anyone mentioning the latter? Why were our intellectuals so one-sided? It is their intolerance masquerading as tolerance or liberalism that has made this uncivil war a battle for the soul of India.

Afzal Guru Event Held under False Pretext

Later that evening, the Press Trust of India (PTI) carried a report of our session.[29] It left out most of what other speakers or I

---

[28]Translated as 'insistence on truth' or 'soul force,' satyagraha denotes a determined but nonviolent resistance to evil. It was deployed on a mass scale against British colonialism by Mahatma Gandhi during India's freedom struggle.
[29]PTI. 'JNU Row: Afzal Guru Event Held under False Pretext, Says Professor',

had said, but highlighted just one thing. The headline said it all: 'JNU Row: Afzal Guru Event Held under False Pretext, Says Professor.' It quoted me as stating, 'It was done on a false pretext. People who wanted to hold that event said they would conduct a poetry reading and that there would be seven people. It was called "A Country without a Post Office". Instead it became a commemoration for Afzal Guru. So it was done on a false pretext.'

The report went on to say, 'Paranjape was critical of the lack of action against the organizers on the part of the university over the use of such "subterfuge" and expressed surprise at the condemnation of the arrest of JNU Students' Union President Kanhaiya Kumar.' What I had actually highlighted was the one-sided coverage of what had happened in JNU. While Kumar's arrest had been condemned, the rally held without proper permission, the slogan-shouting and separatism of one small group of students had hardly been mentioned, let alone criticized. Wasn't this an example of the one-sidedness of our public culture?

PTI quoted me as further stating:

> I am a member of JNUTA. No resolution was passed condemning that misuse, that subterfuge which was used....
> I don't want to wash dirty linen in public but many people and their families were displaced and driven out of their homes in Kashmir. There were no protests in JNU when that happened. But to commemorate Afzal Guru there were protests.
>
> Whether you accept capital punishment or not is a different issue. You are using the ideas of democracy and dissent to justify the commemoration of those who want to destroy the Indian democracy. So are we trying to say that when we do not 'tolerate' the commemoration, the

---

Hindustan Times, 19 February 2016, https://www.hindustantimes.com/india/jnu-row-afzal-guru-event-held-under-false-pretext-says-professor/story-B6sMeFcKqDkh08LGmHWi3H.html. Accessed on 27 August 2021.

deification of a person such as Afzal Guru, we are being intolerant?[30]

The report continued by mentioning how I wanted students to study, not just do politics:

> Paranjape asserted that it was important for the students at JNU, which is considered an institution of 'national integration', to study and not do politics or they will be 'neither here nor there'. 'I tell my students, "have you come to JNU to do politics or to study because in the end you will be neither here nor there. The cadres will be picked up and patronised but what about the majority of you from the middle and lower middle class who have to earn a living?"' He claimed that most students spend four to five years in the university but don't attend classes because 'attendance is not compulsory', and by the time the course ends they 'are incompetent to face the world because they don't have any skills.'[31]

It is this report of the PTI that got me implicated in the JNU controversy. Colleagues and students started accusing me of betraying JNU and its much-vaunted 'democratic spirit'. I was subjected to a barrage of invectives, tirades and diatribes, many in the form of 'open letters'.

There was, however, a lighter side to the 'Country without a Post Office' poster. The vice president of India, M. Venkaiah Naidu, then minister for Housing and Urban Affairs, was prompted to ask in Parliament, 'Is India without a post office?' He said, 'The entire world is looking towards India under the great leadership of Shri Narendra Modiji today. The world wants to invest in India.'[32] Obviously, the title of the poem that was appropriated

---

[30]Ibid.
[31]Ibid.
[32]Zargar, Safwat. 'Within India, There's a "Country without a Post Office" and It

in the poster was not meant to be taken literally.

That, however, was precisely what Kanumuri Manikanta Karthik, a Hyderabad-based engineer and Right to Information (RTI) activist, did. He filed an RTI application asking if it was indeed true that Kashmir did not have a single post office. To that he added other questions, 'First, what percentage of Kashmir is covered by the postal department? Second, how many post offices are there in Kashmir?'

Karthik was innocent of Shahid's poem. Seeing the poster on the Internet, as a patriot, he wondered 'if the protesting students were trying to misguide others into believing that Kashmir was backward enough to not have a single post office.' What is even more noteworthy is that he received a quick revert from J.R. Angural, the assistant director of Postal Services, Jammu and Kashmir: 'Postal facilities are provided in every nook and corner of Kashmir Valley... A total of 1,699 post offices function in the J-K Circle, of which 705 post offices function in Kashmir Valley.'[33] Though he received a prompt response, Karthik was 'mercilessly trolled' for his RTI application.

Guru's and Bhat's Hangings—Why Separatism Could Not Be Taken Lightly

The outbreak over the protest march against Afzal Guru and Maqbool Bhat's hangings had happened on 9 February. My intervention in the matter came a good 10 days after, on 19 February, at the Sahitya Akademi's annual Festival of Letters. But

---

Is Now Being Debated in Parliament', *ScoopWhoop*, 26 February 2016, https://www.scoopwhoop.com/The-Country-Without-A-Post-Office-A-Poem-Only-JNU-Got-Right/. Accessed on 27 August 2021.
[33]Saha, Abhishek. 'Twitter Laughs Out Loud as JNU Row Inspires RTI Application', *Hindustan Times*, 21 February 2016, https://www.hindustantimes.com/india/twitter-laughs-out-loud-as-jnu-row-inspires-rti-application/story-QCg25h7xO5o0VxIazl5mFN.html. Accessed on 27 August 2021.

in the intervening period, JNU had changed irrevocably.

On 13 February, JNUSU President Kanhaiya Kumar was arrested on charges of sedition. Five days later, on 18 February, just a day before my talk, he was produced before the magistrate at the Patiala House District Courts. Regrettably, there was an altercation between those who supported him and others who opposed him. Some lawyers, joining the melee, actually beat him up, right there on the premises of the court.[34]

Frankly, at that time, I was not following these events as they unfolded daily. At the Sahitya Akademi conference, I had merely wanted to point to the one-sided reporting and the selective outrage over the JNU incidents. I was trying, so to speak, to right the narrative because I felt it was so slanted in favour of the Left.

In addition, I was keen that the truth come out, in all its complexity and nuances. How well planned the separatist assault on the Indian state in the guise of free speech and dissent had been. Such events had been planned and executed all over India year after year since Guru's hanging on 9 February 2013.[35]

Guru had been tried and convicted for his involvement in the 13 December 2001 terrorist attack on the Indian parliament. In that attack, five professional killers of the Pakistani Jihadi outfit, Jaish-e-Mohammed (JeM), had stormed into the premises of the Indian parliament complex in cars with fake Home Ministry labels.

---

[34]'Kanhaiya Wet His Pants While We Beat Him Up in Police Custody, Say Lawyers Behind Patiala House Assault', *India Today*, 22 February 2016, https://www.indiatoday.in/india/story/exclusive-kanhaiya-wet-his-pants-while-we-beat-him-up-in-police-custody-say-lawyers-behind-patiala-house-assault-310008-2016-02-22. Accessed on 27 August 2021.

[35]'Afzal Guru: Kashmir Anger over Hanging', *BBC News*, 11 February 2013, https://www.bbc.com/news/world-asia-india-21406874. Accessed on 27 August 2021; PTI. 'Afzal Guru Hanging: AMU Students Bring out Protest March', *First Post*, 11 February 2013, https://www.firstpost.com/india/afzal-guru-hanging-amu-students-bring-out-protest-march-620880.html. Accessed on 27 August 2021.

They had crashed into the vice president's parked car and thereupon started firing indiscriminately with automatic weapons. The area was quickly cordoned off by Indian security personnel. No Member of Parliament died, but eight cops and one gardener were killed in the shoot-out. All five of the terrorists were gunned down. A horrified nation watched much of the action live on television.

A special cell of the Delhi Police fast-tracked the investigation. Four suspects, Guru, his cousin Shaukat Hussain Guru, the latter's wife, Afsan and Arabic lecturer at Delhi's Zakir Husain College, S.A.R. Geelani, were arrested. The evidence included cell phone records, the car used in the attack, exchange of money between them and the killed terrorists, and so on. The accused were tried under the Prevention of Terrorism Act (PoTA) for waging war against the State, conspiracy, murder and attempt to murder.

Guru confessed to his involvement, but later retracted. The trial went on for over six months. Some 80 witnesses were examined. The court ordered capital punishment to Guru, Shaukat and Geelani. Afsan, Shaukat's wife, was sentenced to five years for concealing the plot. In their appeal in the High Court, senior celebrity lawyers, Shanti Bhushan and Colin Gonsalves, represented the accused. Afsan was spared capital punishment on 29 October 2003.

Guru, Shaukat and Geelani appealed to the Supreme Court. Nearly two years later, on 4 August 2005, the Supreme Court acquitted Geelani and reduced Shaukat's sentence to 10 years imprisonment.

But Guru's conviction was upheld. He filed a review petition, which was dismissed on 22 September 2005. His wife, Tabassum, then submitted a mercy petition on 3 October 2005 to the then president of India, A.P.J. Abdul Kalam. He also filed a plea with the Supreme Court to review his death sentence. That petition was dismissed on 12 January 2007.

In the meanwhile, the case had attracted national and

international attention. Several human rights groups, prominent intellectuals, Valley as well as mainstream politicians tried to pressurize the government into commuting Guru's death sentence. His co-conspirator and cousin, Shaukat, was released from Tihar jail on 30 December 2010 for good conduct.

On 10 December 2012, the then home minister Sushil Kumar Shinde said in Parliament that he would personally look into the file. Next year, on 3 February 2013, the then president of India, Pranab Mukherjee, rejected Tabassum's long pending mercy petition. Guru was finally hanged on 9 February 2013, a good 12 years after the attack on India's parliament.[36]

Nine years earlier, Maqbool Bhat, the founder of the terrorist group National Liberation Front of Kashmir, had been hanged on 11 February 1984. Charged and convicted in the hijacking of an Indian Airlines flight in 1971, he too had taken every possible judicial recourse, including a mercy petition to the then president of India, Zail Singh. On 3 February 1984, an Indian diplomat, Ravindra Mhatre, was kidnapped in Birmingham. The kidnappers demanded Bhat's release in exchange for releasing Mhatre. But Mhatre was murdered. Bhat's clemency petition was thereafter rejected and he was hanged.[37]

The two hangings had occurred in February, albeit nearly three decades apart. Both Bhat and Guru had waged war against India; both were Kashmiri separatists. Those who sought to make heroes or, worse, martyrs of them, were clearly mistaken if not downright treacherous. While they accused the Indian state of

---

[36]Anand, Utkarsh. 'The Legal Journey of Afzal Guru', *The Indian Express*, 10 February 2013, http://archive.indianexpress.com/news/the-legal- journey-of-afzal-guru/1072029/0. Accessed on 27 August 2021.

[37]Bobb, Dilip. 'Brutal Killing of Indian Diplomat Ravindra Mhatre Resurrects Kashmir Issue Once Again', *India Today*, 29 February 1984, https://www.indiatoday.in/magazine/cover-story/story/19840229-brutal-killing- of-indian-diplomat-ravindra-mhatre-resurrects-kashmir-issue-once-again-802840-1984-02-29. Accessed on 27 August 2021.

'judicial murder', these protesters said nothing of the brazen murders and killings that terrorists such as Guru and Bhat had carried out or supported.

What, moreover, was the logic of raising the issue of justice from a state whose sovereignty itself some of the protesters did not recognize? How or why did they seek justice from that very state that they were working to overthrow or undermine? Whether the trial of Guru had been entirely just or not was a question of complicated legal niceties, not a clear case of 'judicial murder' as it was being projected.

That our top universities were hosts to anti-state 'separatist cells', which turned enemies of the state into heroes, was certainly not a healthy practice in my view. Such groups were reportedly functional in several Indian universities, supported by Leftist student organizations and intellectuals. They were ideologically bolstered by famous writers and public intellectuals, such as Arundhati Roy, who shamed India in the foreign media.[38]

Many ill-informed students, who wished to be 'cool' in an anti-establishment way, backed these protests against the death sentencing of Guru and Bhat. As a responsible teacher at JNU, I thought it was my duty to make them better aware of the facts and circumstances of the case.

Our Kashmiri student leaders never protested against the genocide and forced eviction of Kashmiri Pandits out of the Valley, but only berated the 'Brahmanical' Indian state for its atrocities against the Kashmiris. The ethnic cleansing of the Hindus in the state was never mentioned; it was assumed that Kashmiris meant Muslims and the State was branded as Hindu and communal.

---

[38]Roy, Arundhati. 'India's Shame,' *The Guardian*, 15 December 2006, https://www.theguardian.com/world/2006/dec/15/india.kashmir. Accessed on 27 August 2021; Parvin Swamy's rebuttal of Roy's 'cherry picking' polemics is worth reading: 'The Vanity of 13/12 "Truth-Telling"', *Hindustan Times*, 11 February 2013, https://www.thehindu.com/opinion/op-ed/the-vanity-of-1312-truthtelling/article4400821.ece. Accessed on 27 August 2021.

This, in turn, revealed how communal, even Islamist these so-called protesters themselves were. In JNU, the Leftist student organizations supported them and their anti-India cause.

What about the Jammu-ites, a majority of whom were Hindus, or the Ladakhis, who were predominantly Buddhist? To ask such questions in JNU was to invite the wrath of the dominant student and teacher bodies. I shall speak later of how critics and dissenters were silenced or sidelined.

What Was Different Now?

Year after year, protests and commemorations of 'such enemies of India' were not uncommon in JNU. This included annual marches and morchas against the hangings of Guru and Bhat.

What was different this year?

For one, the government at the Centre had changed in 2014. A new prime minister, Narendra Modi, heading a BJP-led National Democratic Alliance (NDA) was at the helm of affairs. In JNU, too, we had a new VC, M. Jagadesh Kumar, who had assumed office in January 2016.

While the earlier VCs had looked the other way, tolerating such campaigns as examples of free speech, the JNU administration was now much more vigilant. The ABVP cadres were also more active and vociferous on campus. They would not take insults to 'Bharat Mata' lying down.

The JNU campus was like a tinderbox. Only a spark was needed to set off a conflagration. The incendiary slogans and the student clashes that ensued provided that provocation.

But at that time, no one—least of all I—had expected how big the flare-up would be. When I spoke at the Sahiyta Akademi against selective reporting and one-sided portrayals of the events at JNU, I didn't imagine that I would soon be in the vortex of the storm myself.

Indeed, I didn't even expect to be invited to speak in the

lecture series on nationalism, which JNUTA had started just two days earlier, on 17 February. I was planning simply to go back, after the Sahitya Akademi panel, to my writing and reading since there was precious little by way of teaching that was going on.

I was, as the subsequent chapters show, sadly mistaken. What awaited me in the coming weeks was an unprecedented period of turbulence and conflict. JNU was indeed the backdrop, but the struggle was for the meaning of India itself.

4
TAGORE, GANDHI, JNU... AND WHAT'S 'LEFT' OF THE NATION

JNU's 'Teach-In'

After the unauthorized rally memorializing and protesting against the hangings of Afzal Guru and Maqbool Bhat on 9 February 2016, JNU was thrown into turmoil. There were clashes between student groups. Anti-India slogans were shouted on campus.[39] Kanhaiya was arrested on 12 February 2016, charged with sedition under Section 124A and criminal conspiracy under Section 12B of the Indian Penal Code.[40]

---

[39]There were several reports on these incidents, including the fact-finding committee appointed by the JNU administration the day after to probe into what had happened. See, for instance, news reports with PTI inputs, 'JNU Orders Probe into Afzal Guru Event', *The Tribune*, 11 February 2016, https://www.tribuneindia.com/news/archive/nation/jnu-orders-probe-into-event-on-afzal-guru-194807. Accessed on 27 August 2021; Rai, Siddharth. 'JNU Students Clash over Event against Afzal Guru Hanging', *India Today*, 10 February 2016, https://www.indiatoday.in/mail-today/story/jnu-students-clash-over-event-against-afzal-guru-hanging-307958-2016-02-10. Accessed on 27 August 2021; and 'JNU Row: Provocative Slogans Were Shouted by Outsiders, Says University's Probe Panel', *ZEE News*, 16 March 2016, https://zeenews.india.com/news/india/jnu-row-provocative-slogans-were-shouted-by-outsiders-says-universitys-probe-panel_1866104.html. Accessed on 27 August 2021.

[40]Shankar, Aranya. 'JNU Student Leader Held On "Sedition" Charges Over Afzal Guru Event', *The Indian Express*, 13 February 2016, https://indianexpress.com/article/india/india-news-india/afzal-guru-film-screening-jnu-student-leader-held-for-sedition/. Accessed on 27 August 2021.

Following Kumar's arrest, five students who had led the 9 February protest march—Umar Khalid, Anirban Bhattacharya, Rama Naga, Anant Prakash and Ashutosh Kumar—disappeared.[41] Or, to put it differently: they fled and could not be traced. All of them belonged to a breakaway faction of an extremist Left-wing group.[42]

After 10 days in hiding, Khalid and Bhattacharya surrendered to the police, while the others said they would make themselves available to be questioned if needed.

Huge demonstrations broke out on campus. Two days after Kumar's arrest, on 14 February, student groups demanded a shutdown of the university. Classes were suspended. The administration building was blockaded and sealed off. Students occupied the space around it, even spending nights there. The whole area was rechristened 'Freedom Square'.[43]

Decorated with festoons, posters and letters of support and solidarity from around the world, it became the rallying site

---

[41]PTI. 'I Have Got to Know Things About Myself Which I Never Knew: Umar Khalid', *The New Indian Express*, 22 February 2016, https://www.newindianexpress.com/nation/2016/feb/22/I-Have-Got-to-Know-Things-About-Myself-Which-I-Never-Knew-Umar-Khalid-895603.html. Accessed 22 September 2021.

[42]They broke away from the Democratic Students' Union (DSU), one of the constituents of the All India Revolutionary Students Federation (AIRSF), which is a front of the Communist Party of India (Maoist). This party believes in the armed overthrow of India's elected government through 'people's war'. Founded on 21 September 2004, it came into being when the Communist Party of India (Marxist–Leninist), People's War (People's War Group) and the Maoist Communist Centre of India (MCCI) merged. The party has been declared illegal by the Government of India under the Unlawful Activities (Prevention) Act (UAPA).

[43]It took the university authorities more than six months to clear the area. Agha, Eram. 'JNU Fences Freedom Square, V-C Says to Solve Parking Woes', News18, 12 December 2016, https://www.news18.com/news/india/jnu-fences-freedom-square-v-c-says-to-solve-parking-woes-1322191.html. Accessed on 27 August 2021.

for anti-administration and anti-government protests. Leading opposition politicians including Rahul Gandhi of the Congress and Sitaram Yechury of the CPI(M) addressed rallies.

On 14 February, when Kumar was produced at the Patiala House Court for his hearing, clashes broke out between his supporters and opponents. Among the latter were lawyers, who participated in the scuffle, attacking Kumar.[44] It was a few days after this incident, on 17 February that JNUTA started what they termed a 'Teach-in' at Freedom Square. The lecture series, focussing on nationalism, was titled 'What the Nation Really Needs to Know'.

Initially planned as a week-long activity, the lectures went on for a whole month, ending on 17 March. In all, some 24 lectures were delivered in the series. The speakers included a galaxy of eminent professors, scholars, academics and activists including Gopal Guru, Lawrence Liang, Achin Vanaik, Jairus Banaji, Tanika Sarkar, Ranabir Chakravarti, Romila Thapar, Harbans Mukhia, Ari Sitas, Mridula Mukherjee, G. Arunima, A. Mangai, B.S. Butola, Anand Kumar, Nivedita Menon, Badri Narayan, Satyajit Rath, Satish Deshpande, Ayesha Kidwai and Suvir Kaul.

The open-air and open-to-all speeches began at 5.00 p.m. and went on for a couple of hours. Not only JNU students and faculty, but several other spectators and listeners, often from distant places and out of Delhi universities, also attended. The audience numbered as high as 4,000, with several hundred people standing around a makeshift stage beside the administration building stairs. Soon, the series began to be watched all over India and abroad through live streaming and YouTube posts.

---

[44] "JNU Row: Rowdy Lawyers Beat Up Kanhaiya Kumar, Journalists in Police Presence', *The Economic Times*, 18 February 2016, https://economictimes.indiatimes.com/news/politics-and-nation/jnu-row-rowdy-lawyers-beat-up-kanhaiya-kumar-journalists-in-police-presence/articleshow/51028524.cms. Accessed 27 August 2021.

Later, a collection of these lectures came out as a book, *What the Nation Really Needs to Know: The JNU Nationalism Lectures*. As the editorial collective observe:

> Soon after 9 February 2016, the country was turned into a choric chamber in which the accusation of 'anti-nationalism' was repeatedly echoed, a pejorative attribute which attached itself to the whole JNU community. It produced great political and intellectual disquiet among the JNU community of students and teachers. But an extraordinarily creative repertoire of protests—talks, music, theatre, artwork, photographs, cartoons—organized by the JNUSU, swiftly followed. They transformed the grand steps and adjoining spaces in front of JNU's Administrative Block into a 'Freedom Square'. The JNUTA's decision to stand with the cause of democratic thinking and justice added to the energetic creativity that was already on display.[45]

I, too, as it happened, came to be invited to give a lecture in the ongoing series.

In the meanwhile, Kumar was bailed out. He returned to JNU to a hero's welcome after spending 18 days in jail. The crowds went delirious. Azadi slogans were chanted aplenty.

How I Made the Cut

The JNUTA collective organizing the sit-ins invited me to deliver a lecture in the series. Exactly how this happened remains a bit of a mystery. But it seems that an interested observer contacted one of the members of the collective to ask why was it that all the talks were so one-sided, almost uniformly anti-state, anti-administration and pro-protest. Weren't there other voices in

---

[45] Azad, Rohit, et al. *What the Nation Really Needs to Know: The JNU Nationalism Lectures*, HarperCollins, 2017, pp. xx–xxi.

JNU? The organizers responded with, 'Such as?' The interested observer asked, 'What about Makarand Paranjape?' Perhaps, this was the inception of an idea, which then took root.

But there's no way to tell why or how they chose me.

It so happened that most of the speakers were historians.[46] From the School of Language, Literature and Culture Studies, the only invitee was the Leftist JNUTA leader and linguist, Ayesha Kidwai. Did they think that I would be a manageable, if not mild, second choice? I also had a considerable record in publishing and scholarship, besides having written extensively on nationalism. Anyhow, one day I got a call from Mallarika Sinha Roy, the then assistant professor, Women's Studies. She was invariably polite and professional, extending all the courtesies of a proper invitation to me. I was persuaded to say yes, even though I anticipated that I would face a hostile audience.

I felt anxious for days. Especially with date and programme changes. I was finally slotted for 3 March 2016. By then, several

---

[46]Some JNU historians had earned considerable disrepute in the Ram Janmabhoomi-Babri Masjid imbroglio. As eminent archaeologist K.K. Muhammed said in his autobiography, *Njanenna Bharatheeyan* (I, an Indian), Leftist historians, many of them from JNU, misled the Allahabad High Court by claiming there was no evidence of a Hindu temple beneath the demolished mosque ('Left Historians Prevented Resolution of Babri Masjid Dispute, Says K.K. Mohammed, Former ASI Regional Head,' *FirstPost*, 21 January 2016, https://www.firstpost.com/india/left-historians-connived-with-extremists-mislead-muslims-on-babri-issue-says-archaeologist-in-new-book-2592188.html. Accessed on 25 August 2021). The landmark September 2010 judgment overturned this. During the testimony, several Leftist historians were exposed as unreliable ('Babri Demolition: How HC Verdict Discredited "Eminent" Historians', *FirstPost*, 6 December 2012, https://www.firstpost.com/india/babri-demolition-how-hc-verdict-discredited-eminent-historians-547549.html. Accessed on 25 August 2021). Subsequent judgments, including the most recent one of October 2019 by the Supreme Court, acknowledged that there were, indeed, Hindu temples and monuments upon whose ruins or remnants the Babri Masjid was erected. Of course, all JNU professors, let alone historians, cannot be dismissed because of the misdeeds of some.

lectures had already taken place and my own talk was pushed back and rescheduled a couple of times. Some of the topics I wanted to touch on had already been covered. But I tried to gather my thoughts and decided to focus on Tagore and Gandhi.

Finally, the day on which I was to speak arrived. I remember it clearly. I was waiting in my office, going over my notes. Just before I was to speak, a sympathetic student messaged, 'Things don't look too good here, Sir. You should be careful.' The time to walk from my office to the administrative building was less than five minutes. That's all I had by way of forewarning. Of course, I could not back down, pretend to be ill or run away.

As I walked to 'Freedom Square', I felt it in the pit of my stomach, the dull sense of being set up. Of walking into a trap. But now it was too late to turn back. When I reached, I saw that the students were holding some sort of event of their own, with Kumar in the lead. I asked Janaki Nair, former professor of History and the master of ceremonies, what was going on. She said, 'It seems this will be a joint JNUSU-JNUTA event.'

'How is that possible?' I asked, 'I thought the whole "Teach-in" series was a JNUTA activity.' She smiled and said, 'But today the two streams have merged.' I looked around. A huge crowd had already gathered. More people were streaming in.

Thereupon, Kumar took the mike and said, '*Hum aap ke lecture ko chair karenge* [I shall chair your lecture].' They had another speaker that day, in addition to me. She was present, seated by my side, the famous politician-activist from Chhattisgarh, Soni Suri.

I said, 'Let her speak, I withdraw.' Kumar said, 'No, no; everyone is eager to listen to you. You are the scheduled speaker. I will conduct the session.' He had no business chairing my lecture, but I didn't want to argue with him. I made up my mind to go ahead, for better or worse.

So, that's how I got embroiled in the turmoil. What follows is the most comprehensive version of my talk, the fifteenth nationalism lecture that I was invited to deliver on 3 March 2016 by the JNUTA. It incorporates parts of the printed text published in the JNUTA book, *What the Nation Needs to Know*, edited by Rohit Azad, Janaki Nair, Mohinder Singh and Mallarika Sinha Roy (HarperCollins, 2017), combined with my notes for the talk, and what I actually spoke. I have retained the flavour of an oral presentation but rewritten and augmented some portions for the sake of clarity.

Ideas Rather than Ideologies: JNU's 'Alternative' Performative

Friends,

Even as we gather for another lecture in our nationalism series, I am quite aware that our university is under siege. Classes have been suspended, buildings barricaded and the administration shut down. Under these circumstances, I stand in solidarity with the JNU community. Like most of you, I too am against state repression and interference in the workings of universities.

But the events of the last few days are indeed matters of grave concern. Should our university be hijacked by a political agenda that is so markedly anti-government? Should it become a platform for the kind of separatist sloganeering and activism that we have witnessed? We may or may not agree with the government arresting our students on charges as serious as sedition and criminal activity. But, regardless of our political beliefs, shouldn't academics be restored to its rightful priority on our campus? These are the questions that confront us today when we talk of nationalism.

JNU is a special place. On this I am sure we agree, but have we considered why? We are known for our vibrant political culture. Some would say it's too vibrant. But what makes us special also is that JNU is a place of imaginative possibilities. Look at the creativity around you—all the buntings, banners, posters, festoons, the singing, dancing, clapping, jeering and cheering. Our response to the current challenge is not merely political and propagandist, but also creative. That is why this platform is as important as political sloganeering, the staging of ideas as important as the theatrics of JNU politics. Here, in Freedom Square, we have the opportunity of highlighting our creativity and conceptual robustness.

I have learned a lot from the previous speakers. You too, I hope, have found them instructive, in addition to inspiring. That is why I wish to thank all our students for attending these talks. Attendance, as we all know, is not compulsory in JNU, but it's heartening that so many have shown up for this 'Teach-in' and have made it such a success.

2

As you know, I am a student and teacher of literature. To me, one of the crucial issues in knowledge production is how we interpret texts. Texts, of course, include words, speeches, statements, as well as religious, political, literary artefacts and all kinds of narratives.

When I travel about the country, I am often asked to defend JNU or held answerable for JNU's brand of politics. I tell those who hate JNU, why do you look only at what the press says, what pamphlets or posters proclaim or the rhetoric and counter-rhetoric bandied about?

Why don't you come to JNU, feel the energy, the body language, the music, the song and dance of our brand of campus activism—how we mobilize, congregate, rally and protest.

In other words, look not just at the enunciative but at the performative dimension of JNU culture. Then you'll see its vibrancy and creativity. It is this that we are also defending, this inspiration, this originality, this vibrancy. Not just the battle between one political ideology or the other.

Of course, it is another matter that often the slogans and the propaganda are sorely lacking in intellectual rigour or content. Or that the dominant, I should dare say hegemonic, Left is totally one-sided, quite intolerant of divergent views, let alone criticism.

But this is not a new charge. The most effective spokesman of this position was a remarkable socialist, some may say Trotskyist intellectual, Jairus Banaji. I dare say you may have the fortune to hear him speak in this very series soon. I am told that an invitation has been sent to him. In 1972–1973, Banaji mounted an intellectual, rather than political, challenge to a person who was possibly JNU's most celebrated political figure, Prakash Karat. Karat lost the 1973 JNU elections to Anand Kumar, who contested as a 'free thinker'. Some would attribute Karat's defeat to the critiques levelled against the SFI and the organized, 'Stalinist' Left by Banaji.

More recently, there was one more moment, which I have myself witnessed, that challenged the hegemonic Left in JNU. It was the remarkable rise of a group called 'Students for Equality', but as it happened, this movement fizzled out rather precipitously.

My point is simple. JNU ought to be known for a healthy diversity of opinions, for true debate and dissent. Not for undemocratic Left-supremacy. The latter will only give an excuse for the world to dub us all as 'Urban Naxals'.

This brings me to my first point.

JNU should be known for ideas, not just ideology. We should be known for an alternative performative, not just the theatre of the absurd that is current politics. We should be recognized for our creativity, not just for our culture of agitation. We should be known for national integration, which is enjoined upon us in the JNU Act, not just for our so-called 'anti-nationalism'.

This is my plea to you.

What JNU Really Needs to Know

When I heard the title of the lecture series, I was somewhat concerned. 'What the Nation Really Needs to Know'. *Really*? It implied that *we* really know, that we have the answers. We would, therefore, tell the nation what *it* really needs to know. The nation would take its lessons from *us*.

Doesn't this smack of a certain kind of intellectual superiority and arrogance? Instead, perhaps, we need to listen to the nation too and what it is trying to tell us. Could we not invert the topic to ask, what JNU really needs to know? What the nation really wants us to know?

We love to libel and pillory those who disagree with us, but when we are branded as 'anti-national', we don't feel good, do we? It is another matter that today some of us have come to wear that label as the red badge of courage (to invoke the title of a famous American novel by Hart Crane). But shouldn't we ask why have matters come to this pass? Why do people misunderstand us and what we stand for? Or, are we, in some ways, responsible for our terrible image in the country today? Why is it that even somewhat sensible people have turned against us?

As Aditya Nigam, a Leftist scholar and thinker, who, writing against the CPM's lapses and excesses in Bengal, remarked, 'You do not ask what ordinary mortals might. You do not ask, "did we do something wrong?"'[47] Similarly, we need to ask ourselves difficult questions. Because our protests have become successful, attracting international attention, isn't there an air of smugness, even complacency, about us?

---

[47]Nigam, Aditya. 'But Prabhat Patnaik Is an Honourable Man', *Kafila*, 13 December 2007, https://kafila.online/2007/12/13/but-prabhat-patnaik-is-an-honourable-man/. Accessed on 27 August 2021:

> We had assumed that given the political history of Stalinist Marxism, with intellectuals who were maligned, denigrated, humiliated and finally put before the firing squad, Patnaik had made his 'existential choice' a la Georg Lukacs. Lukacs, one of the most brilliant philosophical minds, decided to remain in the ranks (the 'camp of the people', in Patnaik's words) and become the voice of Stalinism for decades thereafter. Need we recall the whole list of such people—intellectuals—who were thus repeatedly destroyed? And do we need to tell you that so far only fascism or Nazism has been able to compete with the communist record.

Some even claim that we are making history. Just because Noam Chomsky sent a message in support of the student agitation? I hope a bit of self-interrogation is not out of place in today's JNU. I hope that it is okay to be self-critical too, not just self-congratulatory.

Some days back, I was touched to find a fellow JNUite carrying a placard on a bicycle: 'I am not an anti-national'. I hope the one who questions or critiques the dominant view in JNU is not forced to carry a placard saying, 'I am not anti-JNU'.

Intermedial Hermeneutics

'Today, we feel encircled by hostility—much of it in fact generated by our own ineptitude and actions.' How true this statement rings today. It was made in *Indian Science and Technology in the Eighteenth Century* by the famous Gandhian and independent scholar, Dharampal.[48]

Following his lead, I would not presume either to tell the nation what it really needs to know or JNU what the nation is trying to tell it. I will steer between these two roles, responsibilities or positions. Instead, my endeavour will be to intermediate between them so that they can talk and listen to each other. That, I think, is the need of the hour when faced with two seemingly opposite, even incommensurable, loci of enunciation. When we find ourselves in such dire straits, we are compelled, as it were, to evolve a hermeneutics of mediality. That is what we need today, especially those of us who wish neither to be ultra-left nor ultra-right.

What is the hermeneutics of mediality? 'Medium', 'medial', 'median' go back to very old Indo-European roots from whence also spring common Indian words like 'madhyam'. Those interested in classical Indian thought will immediately see the connection

---

[48]Dharampal, *Collected Writings*, Vol. 1, Other India Press, 2000, p. 11.

with the Mahayana Buddhist school, *madhyamaka* (मध्यमक).

It is a rather powerful tradition, with hundreds of years of continuity and development, from the famous master Nagarjuna (third century, 250 CE), to our own contemporary, the Dalai Lama, who is perhaps its most famous living exponent. Shouldn't we learn from such traditions to mediate between polarities? That is the kind of hermeneutics we need for mediation—call it an intermedial hermeneutics, if you will.

We must recognize the imperative to stand between, stand under or understand the two opposite poles of the ideological spectrum, its bipolar ends as it were, so as to negotiate our course between them. We must see how the two sides can speak to one another without one necessarily defeating the other. What ensues then is dialogic rather than dialectic.

To begin with, then, our project will be intermedial. But if it is truly to succeed, it must also be remedial. Being in good health (*svasthya*) means abiding in our self-state or our natural state of well-being (*svastha*).[49] Returning to a healthy state, likewise, is predicated upon restoring equilibrium, which, of course, can be very difficult to do in these times. That is why I want to propose intermedial hermeneutics as the need of the times. A hermeneutics of remedially, of generosity. Not of antagonism and hostility.

I derive my inspiration for such a methodology from the Portuguese social scientist and thinker, Boaventura de Sousa Santos. Santos proposes diatopical hermeneutics as a way of compassionate detachment from settled and reductive ideological positions.[50] Diatopical hermeneutics calls for 'placing oneself

---

[49] Which, in a slightly modified form—*swasdee*—is a common Thai greeting.

[50] The phrase 'diatopical hermeneutics' actually derives from the work of the Indo-Catalan theologist, Raimundo Panikkar (see http://www.raimon-panikkar.org/english/gloss-diatopic.html). The two Santos essays that I am referring to are: 'Public Sphere and Epistemologies of the South', *Africa Development*, Vol. 37, No. 1, 2012, pp. 43–67, and 'Toward a Multicultural Conception of Human

simultaneously inside and outside what one critiques, and thus making possible ... the doubly transgressive sociology of absences and emergences...'[51] In today's charged and contentious environment, however, it is much easier to relate to reductive formulations.

On the battlefield, you already know who the enemy is. You are ready to pit yourself against them. But when we are conducting a different kind of discourse—academic, rigorous and intellectual, rather than polemical—we must open our minds to both sides. Rather than being purely polemical or obtusely oppositional in a depleted and scaled down manner.

As Santos puts it:

> Diatopical hermeneutics is based on the idea that the *topoi* of an individual culture, no matter how strong they may be, are as incomplete as the culture itself. Such incompleteness is not visible from inside the culture itself.... The objective of diatopical hermeneutics is, therefore, not to achieve completeness—that being an unachievable goal—but, on the contrary, to raise the consciousness of reciprocal incompleteness to its possible maximum by engaging in the dialogue, as it were, with one foot in one culture and the other in another. Herein lies its *diatopical* character.[52]

According to this view, no topos, no ideology is complete in itself. It is only when we accept that there are some difficulties, problems, absences, misunderstandings and factual errors in our own position that we can engage in this kind of diatopical

---

Rights', *Moral Imperialism: A Critical Anthology*, edited by Berta Hernández-Truyol, New York University Press, 2002, pp. 39–60.

[51]de Sousa Santos, Boaventura. 'Public Sphere and Epistemologies of the South', *Africa Development*, Vol. 37, No. 1, 2012, pp. 43–67.

[52]de Sousa Santos, Boaventura. 'Toward a Multicultural Conception of Human Rights', *Moral Imperialism: A Critical Anthology*, edited by Berta Hernández-Truyol, New York University Press, 2002, pp. 39–60.

understanding or dialogue. You may call this an epistemology of dispassionate compassion rather than the 'epistemicide' that passes in the name of ideology.

According to Santos, diatopical hermeneutics demands 'placing oneself simultaneously inside and outside what one critiques, and thus making possible ... the doubly transgressive sociology of absences and emergences'.[53] I prefer 'intermedial' to diatopical because the latter implies *two*. Thus, it takes us back to negotiating binaries. To me, intermediality can negotiate not just two, but multiple positions or points of reference. It is, thus, more rebust and beneficial, especially in a complex culture such as India.

Intermedial hermeneutics is nothing less than a new satyagraha. Though it is a way of reading texts, it actually calls for a combination of dispassion and compassion. It is a new satyagraha, too, in that it can pave the way for sahitya, the common good, and the welfare of all, sarvodaya.

This new satyagraha—what would it entail? A politics that is both intermedial and remedial. It is intermedial because it helps us to consult, parley, palaver, moderate, conciliate and settle difference. In restoring us to health and well-being, it also becomes remedial at its best.

Shall we give it, this satyagraha of intermediality, a try?

Tagore, Gandhi, JNU ... and What's 'Left' of the Nation

Let me now come straight to my topic—Tagore, Gandhi, JNU... and What's 'Left' of the Nation.

Tagore, Gandhi, JNU—that's fairly straightforward. At least seemingly so. It is a sequence of words, of proper nouns, suggesting progression, connection, even causality.

But then what of the ellipsis afterwards, followed by the second

---

[53]Ibid.

half of the topic, 'and What's "Left" of the Nation'?

So, it's a little bit more complicated than it may look at first.

On one side of the nationalism debate we have Tagore and Gandhi. Both have been universally recognized as key figures in the making of modern India. On the other side, we have what's *left* of the nation. What does that mean? Left, here, is obviously a pun. It refers, first of all, to the Left as an ideology. But also to what remains of the nation. The implication is that by the time the Left is done with the nation, there would be very little left of it. Why do we say this? Because the Left doesn't, ostensibly, believe in the nation. Certainly, not of the Indian nation.

They think, at least some of them do, that India is a multinational country, which may as well become many nations. That way the revolution would be easier to provoke. A weak state suits those who want to overthrow it. Whether these be Kashmiri separatists or Maoists. As it happens, a weak, truncated, or internally divided India also suits our enemies. Even some of our so-called friends, who would like to exploit the growing Indian market for their own profits.

So I hope the broader implications of my title are clear at the outset.

But to return to the Left, there's very little left of the Left itself. They've lost ground everywhere. Their ideas of history and, also of economics, don't work. There is, of course, China, the behemoth and hyperpower. But it is not communist in the traditional sense. Only political power vests firmly in the hands of the Chinese Communist Party (CCP). But they are very much a part of global capitalism. In fact, they wish to present themselves as an alternate system to democracy.

But we'll come to that later.

Back to the title of my talk, 'Tagore, Gandhi, JNU... and What's "Left" of the Nation.'

Bang in the middle of both sides of the debate is JNU. Why? Because what's going on here is at the very heart of the current contestation over the idea of India. One might as well ask if JNU's protests are allowed to run rampant, what will remain of the nation, of the idea of India?

In this regard I am reminded of a witticism attributed to John (also known as Jack) Gallagher, professor of Imperial History first at Oxford, then at Cambridge: 'Revolutions devour their children, nationalism eats its parents.'[54] You know, of course, that the source of the first part of the quotation is Jacques Mallet du Pan's remark, 'like Saturn, the Revolution devours its children', on the French Revolution.

In today's altered state it seems as if revolutionaries are eating their parents and nationalists eating their children! On the one hand, nationalists are attacking the very universities in which their children are studying in independent India. On the other hand, these truant offspring, the so-called revolutionaries, are eating their nationalist parents. It is somewhat of a reversal of Gallagher's quip, but quite expected in norm-defying India, whose nationalism is as unusual as its post-nationalism.

If, however, we are not cannibalistically inclined in either direction, where do we stand? If we are neither ultra-nationalists nor self-styled revolutionaries, naturally, we might feel distressed to find our entire lives, including our academic pursuits, not to speak of this campus itself, being held hostage, being hijacked, by a small minority of agitators whose positions we do not share even if we respect their right to voice them.

What is lost is precisely the nation that our forefathers and mothers, from Ram Mohan Roy to Mahatma Gandhi, strove so hard to build. Indeed, the sort of 'anti-nationalism' that has been

---

[54] Cited as the epigraph of John Garrard, 'The Challenge of Glasnost: Ogonek's Handling of Russian Antisemitism', *The Journal of Nationalism and Ethnicity*, Vol. 19, No. 2, 1991. Jacques Mallet du Pan's remark originally appeared as 'A l'exemple de Saturne, la révolution dévore ses enfants' in his widely circulated 1793 essay, 'Considérations sur la nature de la Révolution de France, et sur les causes qui en prolongent la durée'.

championed in JNU would also go against the 'Hindutva' idea of India as a religio-cultural entity.[55]

It is the imagining of this India that I tried to convey in my book, *Making India*.[56] It is this India that we stand to lose, that needs so sorely to be recuperated. Very little of this idea of India is left after we're done demolishing the notion of the nation.

Tagore's 'No-Nation'

In keeping with such a line of thinking, the challenge of intermediality is arriving at non-reductive understandings not just of Rabindranath Tagore and M.K. Gandhi, but of issues such as nation and nationalism. What I try to do in *Making India*, consequently, is trace the genealogy of that middle ground we are trying to retrieve today, the middle ground that made India as we know it possible.

Starting with Tagore, we may understand him better as an *alter*-nationalist than *anti*-nationalist. The latter characterization is an overdone simplification, based on a reductive misinterpretation of his complex ideas and the contexts in which they were circulated. We might need to coin new phraseology such as 'no-nation-ism' (after E.P. Thompson's 'Introduction' to *Nationalism*),[57] or 'vernacular' nationalism or alter-nationalism as the more apt way to describe the poet's views. If Tagore's refusal to yield easy conclusions on nationalism is our opening caveat, then our own reluctance to engage with his limitations may also detract from

---

[55]Though I later mention one of its chief proponents, V.D. Savarkar, this trajectory of Indian nationalism would require a detailed, separate treatment.

[56]Paranjape, Makarand R. *Making India: Colonialism, National Culture, and the Afterlife of Indian English Authority*, Springer, 2013; An Indian edition was published by Amaryllis in 2015. There is another idea of the nation, as a religio-cultural body, which I am not engaging with here.

[57]Thompson, E.P. 'Introduction', *Nationalism* by Rabindranath Tagore, Macmillan, 1991, pp. 1–17.

a richer engagement with his lifeworld.

When we do not wrestle with such towering personalities as Tagore or Gandhi at their limits, we risk repetition or homage, both of which obstruct the dharma of scholarship. How can we forget that through his long and ferociously fecund career, as also through the variety of creative genres and media that he practised and mastered, Tagore grew, expanded and changed with time? This evolution of views, if not merely choronological or teleological, is still progressive in its unfolding and self-fashioning.

Let us, thus, look a bit closer at Tagore's idea of nationalism by focussing on two moments in his very complex life and creative career. These two moments, though part of a space-time continuum, are also intermedial in that one represents the poet as an idealist, if not ideologue, while the other as a creative artist and novelist.

Let us start with the former, though it comes later in time. During Tagore's trip abroad in midsummer 1916 when, at 55 and in the middle of the Great War, he gave a series of lectures on nationalism in Japan and then in the US. Soon after, these were published as a book with the same title by Macmillan, London, in 1917. In these lectures, Tagore takes an unequivocal stand against nationalism: 'Nationalism is a great menace. It is the particular thing which for years has been at the bottom of India's troubles'.[58] The poet contends that the Nation (with a capital N) is an inhuman, predatory and terrifying monster:

> Have you not seen, since the commencement of the existence of the Nation, that the dread of it has been the one goblin-dread with which the whole world has been trembling? Wherever there is a dark corner, there is the suspicion of its secret malevolence; and people live in a perpetual distrust of its back where it has no eyes. Every sound of a footstep,

---

[58] Tagore, *Nationalism*, Macmillan, 1917, p. 133.

every rustle of movement in the neighbourhood, sends a thrill of terror all around. And this terror is the parent of all that is base in man's nature. It makes one almost openly unashamed of inhumanity.[59]

Clearly, this idea of the 'Nation' signals a harsh critique of totalitarian, authoritarian and imperialistic regimes. Conflicts between them were not only threatening the peace and stability of the world, but had caused World War I. Tagore was, in fact, travelling during its outbreak, albeit away from its principal theatres.

Six months after Tagore reached the US in October 1916, America also entered the 'war to end all wars.' Tagore was, thus, amply aware of the dangers of nationalist ideology, which according to him, was the main cause of the war. It had become almost a religion, full of lies, propaganda and jingoism:

> Clever lies become matters of self-congratulation. Solemn pledges become a farce... The Nation, with all its paraphernalia of power and prosperity, its flags and pious hymns, its blasphemous prayers in the churches, and the literary mock thunders of its patriotic bragging, cannot hide the fact that the Nation is the greatest evil for the Nation, that all its precautions are against it, and any new birth of its fellow in the world is always followed in its mind by the dread of a new peril.[60]

No wonder, after reading this book, we might think that Tagore was a staunch anti-nationalist.

Yet, this would be a one-dimensional reading of one text where nationalism, as Thompson points out in his 'Introduction', mostly stands for imperialism. But on the strength of these lectures and

---

[59]Ibid. 41–42.
[60]Ibid.

a few other texts quoted out of context, many have appropriated Tagore's legacy to the cause of post and anti-nationalism.[61]

In a salutary corrective, the late Professor Sabyasachi Bhattacharya shows at least five distinct phases, not necessarily developmental in a unidirectional sense, of the deepening and enlarging of Tagore's views on nationalism: 1890–1904 (conventional nationalism), 1904–1907 (Swadeshi agitation), 1907–1916 (disillusionment and criticism of militant nationalism), 1917–1930 (critique of imperialism) and 1931–1941 (reconciliation of antinomies).[62]

To this we might add Narasingha P. Sil's caveat that Tagore's positing of 'the India of no nations' and of 'we, who are no nation ourselves' is not historically founded, but fundamentally flawed and romantic, if not strategic and motivated.[63] In San Francisco, for instance, Tagore was denounced by members of the Ghadar faction, a revolutionary organization which advocated an armed overthrow of British Raj in India. In a letter published in the *San Francisco Examiner*, Ram Chandra Bhardwaj, a Ghadar leader, who was later murdered, wrote, 'For all the appreciation directed towards Tagore, he now stands for Old India.' Ram Chandra condemned Tagore for accepting knighthood and collaborating with the British.[64] It was thought that Tagore's life was under threat and therefore Indians, then called Hindus in the US, were debarred

---

[61]I develop such an argument at greater length in my essay, 'Tagore's Nation: Swadeshi Samaj and the Political Novel', in *Tagore and Nationalism*, edited by K.L. Tuteja and Kaustav Chakraborty, Spinger, 2017.

[62]Bhattacharya, Sabyasashi. 'Antinomies of Nationalism and Rabindranath', *Economic and Political Weekly*, Vol. 51, No. 6, February 2016, pp. 39–45.

[63]Sil, Narasingha P. 'Rabindranath's Nationalist Thought: A Retrospect', *Alternatives: Turkish Journal of International Relations*, Vol. 11, No.1, Spring 2012, pp. 127–140.

[64]Kumar, Anu. 'On His Second Visit to the USA, in 1916, Rabindranath Tagore Was an Assasination Target', *Scroll.in*, 4 April 2020, https://scroll.in/article/958079/on-his-second-visit-to-the-usa-in-1916-rabindranath-tagore-was-an-assassination-target. Accessed 18 December 2021.

from attending his talks. No wonder Ellsworth Huntington, reviewing *Nationalism* in *Yale Review*, sneered, 'Tagore seems to oppose the idea of a nation because he belongs to a race which has no nation of its own. Such a race is to be pitied, not blamed'.[65] Tagore's critique of nationalism was seen as the recourse of the weak and colonised.

In his two Bangla essays, '*Rabindrik Neshan Ki* [What is Tagore's Nation]?' (2003) and '*Rabindrik Neshan Prasange Aro Du-Char Katha* [A Couple of More Thoughts on Tagore's Nation]', *Baromas, 26* (2004), Partha Chatterjee points to several other limits to Tagore's idea of nationalism, but especially Tagore's inability or refusal to imagine the organization of a polity of the scope and dimension befitting the geo-cultural scale of India.

Indeed, Tagore's thinking on nationalism is cautionary and critical, rather than constructive or pragmatic. In addition, there are at least two different, though interrelated, personae that operate through his vast and complex oeuvre—the English, outward-facing, international Tagore and the distinctly Bengali Tagore, more inward and Indian. In addition, there are two other contending Tagores at play, an aesthetically reflective creative artist and spiritual seeker contrasted with the socially and politically conscious public intellectual and international celebrity.

Tagore demands a methodological anti-essentialism, akin to the hermeneutics of intermediality that I discussed earlier. We must resist the temptation of pigeonholing or slotting him according to our requirements. We ought to remember also Tagore's more constructive nation-building essays on swadeshi samaj, where he believes that a self-sufficient and self-supporting village society would be the backbone of new India.

The bottom line? Tagore was deeply distrustful of all ideologies that destroy the human spirit, the finer qualities and inner creativity that define us as individuals. Excessive or hyper-

---

[65]Huntington, Ellsworth. 'Nationality', *Yale Review*, March 1919, pp. 444–48.

nationalism was one of them. It caused conflicts, led to wars and was no different from imperialism when it expanded outward to conquer other nations and territories.

This brings us to the second part of my discussion on Tagore.

The intermedial challenge in reading Tagore is not only to reconcile the diachronic and paradigmatic but also to cross several genres, languages and creative media. Tagore's oeuvre ranges across not just novels and non-fiction, but stories, plays, songs, not to mention an astonishing range of art works, from doodles and cartoons to the mysterious oil paintings. All these need to be taken into account, along with their mutually influencing interactions, to form a more comprehensive picture of his notions of nationalism.

This is a huge challenge but must be undertaken if we wish to understand Tagore properly. From such a perspective, if we examine Tagore's creative output, we see at work, especially in his significant texts, a careful and critical mediation between political extremes. To illustrate, let us consider his three major political novels, *Gora* (1909), *Ghare Baire* (1916) and, finally, *Char Adhyay* (1934), the last of his 13 novels.

In *Gora*, which was serialized in *Prabasi*, soon after the partition of Bengal, through his eponymous protagonist, Tagore rejects both the extremes of religious ultra-nationalism and comprador elitism. While the first part of the book shows the inadequacy of the former, British imperialism comes under severe condemnation later.

It is only when Gora goes to the countryside that he discovers the brutal force and ugly face of British rule. The oppression of the peasants and the economic pauperization of the villages open his eyes to the structural inequalities and cruelty of imperialism behind the rather polite façade of paternalistic inclusion offered to the native bourgeoisie. From being a 'good' subject, Gora becomes a 'bad' objector and finds himself in jail. When he returns, he is disgusted to discover that he has become a 'national' hero. The very middle class which refuses to move a muscle to help the poor has now transferred the guilt of its apathy into adulation for him.

Gora's long disappearance from the text serves to give the other characters the space to resolve their complicated personal and social relationships. He, in turn, understands what have been his own fatal flaws—first, the neglect of and ignorance about the peasantry, but equally so, the suppression and disregard of the other half of India, its women.

It is now that Suchorita's face appears in his mind's eye, merging with that of his mother, Anandamoyi, who is, of course, Mother India herself. He clearly understands that a new India can only be created by including and recognizing its women. This will have to be a collaborative and cooperative project, harnessing the agencies and energies of both the sexes, not a hyper-masculinist imposition of the will of a strong man on the passive and compliant masses.

Tagore uses two couples to work out his vision of a new India. Binoy and Lalita serve not only as foils to Gora and Suchorita, but are, perhaps, the mainstay of the book. Binoy, not Gora, is the real hero, because Binoy is closer to the average person. Gora's extremism comes for disapproval.

In *Gora*, Tagore tells us that what appears to be most Hindu is actually least so. It is a foreign element masquerading as the authentic internal one. The West that we internalize is the real enemy, more dangerous than the West out there. Tamed of its Semitic zeal, such an element may coexist with the others in a larger rainbow of many cultures that is India. But when it strives to dominate, taking over the whole spectrum of political and cultural possibilities, it must be tamed and neutralized. This only Suchorita's feminine sexual energy can do. Without her, Gora's cultural nationalism would turn pathological and destructive, not only to his own household, but to the nation in the making.

Gora ends with the major characters preparing for a long journey away from Calcutta, then capital of British India. Their actions have raised a storm which must be allowed to subside before they can return. The seeds of a new society are to be nursed in another soil before they can be transplanted back. Where do they repair? Interestingly, to Shimla, the summer capital of the Raj. In the Himalayas, where the deities and masters reside, safeguarding ancient Indian religion and culture. Again, the suggestion is unmistakable. The new India, despite its age-old mountainous inspiration, must be blended with modern, western, liberal values.

Tagore explores three formulae of nationalism in *Gora*. Hindu nationalism, born of revivalism and based upon an unrepentant and unreformed tradition. This is rejected as is the slavish and imitative subordinative collaboration with the British Raj that is represented by Varadasundari and Pani Babu. The latter is an especially inapt, not to speak of inept, prospective groom for Suchorita. She knows he will stifle and suppress her soul, not for some higher cause but for the sake of his own, already bloated, ego. Such idolatry is intolerable to Tagore.

Gora's own formula for what constitutes a true Indian is not cumulative. It is not the Punjab plus Sind plus Gujarat plus Maratha and so on that we celebrate in our national anthem penned by none other than Tagore himself. Instead, it is arrived via negatives, *neti neti*—neither Punjab, nor Sind, nor Bangla, nor Brahmin, nor Dalit and so on. What is left, of course, is a sort of basic common denominator of humanity, shorn of all caste marks or identity tags.

The real Indian is simply the essential man or woman. Paresh Babu, Anandamoyi and the two young couples qualify as the inheritors of an authentic Indian tradition as well as the progenitors of the new Indian nation. Together they form the basis of a new society that is yet to emerge as the novel ends. India, to Tagore, is still a nation in the making. It is not yet fully formed. That is true even today.

Gora is an earlier text than *Ghare Baire*, but anticipates it. Gora becomes Sandeep in *Ghare Baire*, while Binoy is changed into Nikhil. More importantly, from being Gora's shakti or supporting power, Suchorita is changed into Bimala. She is at the centre of *Ghare Baire* as Nikhil's wife and Sandeep's object of desire. Instead of two couples, we have a triangle. While the device of two couples in *Gora* reduplicates the ideal of masculine–feminine bonding and partnership out of which the new India will be born, the love triangle in *Ghare Baire* ends in catastrophe.

Two men, representing different forces of history compete for her. She is Bengal—or even India. Nikhil, virtuous, generous, decent and devoted, is also effete, condescending, and somewhat apathetic. He lacks Sandeep's virility and vitality. Sandeep too, because he is mendacious and unscrupulous, is unworthy of her. He represents the new emerging leadership of India drawn from the middle classes, while Nikhil stands for the dying, feudal aristocracy, which is losing its power.

Bimala is 'seduced' by the emerging forces of history, which seem irresistible. She is deceived by the mask of idealism and national service that Sandeep wears, unable to fathom behind it his megalomania and hunger for power. Sandeep is exposed to be a selfish demagogue, a trickster ultimately, who unleashes vastly destructive forces before fleeing from the scene of his misdeeds.

The novel and the film, in Satyajit Ray's adaptation, end rather differently. While the former is somewhat open-ended, leaving the final outcome ambiguous, Ray's film is tighter, showing the almost inevitable death of Nikhil. Ray begins the film at the end of the book, thus intensifying, as Andrew Robinson says, its 'sense of predestination': 'From its outset we know that Nikhil and the woman he loves are doomed.'[66]

Interestingly, this is the reverse of how Ray treats Tagore's *Nashtanir*. In his cinematic adaptation, *Charulata*, he shows a more hopeful ending than Tagore's novella. Ray's moral code,

---

[66] Robinson, Andrew. *Satyajit Ray: The Inner Eye*, Andre Deutsch, 1989, p. 269.

moreover, is more stringent than Tagore's. While Amal's innocence saves Charu, Sandeep's corruption dooms Bimala, who must share its guilt for consciously giving herself to his seductions against the codes of her wifely dharma.

While *Ghare Baire* has been read as Tagore's critique of the swadeshi movement, it shows a more general suspicion and distaste of politics. The novel's depiction of amoral and often violent pursuit of power is an indictment of politics itself. It is also a commentary on the dynamics and tensions between the inner, more enclosed worlds of the domestic sphere and the rough and tumble of life on the outside. In the end, the latter invades the former and overruns it. Yet, the political implications of the love triangle show a clear, albeit indirect, denunciation of colonialism.

What, after all, is wrong with the marriage of Nikhil and Bimala? While the former is determined to educate his wife and give her the freedom to grow both intellectually and emotionally, this seems actually to be a ruse to evade the crucial problem of a lack of sexual passion or gratification in the marriage. I interpret this to mean, in contradistinction to Partha Chatterjee, that the political invades the personal long before Sandeep, with his fiery brand of nationalism, physically enters this sheltered household.

Under colonialism, the subjugated male invariably suffers a symbolic castration and emasculation. The comfort, even luxury, of the life of a zamindar's wife is still, as Bimala realizes, bordering on the insipid and sterile. The large house is, after all, childless and heirless.

Even an average marriage in 'colonised' times cannot be entirely satisfying or fruitful. The inequality institutionalized in the political sphere blights the marital bed of the protagonists. The novel, like many others set in those times, such as *Devdas* or *Sahib, Bibi, Golam*, depicts the impossibility of a mutually satisfying and joyous relationship during colonial rule.

It is as if colonialism thwarts and frustrates Eros and spurs Thanatos. Sandeep, if only he had been noble, faithful and sincere, might actually have been the better partner for Bimala. However, neither Tagore nor his times would condone adultery. The love triangle ends in calamity.

What happens in *Gora* and later in *Ghare Baire* prefigures the ruin that the passion of politics and the fanaticism of nationalism cause. Tagore had observed and experienced these first hand during Bangabhanga or the partion of Bengal in 1905. Though the agitation that followed forced the reunification of the province in 1907, the deeper damage was already done. The seeds of the partition of the subcontinent were sown during those years. It was also the start of communal politics, with the foundation of the Muslim League in Dhaka in 1906 and the Sarvadeshak (All India) Hindu Sabha at the Kumbh Mela in Haridwar in 1915.

The protagonists who embody hyper-nationalism in Tagore either correct themselves as in *Gora* or come into disrepute as in *Ghare Baire*. In *Char Adhyaya*, Sandeep resurfaces as Indranath, even more coldly calculating, self-serving, unscrupulous and manipulative.

In *Ghare Baire*, Bimala is misled, her marriage destroyed. She offers her jewels to the national cause but when Amulya, her ardent admirer, almost a foster son, also loses his life, she is shocked into realizing how big a moral and political blunder she has made. Not only does Sandeep's ideological posturing and chicanery come under attack, but political passion is also shown to be a dangerous and deranging narcotic, which can turn our minds and mislead us. Bimala falls prey to someone who has been insincere and opportunistic in the first place.

Georg Lukacs, the famous Marxist critic who reviewed *Ghare Baire*, dismissed it with a telling, if unjust epithet. He called it 'a petty bourgeois yarn of the shoddiest kind'.[67] His article was

---

[67] Lukacs, Georg. *Die rote Fahne*, 1922, https://www.marxists.org/archive/lukacs/works/1922/tagore.htm. Accessed on 9 January 2022.

published in *Die rote Fahne* in 1922, when the liberal world's honeymoon with Soviet socialism was far from having ended.

Lukacs was only voicing what most Leftists felt about Tagore:

> The author portrays the beginnings of the national movement: the struggle to boycott British goods, to squeeze them out of the Indian market and to replace them with native products ... The hypothesis is that India is an oppressed, enslaved country, yet Mr. Tagore shows no interest in this question ... Let the British come to terms as they wish and in their own way with the damage done to their souls through their use of violence: Mr. Tagore's task is to save the Indians spiritually and to protect their souls from the dangers posed by the violence, deceit, etc. with which they are waging their struggle for freedom.[68]

Lukacs has no patience for such spirituality.

Thus, Tagore becomes the butt of his denunciation:

> This stance represents nothing less than the ideology of the eternal subjection of India. But Tagore's attitude is even more blatantly manifest in the manner in which he shapes this demand in the action and the characters of his novel. The movement which he depicts is a romantic movement for intellectuals... Romantic Utopianism, ideological exaggeration and the crusading spirit are an essential part of all these movements ... He turns this crusading romanticism, whose typical representatives were without question motivated by the purest idealism and self-sacrifice, into a life of adventure and crime. His hero, a minor Indian noble who advocates the current doctrine, is destroyed both inwardly and outwardly by the rapacious excesses of such a

---

[68]Ibid.

'patriotic' criminal band. His home is destroyed. He himself falls in a battle that was sparked off by the unscrupulousness of the 'patriots'.[69]

Lukacs accuses Tagore of not giving any narrative space to voice the aspirations of an enslaved people rebelling against imperialism. '*Mr. Tagore's task is to save the Indians spiritually and to protect their souls* [emphasis in the original] from the dangers posed by the violence, deceit etc. with which they are waging their struggle for freedom.'[70]

Lukacs's calling Sandeep a caricature of Gandhi is obviously mistaken because the novel was written before Tagore had met Gandhi in 1915. Was Tagore really anti-national when every Indian sees him not only as a great patriot, but as one of the founders of modern India? As Brojendranath Seal remarked to Thompson on Tagore's critique of nationalism, 'Yes, but he has a right to criticise us. He has been a nation-builder'.[71]

The same paradox might explain how, in *The Creative Ideal*, Tagore is so sarcastic about patriotic or religious poetry:

> When some storm of feeling sweeps across the country, art is under a disadvantage. In such an atmosphere the boisterous passion breaks through the cordon of harmony and thrusts itself forward as the subject ... For a similar reason most of the hymns used in churches suffer from lack of poetry. For in them the deliberate subject, assuming the first importance, benumbs or kills the poem. Most patriotic poems have the same deficiency.[72]

---

[69] Ibid.
[70] Ibid.
[71] Dasgupta, Uma. *A Difficult Friendship: Letters of Edward Thompson and Rabindranath Tagore 1913–1940*, Oxford University Press, 2003.
[72] "The Creative Ideal', *The Complete Works of Rabindranath Tagore*, http://tagoreweb.in/Render/ShowContent.aspx?ct=Essays&bi=72EE92F5-BE50-40D7-AE6E-0F7410664DA3&ti=72EE92F5-BE50-4A47-5E6E-0F7410664DA3.

This coming from the author of two, perhaps three, national anthems and innumerable devotional poems shows the complexity of human creativity. So easy to read, so hard to pin down. Thus, an engagement with Tagore inevitably leads to an unsettling of easy certitudes or conclusions.

Let us return to our initial question. Was Tagore an anti-nationalist?

A naïve and motivated reading of his lectures on nationalism would certainly suggest so. Mostly on the strength of these lectures and a few other texts, he has often been (mis)construed as an anti-nationalist. While there is little doubt that several of his works show a considerable discomfort with nationalism, would it not be more accurate to consider him an anti-imperialist and a cautious nationalist?

Could it also be that he was sceptical of revolutionary ideologies, especially those that sacrificed the well-being of human beings to impersonal ideologies? If he was sceptical of the nationalist project, what was his idea of a good society? What, furthermore, was the relationship between nationalism and cosmopolitanism in his works? Are his creative and critical writings in consonance on this theme? We must admit that there are no conclusive answers to such questions.

But if we were to shift this argument slightly to suggest that Tagore was not anti-nationalist so much as anti-revolutionary, it would certainly trouble many admirers of the poet. Naturally, such an inquiry remains inconclusive. But what might be salutary even so late in this excursion is the reminder that Tagore does not allow us the respite of any simplistic or comforting redaction of his major ideas, including, in this case, nationalism.

I do not wish to take sides in such a critique of Tagore because that is not how I see my function. My function, as I mentioned earlier, is to understand things deeply, not come to quick and reductive judgements. But, from the foregoing discussion, even if Tagore's grave scepticism, even criticism of all soul-crushing ideologies, including misguided nationalism, is evident, we should have no doubts about one thing—Tagore's critique of nationalism was quite different from JNU's negativism and negationalism. Tagore would have very little sympathy for terrorists, separatists and members of the tukde tukde gang. In fact, Rohith Vemula's tragic death by suicide, from a Tagorean viewpoint, would be precisely the sort of irreparable harm and damage that extremist ideologies do to sensitive and impressionable minds.

Gandhi's *Hind Swaraj*

Mohandas Karamchand Gandhi spent three years, 1888–1891, in England. During this period, he not only passed the London matriculation examination, but qualified as a barrister. As it happened, Tagore, too, was in London from 1879 to 1880, 10 years earlier, but returned without a degree. This bit is well known. But few care to remember that Tagore went to England again in 1890 when Gandhi was there. But, of course, they didn't meet. Neither of them was famous then. There was no reason for their paths to cross.

A little over 20 years after his first visit to London in September 1888, Gandhi returned to England from South Africa in July 1909. This is the first of the two crucial moments in his life that I intend to highlight.

During this visit, he met every shade of Indian freedom fighter and revolutionary. One or two of these meetings took place at the India House, founded by Shyamji Krishna Verma. Verma, who wanted to train young Indians in firearms and bomb-making so that they could overthrow the British rule. From 1905 to 1910, until it was shut down by the British authorities, India House offered a platform to Indian revolutionaries, both from the Left and the Right.[73]

---

[73]The divisions between the Left and the Right back then were not as marked

What is more germane to our discussion is that Gandhi probably met V.D. Savarkar at India House. Savarkar, an avowed revolutionary, was also the author of *India's First War of Independence*, offering a counter-narrative to the established school of imperial historiography on the Great Revolt of 1857. Incidentally, like *Hind Swaraj*, Savarkar's seminal work was also published in 1909, in a clandestine edition in the Netherlands, reportedly with *The Pickwick Papers* as the false dust jacket. It too was banned by the British colonial authorities.

Not surprisingly, while Savarkar believed in armed revolution, Gandhi abhorred the use of violence for political ends. Perhaps, this was the beginning of a lifelong antagonism between the two that persisted right till Gandhi's assassination at the hands of Nathuram Godse, an admirer of Savarkar.

Another of Savarkar's protégés, Madan Lal Dhingra, shot Sir Curzon Wyllie at point-blank range, on 1 July 1909. Wyllie was the political aide-de-camp to the secretary of State for India. He also happened to be a friend of Madan Lal's father. Madan Lal, then an engineering student at University College, London, had tried to kill Lord Curzon before he shot Wyllie. Gandhi had arrived in London just nine days later, on 10 July.

Dhingra was arrested, tried at Old Bailey and sentenced rather swiftly. He was hanged on 17 August 1909 when Gandhi was still in London. Returning to South Africa, Gandhi wrote his handbook on non-violent revolution in just nine days aboard the S.S. *Kildonan Castle*.

Hind Swaraj was written between 13 and 22 November 1909, in 275 manuscript pages of the ship's stationary, 40 of which were

---

and antagonistic. The founder of the Ghadar Party, Lala Har Dayal, who was an Arya Samaji, wrote a fascinating book called *Karl Marx. A Modern Rishi*. Madan Lal Dhingra could also be considered to belong to the ideological Right, while India's most celebrated revolutionary, Bhagat Singh, was clearly a communist. But they all saw themselves working together for the same anti-imperialistic cause. Today, we have almost forgotten those historical conjunctures.

written with the left hand. Yes, Gandhi was ambidextrous. Only 16 lines were scratched out of the 275 pages. In a letter to his friend, Hermann Kallenbach, Gandhi said that he had had a 'profound experience of illumination' and had produced 'an original work'.

Like many great ancient Indian texts, including the Upanishads and Gandhi's favourite go-to scripture, the Gita, *Hind Swaraj* is dialogic, not dialectical. What was Gandhi's great discovery? Simply put, it was this: the way of violent revolution was not India's way.

Why?

On one level, that was because the British Empire was too powerful, almost impossible to overthrow, given that Indians were not just unarmed or disunited, but because they were dispirited and mentally defeated. But at another, more significant level, Gandhi believed that the only way to energize this defeated people was through atmabal (soul force), not bahubal (force of arms) or even buddhibal (strength of mind).

But how were Indians to empower themselves in this manner?

Through satyagraha. For the goal was not political independence alone, but swaraj. Swaraj has two senses: self-restraint, which prevents one from oppressing others, and self-assertion, which makes one resist those who oppress. It is the proverbial shurasya dhara, the razor's edge.

Hind Swaraj, written in Gujarati, was first published in the *Indian Opinion*, a broadsheet that Gandhi edited. It was then translated into English by Gandhi himself and published in early 1910. It soon ran into many editions and was banned by the British authorities in India.

Swaraj meant not just political freedom, but complete self-mastery and emancipation. Gandhi offered the blueprint of a new India and, indeed, a new world order, based on self-restraint, non-aggression, cooperation, limited consumption and moral, as opposed to material, development.

Gandhi tried and tested satyagraha, or non-violent non-cooperation, in his struggle for the rights of Indians in South

Africa. Heeding his call, many, including women, went to jail and endured untold privations and suffering.

The fight culminated in the long march that Gandhi led of over 2,000 striking miners and sugar plantation workers, along with 127 women and 57 children, from Natal to Transvaal in November 1913. This great satyagraha led to the Indian Relief Act of 1914, the repeal of harsh taxes and recognition of native marriages.

Gandhi left South Africa the following year, but his struggle for the oppressed Indians in that theatre of resistance also saw the making of the Mahatma. In India, too, Gandhi's ideas met with widespread support. Indians were divided, disarmed and demoralized; they might never have beaten the British at their own game had it not been for Gandhi's mass movement. The British Empire was an efficiently-run police state, the primary purpose of government being to exploit the colonies economically and suppress them politically. The British spared no effort or cost to maintain their hegemony in India. Every single major opponent of the Raj was hanged, transported, exiled or neutralized some other way. Bal Gangadhar Tilak was sent to Mandalay, Aurobindo jailed in Alipur, Savarkar transported to the Andamans and Bose forced to flee under disguise. Several thousand less prominent opponents were hanged or incarcerated. The coercive power of the British imperial machinery, with its highly-effective intelligence-gathering apparatus and wide participation from diverse groups and classes of India, would have been virtually impossible to overthrow. At least, so this argument runs. Others dispute it to claim that it is Bose and his Indian National Army who precipitated the British withdrawal.

Perhaps, that was the reason why millions of Indians supported Gandhian methods so ardently. What Gandhi did was not so much to kick out the British, but make India very difficult, no longer very worthwhile, to hold, let alone govern. He also taught Indians to govern themselves democratically, obeying the rule of law.

After World War II, the empire ceased to be profitable and was scarcely viable even politically. The age of global imperialism was finally over. The British, moreover, were sapped and exhausted by the war, winning which had brought them to their knees. The freedom struggle led by Mahatma in the loin cloth, on the other hand, seemed to empower Indians enormously, making them—partly through their suffering and partly through their rulers' discomfiture—ethically superior.

Justice was on our side; our rulers, the invincible white sahibs, were no longer gods with clay feet, but more like asuras, oppressive villains and wrong-doers. Gandhi, through ahimsa and satyagraha, had wrested the moral and media advantage, robbing the Raj of much of its sheen. Indians lost not only their respect for their rulers, but more importantly, ceased to fear them.

Gandhi proclaimed that satyagraha could be practised by anyone at any time, with women being even better suited temperamentally to adopt it than men. While feminists may consider such a notion sexist, Gandhi thought that the virtues of patience, suffering and resistance had been perfected by our womenfolk over generations of living in a male-dominated society.[74]

Hard-headed votaries of *realpolitik* may well scoff at these Gandhian ideas, but the victories he achieved in the realms of the spirit bore concrete results in the material, political plane. Mass awakening, non-cooperation, widespread civil unrest, complemented by a string of rebellions, mutinies and finally Subhas Chandra Bose's assault with his Azad Hind Fauj—albeit repulsed on the Northeast borders—all these not only shook the very foundations of the British Empire in India, but made freedom and political independence seem imminent, inevitable.

Gandhi's great discovery, as revealed in *Hind Swaraj*, was quite

---

[74]Patel, Vibhuti. 'Gandhiji and Empowerment of Women,' *My Life Is My Message* by M.K. Gandhi, https://www.mkgandhi.org/articles/womenempowerment.htm. Accessed on 18 September 2021.

contrary to Marx's. The latter believed that British rule in India was a regrettable but necessary phenomenon in that it fulfilled 'a double mission ... one destructive, the other regenerating—the annihilation of old Asiatic society and the laying of the material foundations of Western society in Asia.'[75]

Marx had little understanding and less respect for India's traditional Hindu civilization, which he regarded as 'a brutalising worship of nature, exhibiting its degradation in the fact that man, the sovereign of nature, fell down on his knees in adoration of Kanuman [sic], the monkey, and Sabbala, the cow'.[76] Notice how this misunderstanding and conflict still persist in India today, not only between 'orthodox' Marxists but also Left-Liberal secularists on the one hand and the pious multitudes on the other.

This is how Gandhi came to pen *Hind Swaraj*, his seminal treatise on non-violent revolution. It contained a blueprint for an alternate nationalism based on truth, non-violence, bread labour, mutual respect, Hindu–Muslim unity, caste and gender equality, village autonomy and empowerment of the people rather than the state. It was, arguably, a neo-traditional if not impractical idea of India because it ignored or downplayed techno-modernity, regarding it as morally bankrupt and ungodly.

Gandhi's model was adopted neither by his closest ally and political heir, independent India's first prime minister Jawaharlal Nehru, nor by the party that he led, the Indian National Congress. We still pay sidelong and piecemeal respect to it when it comes to village industries or panchayati raj, but it would be safe to say that India never gave Gandhi's idea of a perfect society a chance. It was considered too impractical to work.

Let's proceed to the second Gandhi moment, which is not of victory but immense failure and sorrow. Bapu, the so-called 'father

---

[75] Marx, Karl. 'On India', *New-York Daily Tribune*, 25 June 1853, http://icwfreedom.org/wp-content/uploads/2014/03/. Accessed on 8 December 2021.
[76] Ibid.

of the nation,' bore witness (*sakshi* and *shahdad*) to Partition, the incredible bloodbath and the largest exchange of populations in human history that accompanied our Independence. I have written in greater detail about this in *The Death and Afterlife of Mahatma Gandhi*.[77]

One of the things I looked at is Gandhi's last 133 days in Delhi.

After he doused the communal conflagration, managing to broker an amazing peace between feuding Hindus and Muslims in Kolkata, the frail and sick-in-the-soul Mahatma arrived in Delhi on 9 September 1947.

It was raining and his normal place of residence, the sweepers' colony, was no longer available to him because of security concerns. He was sent to Birla House, to be shot dead on 30 January 1948, bringing this last and quite remarkable phase of his life to a premature and tragic close.

If you go to Birla House, now Gandhi Smriti, you see the little room in which he lived with the bare minimum of comforts and possessions, sleeping on the floor. It's almost as if he's telling the world, I was in, but not of, this place.

During these days, Gandhi performed his last yagna or sacrifice, saving India from perpetual, never-ending civil war, a partition that would otherwise keep recurring in endless and mimetic cycles of internecine bloodletting. He was prepared to die to prevent this and actually offered his own life as ahuti, oblation, to this sacred task.

One the one hand, Gandhi appeals to Hindus not to drive Muslims out of Delhi just because the Hindus and Sikhs were driven out of Pakistan: 'You cannot secure justice', he says, 'by doing injustice to the Muslims.'[78] On the other hand, he exhorts

---

[77]Paranjape, Makarand R. *The Death and Afterlife of Mahatma Gandhi*, Penguin Random House, 2015.
[78]Quotations that follow are from Volume 99 of *The Collected Works of Mahatma Gandhi*, Government Publications Division, 1999.

Muslims in Delhi to 'unequivocally condemn the Pakistan government where it had departed from the civilised conduct and demand that all those Hindus and Sikhs who had to leave their homes in Pakistan should be invited to return with full guarantee of their safety and self-respect.'

He insists on replacing the cycle of reciprocal violence with one of reciprocal peace. In making such a demand, Gandhi admits: 'I am told that the whole thing was started by the Muslims. It is true.' In the very next breath, he adds, 'But what is the point in harping on it all the time?' Isn't it better to stop this mutual destruction? To dwell on others' wrongdoing repeatedly only foments hatred and counter-violence.

Though exhausted and deeply distressed, Gandhi devotes all his energies to save the fragile and newly independent nation, which he likens to a wrecked boat. Partition, he acknowledges, was a big mistake: 'I realise what a blunder we have committed in partitioning the country,' but as if that was not enough, 'we continue to make more and more blunders'.[79]

In a letter to an unnamed correspondent, he cries out in anguish, 'If heart unity is not restored in Delhi, I can see flames raging all over India.'[80] Describing the plight of India, Gandhi prays, 'Hence, night and day, I turn to Him. I say: "O God, come. Gajaraja is sinking—India is sinking—save her."'[81] He is sure that if Delhi is won, Pakistan will also turn: 'When I go to Pakistan I will not spare them. I shall die for the Hindus and the Sikhs there.'[82]

Before he was assassinated, Gandhi went on a five-day fast, his last. The doctors predicted that it would kill him, but that did not deter him. Only a solemn, written pledge from all of Delhi's warring factions to end violence persuaded him to break it.

---

[79]Ibid. Vol. 97, p. 389.
[80]Ibid. 343.
[81]Ibid. Vol. 86, p. 387.
[82]Ibid. Vol. 96, p. 388.

Delhi's Muslim citizenry, which had fled from Chandni Chowk and Daryaganj, now returned to their homes. Eyewitness accounts are available attesting to the miraculous change in atmosphere. Delhi, nay, India was saved.

A few days later, cleansed in body and spirit, as peace restored to the capital of newly independent India, Gandhi fell to his assassin's bullets.

Gandhi's critics—and their tribe is growing by the day—will be quick to declare that this was also the moment when Gandhian ahimsa or non-violence, whether as state policy or national ideal, was also recognized to have failed. We already had an invasion in Kashmir on our hands, not to mention three wars with Pakistan to follow. Religious intolerance and violence still stalked the land.

But if you take a long view of human history, you will see that all great prophets and visionaries, including the Buddha and Jesus, right down to our own Mahatma, failed. Why? Perhaps, they always saw humanity at its highest potential, rather than its lowest depths of depravity. Are these great forerunners to be dismissed as deluded dreamers?

If so, as Indians, we should no longer take credit for such lofty maxims as 'ahimsa paramo dharma'—non-injury is the highest moral duty. We should renounce the great advances of Jainism, Buddhism and Hinduism in fostering peace cultures. On the other hand, the failure of a lofty ideal does not mean we must give up on it. Perhaps, we will reach there one day. There is still hope for humankind.

JNU and What's Left of the Nation

With the first part of our topic now covered, let us now, using Gandhi as our link, return to JNU and our present situation. From his lifelong avowal of ahimsa, Gandhi in his final phase came to admit that very few had understood non-violence. We find Gandhi preferring the immediacy of violence-regulation by the government rather than riots and mob rule in the larger interests of the common good and in order to uphold the ultimacy of non-violence.

For most Indians, however, ahimsa was merely passive resistance, the preferred path of an unarmed and fearful subject to overthrow a vastly superior adversary. But when the authority of the colonial state was suspended, Indians fell upon each other with shocking barbarism and hatred, forgetting all about non-violence.

Gandhi was forced to settle for the limited violence of the state in maintaining law and order. That, to him, was preferable to indiscriminate mass violence. He even approved the sending of troops into Kashmir to protect innocent civilians and combat the invading mercenaries led by Pakistani Army generals, who had already pillaged several towns, raping and killing thousands.

Perhaps those advocating azadi for Kashmir today have forgotten those days of terror, when some of their own ancestors in the Valley were saved from great harm by Indian troops. Muslim Kashmiri separatists from the Valley, on behalf of whom some of our students have been shouting slogans, would also do well to ask where they were when their Kashmiri Pandit brethren were driven out of the Valley, just for being Hindus. When the Kashmiris treated their own minorities so badly, didn't they damage their moral right to be treated better as minorities themselves? When the Kashmiri Pandits were evicted out of Kashmir at gunpoint, their lives and properties threatened, why were there no protests in JNU?

How is it that when our JNU Muslim Kashmiri students shout, 'Kashmir *hamara hai* [Kashmir is ours]', no one asks them, '*magar* Kashmiri Pandit *aap ke kyon nahin*? [but why are Kashmiri Pandits not yours too]?' Why are there no agitations when Sujith—and hundreds of other RSS/BJP workers—are lynched in Northern Kerala? Why no morcha for Hindu girls who are abducted, raped, killed or converted in Pakistan? Or against the slaying of Hindu priests and leaders in Bangladesh?

Let us also remember Taslima Nasrin, the author of *Lajja*, who defended the rights of religious minorities in Bangladesh. Wasn't she hounded out of Kolkata in 2007 under the Left Front government?[83] Let us remember T.P. Chandrasekharan, a dissident CPI(M) leader in Kerala, murdered in 2012 for setting up an alternative Left group. He was stabbed over 50 times, his face mutilated beyond recognition.[84]

Clearly, many of our Leftist agitators conveniently forget these uncomfortable truths. Not only are they not fair and even-handed, but they are actually divisive and harmful to India's social fabric and unity. They lack integrity, whether ideological or ethical.

Whether we agree with the Supreme Court verdict or not, Afzal Guru received due process in the Indian legal system. His trial went on for eight years; his relatives even appealed for a presidential pardon after he was awarded the death sentence. What due process do Maosits, militants, religious fanatics and terrorists give to their opponents?

According to Home Ministry sources, 'As many as 12,000 people have lost their lives in Maoist violence over the last two decades, including 2,700 personnel of the security forces.'[85]

These are not just figures, but real people. For example, Maoists murdered two policemen who were in their custody—both of them from local indigenous communities—Francis Induwar (beheaded in 2009) and Lucas Tete (shot in 2010).

---

[83]"Taslima Nasreen: Controversy's child", *BBC News*, 23 November 2007, http://news.bbc.co.uk/2/hi/south_asia/7108880.stm. Accessed on 27 August 2021.
[84]Babu, Ramesh. 'Ex-CPM Leader's Murder Rocks Kerala', *Hindustan Times*, 5 May 2012, https://www.hindustantimes.com/india/ex-cpm-leader-s-murder-rocks-kerala/story-wDrUThMAFlh7LLlGwgL5gK.html. Accessed on 27 August 2021.
[85]'Naxal Violence Claims 12,000 Lives in 20 Years', *The Economic Times*, 14 July 2018, https://m.economictimes.com/news/defence/naxal-violence-claims-12000-lives-in-20-years/articleshow/59521195.cms. Accessed on 27 August 2021.

Kenduka Arjun, secretary of the Chasi Mulia Adivasi Sangh in Odisha, was murdered by Maoists in 2010. They also beat to death Niyamat Ansari, a Mahatma Gandhi National Rural Employment Guarantee Act (MGNREGA) activist, in front of his family in 2011. I will not even go into the implications of the derailment of the Jnaneswari Express in 2010, which resulted in the loss of 148 lives.[86]

These same radical groups, who attack Indian democracy, claim the right to dissent and free speech, guaranteed by the very State and its Constitution that they do not respect and intend to overthrow.

Actually, which communist state has given any separatist group the right to secede? They have, in fact, been imperialist, taking over other people's territories and nations. There is no protest against them and their atrocities here. Surely, this is a major contradiction that should be evident to all thinking people.

A lot of you have been shouting slogans for azadi. I invite you to consider the difference between Gandhi's idea of swaraj and the separatists' call for azadi. Swaraj is based not just on the demand to be freed from some external power but on self-restraint and self-mastery.

Azadi, a word of Persian origin, has the original sense of manumission, of being freed from slavery.[87] Swaraj, on the other hand, implies a highly responsible, highly evolved social arrangement. It was not just anti-this or anti-that, it is not just licence and unbridled freedom, but a commitment to oneself and to others.

---

[86] Unconventional Commando Combat Academy, https://www.commandokill.com/world-terrorism/naxalism/index.html. Accessed on 27 August 2021. Union Minister and Amethi MP Smriti Irani's recent novel, *Lal Salaam* (2021) is based on the slaughter of 76 CRPF personnel by Maoists in Dantewada in April 2010.
[87] This paradox is evident even in the name of an important Congress politician from the Valley, whose first two names mean 'the slave of Nabi (Prophet Mohammad)', while his last name means 'free'.

Swaraj, clearly, does not end with political independence; it's an ongoing struggle. It is a daily plebiscite, as a previous speaker rightly said.

What was Gandhi's method to attain swaraj? It was satyagraha, insistence on truth. We must deeply ponder over this because today it seems as if truth is our first casualty. An unprejudiced pursuit of truth is what is meant by the famous phrase, 'scientific temper', that Jawaharlal Nehru, Gandhi's chosen heir and India's first prime minister, advocated.

I needn't remind you that our university, named after him, includes 'scientific temper' in its mission statement. It also figures in the directive principles of our Constitution. But do we maintain and pursue a scientific temper here or, more often than we care to admit, resort to half-truths, cover-ups, even outright lies to achieve our ends?

Closer home, let us not forget that those who led the processions against the hanging of Afzal Guru in JNU did so under false pretexts. They took permission for a poetry reading, but always intended it to be an anti-government demonstration. After the university authorities got wind of their real intent, seeing the flagrantly separatist posters and withdrew permission these students, along with several unidentified outsiders, went ahead with their programme, shouting inflammatory, if not seditious, slogans. The rest, as they say, is history—its deceits and deceptions as easily cotton-balled in disinformation and false propaganda, and as soon forgotten.

Can any ideology justify deceit, duplicity, hypocrisy and insincerity? In the name of perfectly good causes such as equality and social justice, aren't we promoting dangerous, divisive and unethical practices? Pitting one community or caste, one class or section of society against the other, aren't we exploiting and misdirecting the gullible, even romantic, idealism of the youth? We must ask such hard questions.

Of course, when we study human beings and the social

arrangements that they engender, we must also have compassion, not just dispassion. That, to me, is the essence of the kind of remedial hermeneutics that I have been recommending as an antidote to the extremes and excesses of our times.

Satyagraha, therefore, actually implies compassionate dispassion, just as ahimsa implies active love, not just passive non-injury. We who seek justice, Gandhi famously said, must learn to do justice.

But today, we are eager to condemn our opponents. Far from doing them justice, we use every occasion to target and attack them. This is a zero-sum game of assured mutual destruction (quite literally 'mad' if you ask me).

I have dubbed this polarized state of constant strife in India as our *un*civil war. It is this culture that needs to change, whether inside JNU or outside, in the body politic of India. Let us, therefore, ask not just 'What the Nation Really Needs to Know', but also what JNU really must learn to acknowledge.

When the JNUSU president thundered, '*Hum unko bataaenge ki rashtravaad kyaa hai* [We will tell them what nationalism is]!' I wanted to ask, '*Kyaa hum subko sunatehi rahenge? Hame kuch bhi sunna nahi hai? Humko sunna bhi chahiye* [shouldn't we listen to the nation too]?'

Coming to our present situation, though much has been said and much ink spilled, thankfully not as much blood has been shed. But the discourse here is one-sided, usually anti-this or anti-that, as our student leaders say, '*Ladenge, sangharsh karenge, yeh-woh hasil karenge, fellowship bhi badhake rahenge* [We will fight, struggle, we will do this, we will do that, we will also ensure that the fellowship amount is increased]!'

Wonderful! That's what it boils down to—extracting the maximum from the system, then abusing it for being unjust, bourgeois, casteist or whatever. But this is our own state; we have elected these people. Even the VC and the university administration are here to serve you.

What is the point pretending to be great revolutionaries in marching from Ganga Hostel to the administration building, shouting slogans against the university? I am afraid that much of what we demand is probably *not* due to us. We congratulate ourselves on being India's best university, but what have we done to implement good academic standards? Which student leader has agitated for better teaching, higher research standards, more rigorous evaluation or any form of intellectual excellence?

Some comrades even go farther to say that they don't believe in this bourgeois democracy. If so, what is left? *Bacha kyaa hai?*

Coming to his criticism of the RSS, let me ask Kanhaiya, didn't you say that Golwalkar met Mussolini?[88] But did you check your facts? It was Dr B.S. Moonje who met Mussolini, not 'Guruji' Golwarkar. Moonje was a Congressman, who later became president of the Hindu Mahasabha. He met Mussolini in March 1931. According to his diary entries, he was impressed by the discipline and organization of the Italian Fascists. I'm not saying that Hindu nationalists did not admire the fascists; they did. No doubt, fascism stands for a certain kind of anti-democratic politics, but so does Stalinism, doesn't it? Why do you condemn one and not the other? So please, let's agree on what is factual and what is not.

For your information, Gandhi also visited Mussolini later in the same year, 1931, after the Second Round Table Conference in London. For that matter, Tagore, the other protagonist of our narrative, also met Il Duce, twice, even earlier, in 1926. Does that make them fascists? Guilt by association is quite a lame way of discrediting your ideological opponent, isn't it? For that

---

[88]M.S. Golwalkar (1906–1973), was the second sarsanghchalak (chief) of the RSS, a position he occupied for over 30 years. The book, *We or Our Nationhood Defined*, published under his name, was, apparently, an abridged translation of *Rashtra Mimansa* by Vinayak Damodar 'Veer' Savarkar's eldest brother, 'Babarao' G.D. Savarkar.

matter, do you know that the father of the Congress president, Smt. Sonia Gandhi, Stefano Maino, served in Mussolini's army and was himself a fascist? In fact, he affirmed his 'unwavering loyalty to Mussolini and Italy's "admirable fascist past"' in an interview.[89]

My point, Kanhaiya ji, is that you have to check your facts. And guilt by association makes a lame argument.

Kanhaiya Kumar has said, '*Humara sabse purana sanghatan hai, aur humne is desh ke liye bohot ladaai kari hai* [Ours is the oldest students' union and we have fought a lot for the nation]'. But I want to ask him of the sordid record of the CPI during our freedom struggle.

S.A. Dange, one of the founders of the CPI, sided with Lenin against Gandhi, publishing a pamphlet titled, *Gandhi vs Lenin*, as early as 1921. When the Congress Leftists formed the Congress Socialist Party in 1934, the CPI condemned it as 'social fascist'. Later, in 1924, Dange wrote a series of letters to the British authorities pleading that he be relased from Kanpur jail. Don't forget this when you attack Veer Savarkar for writing mercy petitions to the British.[90]

---

[89]Laiq, Jawid. 'Meeting Mr Maino', *Outlook*, 23 February 1998, https://www.outlookindia.com/magazine/story/meeting-mr-maino/205112; https://hidf1.wordpress.com/tag/mr-maino/; https://swarajyamag.com/news-brief/fact-check-was-rahul-gandhis-maternal-grandfather-stefano-maino-a-fascist. Accessed 20 December 2021.

[90]Saha, Murari Mohan. *Documents of the Revolutionary Socialist Party: Volume One 1938–1947*, Lokayata Chetana Bikash Society, 2001, pp. 21–25. The booklet containing these letters, *Dange Unmasked: Repudiate the Revisionists*, was used in 1964 by those who broke the party to form CPI-M, (https://www.marxists.org/subject/india/cpi(m)/1964-dange-unmasked.pdf). Later, at 83, Dange was expelled from the CPI, a party he had helped form in 1925, for supporting Indira Gandhi's Emergency (https://www.indiatoday.in/magazine/indiascope/story/19810430-cpi-central-executive-for-expelling-sripad-amrit-dange-from-primary-membership-772864-2013-11-21). Accessed 20 December 2021. No surprise that Kumar himself left CPI and joined the Congress in 2021.

What about the flip-flop of the communists in 1942 when, at their Soviet masters' behest, they declared practically overnight that the Imperialist War was suddenly the Peoples' War? The CPI made a secret pact with the British during the Quit India movement. They pledged 'wholehearted cooperation in the war efforts with the present Government' in exchange for a number of concessions, including release of communists from jail.[91] All too well-documented, why don't JNU Leftists never mention this great betrayal?

The CPI leadership also failed to oppose the Partition. Gangadhar Adhikari's 1943 thesis *Pakistan and Indian National Unity* is well known for its advocacy of the Muslim right to self-determination, including secession. Many communists, in fact, joined the Muslim League. Some even moved to Pakistan after Partition, only to be so disillusioned that they returned.[92] Dr B.R. Ambedkar, too, was unsparing of communists, calling them 'a bunch of Brahmin boys.'[93]

Soon after Gandhi's assassination in 1948, didn't B.T. Ranadive, the Communist Party supremo, coin the slogan, '*Yeh azadi jhooti hai* [this freedom is fake]', and advocate an armed overthrow of the elected government?[94]

---

[91] Arun Shourie, for instance, documents this with great relish and detail in *The Only Fatherland: Communists, 'Quit India' and the Soviet Union*, HarperCollins, 2015.
[92] See Habib Manzer, 'Communists in the Muslim League', *Proceedings of the Indian History Congress*, Vol. 69, 2008, pp. 563–573; and Ishtiaq Ahmed's 'How Far Left of Partition?' *The Friday Times*, 25 September 2015, https:// www.thefridaytimes.com/how-far-left-of-partition/; Also see Ben Fowkes and Bülent Gökay, 'Unholy Alliance: Muslims and Communists—An Introduction', *Journal of Communist Studies and Transition Politics*, Vol. 25, No.1, 2009, pp. 1–31.
[93] *Dr Babasaheb Ambedkar: Writings and Speeches, Vol. 17 (Part-1)*, Dr Ambedkar Foundation, 2014, p. 406.
[94] Khanna, Rohit. 'CPM to Hoist Tricolour 74 Yrs after "Ye Azadi Jhoota Hai" Days', *The Times of India*, 9 August 2021, https://timesofindia.indiatimes.com/city/kolkata/cpm-to-hoist-tricolour-74-yrs-after-ye-azadi-jhoota-hai-days/articleshow/85163560.cms. Accessed on 8 December 2021.

Again, in 1962, when the Chinese invaded India, didn't E.M.S. Namboodiripad, the communist leader, support the cause of China, branding India as the aggressor? If you don't believe me, go check the record for yourselves. Rudrangshu Mukherjee sums it up well:

> Given its track record, the Left's attempt to see itself as a protector of India's national sovereignty and autonomy is a disgrace. Communists in India have acted, at critical periods, at the behest of the Soviet Union or China. In so doing, communists have sacrificed India's national interests.[95]

Today, communists and Maoists are collaborating with Islamists. Naxal leader Kishenji (Mallojula Koteswara Rao) is quoted as saying, 'The Islamic upsurge should not be opposed as it is basically anti-US and anti-imperialist in nature. We, therefore, want it to grow.'[96]

Another leader, the supreme commander of CPI (Maoist), Muppala Lakshmana Rao or Ganapathy, told Rahul Pandita of *Open*: 'Our party supports the struggle of Muslim countries and people against imperialism, while criticising and struggling against the reactionary ideology and social outlook of Muslim fundamentalism.'[97]

Isn't it important for us in JNU to pay attention to these facts and question such a deadly nexus? Similarly, when you advocate

---

[95]Mukherjee, Rudrangshu. 'The Red Blunders: The Communists Have Consistently Betrayed National Interests', *The Telegraph*, 21 August 2007, https://www.telegraphindia.com/opinion/the-red-blunders-the-communists-have-consistently-betrayed-national-interests/cid/1027877. Accessed on 27 August 2021.
[96]Bhattacharya, Snigdhendu. 'We Support Islamic Terrorism', *Hindustan Times*, 9 June 2009, https://www.hindustantimes.com/india/we-support-islamic-terrorism/story-2Ec3a6rwPKTyyF9dEACKiN.html. Accessed on 27 August 2021.
[97]Pandita, Rahul. 'We Shall Certainly Defeat the Government', *Open*, 15 October 2009, https://openthemagazine.com/features/india/we-shall-certainly-defeat-the-government/. Accessed on 27 August 2021.

communism, what do you make of the conundrum that the Chinese state, run by the Communist Party of China, recreated private property after abolishing it under Mao? Deng Xiaoping recognized that communism simply didn't work as an economic system and turned China into a capitalist powerhouse, without the labour unions and other safeguards that western democracies have.

Aren't such paradoxes of history and ideology worth exploring rather than mouthing the same tired slogans and shibboleths over and over again, as if we are stuck in a time warp?

Wake-up, comrades; the world has moved on!

For my part, I am proud to belong to a country where one so-called 'judicial murder' created such a huge ruckus. Do you know how many judicial murders were committed from 1920 to 1950 in Stalinist USSR? There were over four million political sentencings, out of which 799,455 were executions! As opposed to this, the non-political judicial death sentences amounted only to 34,228 in the same period. And how many people do you suppose were sent to gulags and concentration camps in Stalinist USSR? According to official Soviet records, over 14 million! How many perished there? About 1.7 million.[98]

My submission is that if fascists were undemocratic, so were the communists. Stalin is believed to have killed everybody who disagreed with him. He had Trotsky murdered as well.[99]

---

[98]See, for instance, Stephen G. Wheatcroft's 'Victims of Stalinism and the Soviet Secret Police: The Comparability and Reliability of the Archival Data. Not the Last Word', *Europe-Asia Studies,* Vol. 51, No. 2, 1999, pp. 315–345.

[99]Apologists claim that Lenin was the 'good', while Stalin the 'bad', communist. But Emma Goodman's account of her meeting with him in 1920 suggests otherwise. Deported from the US, she and her anarchist friends looked to the Soviet Union as a beacon of hope and freedom. She was sorely disappointed. In Petrograd she heard that free speech was a 'bourgeois superstition'. Lenin himself reportedly said, 'There can be no free speech in a revolutionary period.' But even after the so-called revolutionary period, was freedom restored? Lenin's

What about China's record? What happened during the 'Great Leap Forward' and the 'Cultural Revolution'? According to Frank Dikötter, chair professor of Humanities at the University of Hong Kong, some 45 million Chinese died because of Mao's misguided and murderous schemes.[100]

Have we forgotten Cambodia's killing fields, instituted by the communist red scourge better known as Khmer Rouge? How many millions perished in such misadventures? I'm not even sure if these unprecedented tragedies of history are properly studied in our Left-dominated JNU.

Consider North Korea, one of the few only communist states, apart from China, that still remains in the world. Find out how many people perish there not just from malnutrition, but from simply trying to cross over to South Korea.

Look around you: we've hung placards and statements from all over the world endorsing our struggle. But can you show me a statement from North Korea, or for that matter, from China? No. Because they don't have the freedom to participate in such protests.

Ruled by the Communist Party, China is a capitalist state as you know. I've been there eight times. I've met many Chinese intellectuals. In a café, over a drink or in private, they can tell you what they really think. But ask them to take out a morcha. They can't. Try to put up a placard or poster in Tiananmen Square. See what happens! Even an ordinary departmental faculty meeting in any

---

unleashing of the 'Red Terror' between December 1917 and February 1922 is well-documented. Tens of thousands were brutally killed. See, for instance, Lincoln W. Bruce's *Red Victory: A History of the Russian Civil War*, Simon & Schuster, 1989: 'the best estimates set the probable number of executions at about a hundred thousand' (p. 384).

[100]See Dikötter's 'People's Trilogy'—*Mao's Great Famine: The History of China's Most Devastating Catastrophe, 1958–62* (2010), *The Tragedy of Liberation: A History of the Communist Revolution, 1945–1957* (2013), *The Cultural Revolution: A People's History, 1962–1976* (2016).

Chinese university must have a representative of the Communist Party present to enforce the party line. Is that democracy?

Do you know that according to a recent survey, a surprisingly large percentage of Hong Kong's population wishes to emigrate?[101] Though the former British colony is now one of the most prosperous parts of the world, with a very high per capita income, many of its citizens don't want to live under an authoritarian regime.

Indeed, closer home, take the trouble to read the joint resignation letter of Umar Khalid, Anirban and their other associates. They quit DSU because there was no room for dissent, no democracy in the so-called *Democratic* Student Union! They felt stifled by the lack of freedom. Are the adherents of such ideologies, with their totalitarian and authoritarian DNA, now suddenly going to be champions of freedom, of azadi, in India?

It was not always that we were so one-sided or unquestioning. If you study the history of JNU itself, in the 1970s, Anand Kumar, standing for the 'Free Thinkers', challenged Comrade Prakash Karat, even wresting the JNUSU presidentship from the SFI. As already mentioned, the erudite and passionate Trotskyist (not Trotsky*ite*), Jairus Banaji, became the leader of JNU's internal Left opposition, tearing to shreds the specious arguments of Stalinist veterans.

The likes of Abhijit Banerjee, Nirmala Sitharaman and S. Jaishankar also studied in JNU. So did hundreds of intellectuals, bureaucrats, diplomats, and media and industry leaders. Their JNU was not so politically hidebound and academically backward.

---

[101] Teh, Cheryl. 'New Poll Shows 60% of Hong Kong Youth Aged 15 to 30 want to Leave the City If They Can,' *Business Insider*, 30 April 2021, https://www.businessinsider.in/international/news/new-poll-shows-60-of-hong-kong-youth-aged-15-to-30-want-to-leave-the-city-if-they-can/articleshow/82321902.cms. Accessed on 9 January 2022.

JNU Today: Myth vs Reality

When Kanhaiya questions the legitimacy of Prime Minister Modi, saying that the BJP polled only slightly over 30 per cent of the votes in the 2014 general elections, might we also not ask where Kanhaiya derives his own legitimacy from?[102]

Kanhaiya secured 1,029 votes out of a possible 8,000 or more, which is the student strength of JNU. That's less than 13 per cent of the votes. The runner up, AISA's Vijay Kumar, got 962. So Kanhaiya won by a margin of just 67 votes. Does that make him more legitimate than the prime minister of India? Who can countenance such egregious and arrogant stupidity?

Similarly, when some of you say that you wish to overthrow the elected government of India, from where do you derive your legitimacy? Is it that all the peasants and workers have been polled to give you the right to speak on their behalf? From where do those who question the sanctity of the Indian state derive their own sanction? It is certainly not from votes or even the support of the people.

Twenty years ago, speaking at the '20th Anniversary Meeting of Marxbadi Path' on 26 August 2000, Prakash Karat said that 'only by applying the method of Marxism and the theory and practise of scientific socialism that the Indian people can emancipate themselves from the vicious cycle of hunger, disease, illiteracy and poverty.' He urged comrades 'not only keep the faith' but asserted, once again, that India 'is essentially a bourgeois democracy limited by the nature of the bourgeois-landlord system.'[103]

I'm not sure his views have changed. Certainly, his party has not garnered any more votes, losing as it has both West Bengal and

---

[102] According to the Election Commission, the BJP increased its vote share from about 31 per cent in 2014 to 37.36 per cent in the 2019 elections.

[103] Karat, Prakash. 'Marxist Analysis of Indian Society', at the 20th Anniversary Meeting of Marxbadi Path, 26 August 2000, https://www.cpim.org/content/marxist-analysis-indian-society-0. Accessed on 27 August 2021.

Tripura. It would appear, therefore, that the communist critique of the Indian State only derives from ideology, not popular support. No wonder he asks his flock to keep their faith! How ironic for Marxists who deride religion as false consciousness.

How is this different from the religious justification of every imaginable crime or misdeed because it is assumed to be true and interconvertible? Ideology is so like theology in this respect, not ratified by plebiscite, vote or any form of social contract. It is considered right and true by blind belief in the veracity of a system that cannot be verified by reason, empiricism or any yardstick that we consider 'scientific'. That is why I invite you to join me in questioning whether JNU is truly as democratic as it is vaunted to be.

Isn't it, rather, a Left-hegemonic space? My own experience in my long stint here is that you are subjected to the five 'b's' (*pancha bakaar*) if you dissent against the dominant ideology—brainwashing, branding, boycotting, bullying and browbeating. It's a form of incremental exclusion, a new untouchability if you will. And if none of this works, there is always, BS or bullshit! That never fails to silence dissent if it is dished out in sufficient measure.

It is well known how the system of patronage works in many centres and schools—you can't go against the ruling ideology or clique. You won't finish your PhD, get a job or a promotion if you do. Such a set-up of academic and ideological inbreeding, not tolerated in any good university abroad, is the norm here. It ensures that deeply entrenched interests reproduce and perpetuate themselves.

Just check the faculty lists in most schools; I would estimate that close to 70 per cent have PhDs, MPhils or MAs from JNU. Some come even earlier—to get their BA—and never leave! A few of our residents have even stuck on without earning a single degree from here, so welcoming is the system. On the other hand, those who are perceived to be ideologically unsuitable don't have an easy time here.

Do we need a robustness of ideas or merely a repetition of shibboleths and slogans? Do we speak truth to power? If so, with the Left being in power in JNU, why are so many truths not spoken here? Do we really ask questions about everything on campus, including its ruling ideologies? If the nation is a daily plebiscite, why isn't JNU a daily plebiscite too? Why do we have so much self-congratulation instead of truly high standards of public discourse?

But before you dub me 'anti-JNU', let me unequivocally express my solidarity with all those who want to protect the autonomy, not just of JNU, but of all educational institutions in our country. I also stand in solidarity with those who demand due process, who believe that democratic institutions, not just within a university, but in the whole country must be nurtured and protected. That is why I thank you all for lending me an ear.

My views have been critical of what I consider Left-hegemonic, bordering on Left-dictatorial, practices right here in JNU. But I love JNU too, no less than any here. Every single book of mine acknowledges JNU, especially my colleagues and my students.

My friends on the Right have wanted me to support calls to take over, if not shut down, JNU. But I have always maintained that what we have here is a unique intellectual, not to mention bio-social, ecosystem, hard-won and worth preserving. We have produced a staggering 20,000 MPhil, MTech, PhD and other such higher degrees. To destroy JNU would be a great loss to the nation.

If you allow me to invoke Freud, not just the Thanatos of politics and propaganda thrives here, but also Eros and jouissance of all that is creative and life-enhancing. In fact, the former flourishes precisely because it is so deeply steeped with the latter. *'Yahan siyasat-bazi ki ek alag masti hain* [There is a different intoxication in politics here].' I too believe that genuine freedom, such as we allow here, even if one must fight for it, is the ultimate prerequisite for human well-being and flowering.

Marxism, at its best, also shares this ideal, whether or not it permits it in actual practice. I do not want JNU to be run over or run down. It is a place where so many aspirations have been fulfilled, so many careers launched. But above all, it is a place where so many young women and men learn how to think for themselves and learn how to live.

I stand here before you because I believe that this performative in which we discuss ideas, uphold each other's right to debate, even disagree, is so important not just for JNU, but for India. It is, therefore, imperative, whether we wish to practise the hermeneutics of intermediality or not, that we don't reduce all politics to unthinking sloganeering or reactive agitation but, instead, venture to interrogate our own positions and critique ourselves.

Who Will Drink the Poison of Divisiveness?

Today Is Shivaratri.[104]

This may mean nothing to many of you, but let us remember that Shiva alone agreed to swallow the poison that the primeval churn of the Ocean of Life threw up. Of all the good things that emerged, both the Devas and the Asuras, who were doing the churning, coveted most of all the nectar of immortality or amrita. Naturally, both parties wanted to wrest control of it.

But when it came to the deadly *halahala*, the toxin that was also spewed out in the process, there were no takers. Shiva, however, quaffed it. It burned his throat, which is why he came to be known as *Nilakantha*, the blue-throated god.

Today, no one wants the 'poison' of patriotism, responsibility, tolerance or service—all that used to go under the notion of 'nation-building'. Now, it seems we only want our own selfish

---

[104]The legend of Shivaratri says that it was during this long night that the fiercest of ascetics, Shiva, united with the great Goddess. He loved her so much that he gave her half his body. Together they became a new entity called *ardhanareeshvara*. So much for the power of Eros over asceticism that we also celebrate in JNU in our own ways.

'nectar', whether it is more liberty, more entitlements, more rights or more unearned privileges.

Who will worry about the common good, the collective well-being, the welfare of all, even risking individual or group interests? Who will unite us and make us work together for a higher ideal? Who will not just lead, but sacrifice, in order to take others along?

Only he or she will be considered 'Shiva', the good, the auspicious, the propitious, the *pro-national*. I can assure you, however, that the 'poison' of such a nationalism, unlike halahala, will not burn your throat, but gladden your heart.

Come, let us sample it.

5
FIVE CONTRARIAN EPISTLES

Animadversions of a Reluctant Public Intellectual

I too was a member, as most JNU professors were, of the JNUTA. The membership is usually by default; the fees are cut from our salaries. In my case, however, moving to JNU from IIT-Delhi had made a difference. I had not been too keen to join the JNUTA. As seen earlier, my guru had warned me against it. Though a member, I didn't vote if I didn't like the candidates. Nor, for that matter, did I habitually attend JNUTA meetings.

But after the events of 9 February 2016, I wanted to make my voice heard. Why had the JNUTA not criticized the 'illegal' rally in support of Afzal Guru and Maqbool Bhat? Why hadn't the 'anti-national' slogan-shouting been condemned? On the other hand, the JNUTA had gone into almost battle-mode to defend Kanhaiya Kumar and to fight the authorities over his arrest. I felt that as a member of JNUTA, I had to make my dissension known. Especially because the association, though it spoke on my behalf, did not represent my views.

When I wrote a letter to the president of the JNUTA on 19 February, after the Sahitya Akademi seminar, I wasn't aware that I was about to enter the vortex of the controversy. But that very evening, PTI put out a report on what had happened earlier in the day at Sahitya Akademi. As mentioned earlier, my talk had been quoted extensively.

Thinking back, I remembered how I had been literally mobbed after the morning session. Several people came up to me, holding out their mobile phones to record my statement, saying, '*JNU ke bare mein kuch kahiye* [Say something about JNU].' I replied, '*Jo kuch mujhe kehna tha, mein keh chuka hun* [I've already said what I had to].' Then, extricating myself from their clutch, I left.

I didn't want to draw unnecessary publicity or add to the narrative war that had begun to erupt. But the very next day, the PTI report was carried all over the country, both in print and electronic media—in practically every major newspaper and portal. I became the instant target of the 'tolerant(s)' who had now branded me as 'intolerant'.

My own colleagues and students from JNU started writing 'open letters' against me. I could clearly see a design emerging. It was to defame, demean and demoralize me. By publicly naming and shaming me, they wanted to damage my reputation and career. And if that didn't work, to bully me into silence.

Should I respond or remain quiet, was a question I asked myself. I was perfectly alone, apparently without the support of any party or group. So I realized that I was perceived as weak and defenceless. But my very vulnerability made me stand up for what I thought was right.

Generally speaking, I don't like being pushed around or intimidated into changing my opinions. I believed that each of us had the right to express his or her point of view without fear. I was the true liberal. My opponents, I understood more clearly than before, were not at all, though they professed to be. They were trying to discipline those who disagreed with them and to muzzle dissent.

I felt someone had to call them out.

This is how my spree of animadversions started. I am reproducing five of them below, with some revisions, additions and corrections, as my own offering to the history of those troubled times.

Epistle I: To the JNU Teachers' Association, 19 February 2016

I wrote this letter to the JNUTA to register my divergence from what I considered the one-sided resolutions of the Left-dominated teachers' body. Though the office-bearers were polite and polished, the meetings were not really democratic.

For instance, I noticed how disagreements, although allowed, were never voted on or recorded in the minutes. After everyone was given a chance to speak, the ring leaders reiterated their positions. The most aggressive ones were usually two or three lady professors, who ruthlessly bullied those who disagreed with them. One of them, a former colleague of mine, was well known for picking on opponents with tremendous verbal firepower, if not argumentative efficacy, augmented by dramatic emotional appeal. On closer examination of her statements, she was often proven to be wrong, false or misleading. She deliberately distorted issues, even misquoting university statutes and ordinances. But no one dared to challenge her.

The entire JNUTA process was overwhelmingly stacked in favour of massaging opinion and creating consensus. Over the years, the Leftists had gotten really good at it. Meetings were orchestrated with masterly tact and subtle threats. It was not as if the solidarity was entirely fake. Only that it was carefully choreographed to sideline or silence disagreement and divergence from the dominant view. We never voted on key resolutions and dissent went unrecorded in the minutes. At least I cannot recall when it was otherwise.

Whenever matters got a bit controversial or heated, members streamed out, as if on receiving a signal, but only after condemning the university administration. High tea being served outside, smaller groups of members would then congregate to confabulate on future strategies.

When the resolutions of the meetings were circulated for approval, they bore little resemblance to what had actually transpired, let alone the diversity of opinions in the meeting. No one cared to challenge these minutes or resolutions either. A show of unanimity and solidarity was created mostly by the fine art of manipulation. The JNUTA leaders were, after all, seasoned politicians. They knew how to manage the members.

When it came to the Afzal Guru march, however, I was convinced that the approach was flawed, even unfair. Both the then president of JNUTA, Ajay Patnaik and Kanhaiya Kumar, the president of JNUSU, belonged to the same political party, the CPI. The two unions were thus in cahoots. This became crystal clear with JNUTA making common cause with the students' union. Such a move, as expected, was not properly discussed or debated. There were, moreover, safeguards in the JNUTA constitution against such collusion, but these were not adhered to.

I surmised that many JNUTA members, other than myself, also thought their divergent views had been brushed aside or not taken into account. I was proven right subsequently because a group of teachers succeeded in splitting the JNUTA. The splinter group, however, by overplaying its hand and fighting amongst themselves, did not quite become an alternative to JNUTA. But what they did highlight was that the teachers were neither unanimous nor united against the administration. This split into two factions of the JNU teachers was formalized three years later in 2019, with the formation of the JNU Teachers' Federation (JNUTF) supported by one-third or more of the total teaching staff.

The major changes that overtook JNU had their roots in the troubles of 2016. It is that sequence of events that my rejoinders to the open letters written against me sought to capture.

19 February 2016

To,
The President, JNUTA

Sir,

I'm sorry to have to miss the important JNUTA general body meeting tomorrow because of a prior commitment. I am to leave early in the morning for Shillong for a conference. But I do wish to table three items for everyone's consideration, as we try to safeguard the reputation, autonomy and sanctity of JNU, as well as protect its students and teachers from state intervention or repression.

1. I would like to move a resolution to condemn the commemoration of Afzal Guru under the false pretexts of holding a poetry reading or to support such a motion in case it has already been tabled in an earlier meeting but not acted upon. I have formed the opinion, after talking to colleagues, that that many share this view.

    Furthermore, I think the hijacking of JNU for the agenda of anti-state actors or separatists is something that many colleagues do not wish to countenance, let alone abet. It would be a perverse kind of logic to argue that in the name of democracy, we support those who launched an attack on democracy (the Indian Parliament). Similarly, why would teachers of JNU let their university, expressly formed with a view to promote 'national integration', be turned into a site of national *dis*integration by a few mischievous elements?

2. This is indeed a time for unity among the JNU teachers and students, but how is unity to be achieved? Surely not by silencing and browbeating those who disagree with the dominant voice on the campus?

    It was shocking and offensive for a *very* senior

professor and dean to pull rank and bully a colleague in his attempt to silence her. Another colleague said words to the effect that she was out of her mind. Doesn't this really smack of a 'witch hunt', both deeply distasteful and sexist? Thankfully, the colleague who made the latter remarks has apologized, but the former *very* senior colleague seems unrepentant.

Let us not resort to name-calling those we disagree with or try to bully them into silence or submission. Surely, that is not democratic.

What we need is a hermeneutics of trust and generosity, not of suspicion or hostility. If we cannot accomplish this on our own campus or put our own house in order so to speak, what right do we have to preach to others about the virtues of tolerance?

3. I am afraid the battle that we are in the midst of is not one between tolerance and intolerance. Instead, I see it as an *un*civil strife between two or more types of intolerance.

We are in the midst of competitive and escalating intolerances, which can be diffused not by attacking each other, but by mutual understanding, harmony and fellow-feeling, even if these may be on the basis of a common minimum programme.

Else, I am afraid we may be facing the prospect of a deep rift, if not a split, in our own ranks.

Yours sincerely,

Makarand R. Paranjape
Professor of English, JNU

In retrospect, I was proven right. My warning was not heeded and JNU hurtled into its most divisive phase in recent memory.

Epistle II: Response to Professor Rajat Datta's 'JNU Students and Free Speech: An Open Letter to Prof. Makarand Paranjape'

A few days after, I was attacked by Professor Rajat Datta, a colleague from the Centre for Historical Studies. His 'open letter' of 2 March 2016 was published not only on his own Facebook page and the JNUTA group page, but also on *India Resists*, a Leftist portal.[105]

He began politely enough and in some respects, he was, of course, right. I had, indeed, not been very active in the JNUTA, nor had gone up to the podium again and again to express my views. But that didn't mean that I agreed with JNUTA resolutions or that my views should not be considered, especially after I had put them in writing. Professor Datta, predictably, ended up calling me an RSS stooge, mentored by the Sangh, because I wanted JNU to be more focussed on academics than politics:

> [T]his is precisely the advice RSS has been giving in its shakhas all these years.
>
> Depoliticize students, but be subversively political yourself. That's the new way forward, isn't it? And if you can't depoliticize, then destroy. I'm afraid that's the cultural project of this new dispensation?[106]

I decided to write back because I thought Professor Datta had not only misunderstood me but, perhaps, deliberately distorted my position. My reply was also posted on the same portal, *India Resists*, after he refused to put it on his Facebook page and the JNUTA didn't publish it either.

---

[105]'#Seditionrow: In Two Open Letters, JNU Professors Paranjape and Datta Debate Kanhaiya's 9 Feb Speech', *FirstPost*, 10 March 2016, https://www.firstpost.com/india/sedition-debate-in-two-open-letters-jnu-professors-paranjape-and-datta-debate-kanhaiyas-9-feb-speech-2667554.html. Accessed on 8 December 2021. Sadly, Professor Datta passed away on 30 October 2021, soon after retiring from JNU at the age of 65.
[106]Ibid.

4 March 2016

To,
Professor Rajat Datta,
Centre for Historical Studies, JNU

Dear Professor Datta,

Not being active on social media,[107] you can imagine how taken aback I was to find myself the subject of a campaign of vilification following your 'open letter' to me of 2 March 2016.

In the first place, that you did me the honour of writing an 'open letter' was itself surprising, if not flattering. I never considered my views of such consequence, but the reactions that followed have, indeed, dismayed, even pained me.

Whatever I may have said at the Festival of Letters of the Sahitya Akademi, to which I was an invited speaker in a panel on 'Freedom of Speech' on 19 February 2016, your 'open letter' has certainly brought me some notoriety. Not only in our own little village of JNU where I was quickly branded as 'the internal enemy', but also in the larger world outside. Especially, through the magnification, even distortion, that usually accompanies such attacks.

The fact that your 'open letter' was also quickly posted on the JNUTA website was even more worrisome. By whose design or authorization did this happen? Did the executive or GBM approve? I have written to the president and secretary of JNUTA to find out, but have received no reply thus far.

Paradoxically, this almost proves the central thesis that I was trying to make in my talk at the Sahitya Akademi. Those

---

[107]This has changed since March 2016. I now have a lively following on Twitter, in addition to a public Facebook page. In those days, I did not have a Twitter account.

who project themselves as the champions of democracy are quite as intolerant of dissent as those they condemn.

What we are in the midst of, hence, is not a battle between those who uphold the freedom of speech and those who seek to muzzle it, but between two opposing and politically charged factions, both of whom silence their opponents by a variety of means such as brainwashing, branding, browbeating, bullying and boycotting.

Our own 'Left-sacred' imagined community of JNU is no exception to this; here too, much intolerance to dissenting views persists.

Now to your 'open letter'.

1. Your *first* charge is that no 'false pretexts or subterfuge were involved' in the seeking of permission for the event on 9 February 2016, which sparked off the unfortunate consequents that have impacted us all. 'You are free', you say, 'to criticise this event and its organisers, but "false pretexts" and "subterfuge" are unfortunately equally false accusations.' Moreover, you quote from the poster announcing the event: 'Against the Brahmanical "collective conscience",' 'Against the judicial killing of Afzal Guru and Maqbool Bhat!', and 'in solidarity with the struggle of the Kashmiri people for their democratic rights to self-determination' as proof that there was no false pretext or subterfuge.

You accuse me of falsehood and distortion.

But surely, Sir, you have made a fundamental error in confusing or conflating two different documents in your line of argument, which I did not expect of you as a historian. Nowhere have I referred to the poster in my remarks on the 'false pretexts' or 'subterfuge' used by the organizers of the Afzal Guru commemoration.

I was speaking of the requisition seeking permission

given to the dean of students, where the event was billed merely as a poetry reading, with an expected audience of seven people. I was going by whatever information was available to me as of 19 February 2016 from the office of the dean of students.[108]

The 'false pretexts' and 'subterfuge' were in this requisition, not in the posters that followed after permission. Although, even in the poster, the commemoration of Afzal Guru is, evidently, in small print, intended to mislead the viewers into thinking that the main purpose is a poetry reading. Indeed, if you had cared to detail the exact sequence of events which might be expected of you as a historian, it was when the said poster appeared that the administration got wind of the real intent of the organizers and withdrew permission. But the organizers went ahead, even after the permission had been withdrawn. Which led to protests by another group of students, following which the whole sequence of subsequent events unfolded.

Not only did you not understand my line of argument, but you misrepresented it; worse, you accused

---

[108]JNU subsequently conducted proctorial and high-level enquiries, imposing fines on the students involved. The students went to the court (see Delhi High Court, 'Aswathi A Nair vs Jawaharlal Nehru University', 12 October 2017, https://indiankanoon.org/doc/104896154/. Accessed on 17 September 2021). In the court proceedings, it became clear that the High Level Enquiry Committee (HLEC) found the students guilty of giving undertaking in the false pretext of poetry reading 'A Country without Post Office' at Sabarmati Dhaba on 9 February 2016 from 5.00 p.m. to 7.30 p.m. Also see Delhi High Court, 'Komal Mohite vs Jawaharlal Nehru University', 12 October 2017, https://indiankanoon.org/doc/127145671/?type=print. It states '...it was discovered that permission was sought from the Additional Dean of Students on the false pretext of holding a poetry reading competition at Sabarmati Dhaba. Despite the alleged "permission" immediately being withdrawn by the DOS, the event was carried on which led to an enormous law and order situation.'

me of lack of honesty based on your misunderstanding or misrepresentation. But as you are my respected colleague, I shall refrain from casting aspersions on your motives.

2. Your *second* accusation against me is that I 'maligned' my own union three days after it passed a resolution, which reiterated that JNUTA 'stands by the Constitution of India'.

You accuse me of distrusting my colleagues and garnering some quick publicity from external platforms.

Allow me to disabuse you on both counts. The latter first. I was, as I mentioned earlier, already an invited speaker in the panel on 'Freedom of Expression' at the Sahitya Akademi's Annual Festival of Letters. My talk was on 'India's Intolerance Wars'.

I had no intention of referring to JNU and would not have, had not the fateful events following 9 February 2016 engulfed us.

It was widely expected of me, I am sure, to say something about JNU. Since it had been in the news continuously from then to the day of my talk on 19 February 2016. In fact, you might recall, not only had the JNUSU president been arrested, but just the day before, on 18 February, he had also been manhandled in the Patiala District Courts.

When I began to speak, I was actually requested by several members of the audience also to bring in JNU. I did. As I was afraid, I was literally mobbed afterwards.

Unfortunately, the only part of my talk that was reported was pertaining to JNU. Everything else was ignored. I had called for a way to reconcile the antinomies of our times. I had said that was the work of sahitya or literature.

None of this was reported. Indeed, I had no idea that

the press was present there. I can assure you I had not the slightest intention of seeking cheap publicity. In fact, in prefacing my remarks on JNU, I even said that I did not wish to wash our dirty linen in public. I too loved JNU and would never wish its name to be besmirched.

Now to the *first* part of your *second* accusation.

The JNUTA resolution that you cite does not specifically condemn the Afzal Guru commemoration event, which I believed had been staged under false pretexts. That was my objection to the one-sided JNUTA approach. In the correspondence that followed between various faculty members, some had made a demand for such an explicit condemnation, but their demand had not been acceded to by JNUTA. Instead, some of these dissenting faculty members had been attacked by other members of JNUTA.

These unseemly attacks had distressed me, but I did not allude to them in my Sahitya Akademi presentation. Why? Precisely because I didn't want to malign my own community and faculty colleagues to outsiders. I only said that the 9 February event, more specifically, the false pretexts under which it had been organized, had not been condemned by my union.

You may or may not know this, but I had explicitly written to the JNUTA president about this precise matter on that very day, 19 February 2016, even as I came to know that an emergency GBM was called for the following morning, on a Saturday.

I wrote because I was already booked on a flight to Shillong on that day for a prior engagement. I requested my letter to be tabled in the GBM. I doubt whether that happened.[109]

---

[109] The letter to the JNUTA has already appeared earlier in this chapter.

3. Finally, to your *third* accusation about 'depoliticization' of students. In my talk I said that politics at the expense of studies would harm the long-term interests of most students, excepting the 'cadres', who would be taken care of and patronized.

We are so full of self-praise about JNU as the 'best university in India', but wouldn't you agree that we have been unable to nurture an ecosystem of academic excellence?

Reorienting our students towards academics is also, thus, a form of de- or reverse politicisation. You claim that 'this is precisely the advice RSS has been giving in its shakhas all these years'. I don't attend RSS shakhas, so I wouldn't know; but perhaps you do, since you speak with such authority about what is said there 'all these years'.

Don't worry. Even if you do attend RSS shakhas, I for one, shall not stop talking with you. I shall not treat you as an 'untouchable'. For I believe that talking and listening to all sections of our ideologically and socially diverse society is one of the demands of our times. Especially, if we wish not to escalate the *un*civil strife that threatens to engulf us.

Yours sincerely,

Makarand R. Paranjape
Professor of English, JNU

Epistle III: How Not to Teach a Class: Is the Left So Short on Substance?

Rejoinder to JNU colleague Ayesha Kidwai, 16 March 2016

The next salvo was fired against me by Professor Ayesha Kidwai, a colleague from the same school, formerly my own department,

Centre for Linguistics and English.

This was subsequent to my nationalism lecture, published in the previous chapter. Fifteenth in the series, 'What the Nation Really Needs to Know', this lecture not only made headlines, but upset the Leftist establishment considerably.

Kidwai, their champion, besides being a very active JNUTA member, became its president later that year. She took it upon herself to hit out at me. Her 'open letter' was published in *Scroll. in* on 14 March 2016.[110] I decided to respond. Two days later, on 16 March 2016, *Scroll.in*, quite decently, not only published my rejoinder the day after I had sent it, but also offered the following headline:

'Not only does Professor Kidwai totally distort what I stand for, but also seems to deny me the basic courtesies due to another human being.'[111]

The header was followed by a brief description, inserted by *Scroll.in*:

> In the on-going series of teach-in lectures on nationalism at Jawaharlal Nehru University, Professor Makarand Paranjape had asked if the campus was a 'democratic space' or a 'Left-hegemonic space' and why Leftists had trouble accepting the 'legitimacy of the Indian state'.

I don't think I could have asked for more; *Scroll.in* had been fair to both sides. I respect the editor, Naresh Fernandes, and his staff for being true to their professed values. The following was my

---

[110]'Here's How Not to Teach a Class: JNU's Ayesha Kidwai Responds to Her Colleague Makarand Paranjape', *Scroll.in*, 10 March 2016, https://scroll.in/article/804879/heres-how-not-to-teach-a-class-jnus-ayesha-kidwai-responds-to-her-colleague-makarand-paranjape. Accessed on 25 August 2021.

[111]'Is the Left So Short on Substance? JNU's Makarand Paranjape's Rejoinder to Colleague Ayesha Kidwai', *Scroll.in*, 16 March 2016, https://scroll.in/article/805002/is-the-left-so-short-on-substance-jnus-makarand-paranjapes-rejoinder-to-colleague-ayesha-kidwai. Accessed on 25 August 2021.

rejoinder to Professor Kidwai:

> I write in response to Professor Ayesha Kidwai's patronising preach on 'how not to teach a class' and how to 'represent both sides of the argument in a fair manner *to the best of your ability*' [emphasis in the original].
>
> It is as if in asking me how *not* to teach, she is arrogantly taking upon herself the mantle of teaching me how to do so. But may I submit that the *purvapaksha*[112] that she demands of me is found sorely wanting in JNU's established and 'revolutionary' Leftists, including her.
>
> So let me ask her directly: did you, or earlier speakers in the 'teach-in', portray the ideas and actions of their ideological opponents, or even the Indian state, '*to the best of your* ability'?
>
> Instead, weren't we subjected to repeated rants against 'fascist Sanghis' and the Modi sarkar, with India itself defamed as imperialistic, even to the extent of alleging that 40 per cent of our country was under armed occupation?
>
> Tell me, Professor Kidwai, was it 'fair' to use the 'teach-in' space for such political propaganda? Where were you when such one-sided polemics was being dished out? Was this silence of yours in consonance with representing both sides in a 'fair manner *to the best of your ability*'?
>
> Even if you were a mute spectator to JNU being turned into an anti-government political platform, which of your comrades-at-arms demonstrated the high standards that you consider obligatory of me?
>
> But let me leave the others aside. If I was one-sided and unfair, I cannot justify myself by others' mistakes. After all, I do not wish to be like those who attack me. My intermediality is neither retaliatory nor expedient.

---

[112] In classical Indian traditions of debate, it was incumbent to present one's opponent at their best before refuting or criticizing them.

So, let me ask all those who heard my talk if I did not fare better than how my esteemed colleague, Professor Kidwai, has chosen to portray me. Did I not declare my solidarity with those who stood for the autonomy of universities and democratic institutions, both within the university and outside?

Did I not condemn acts of violence by extra-state actors against their ideological opponents? Have I not defended my colleagues on national television when news anchors asked if legal proceedings be instituted upon them for their beliefs? Have I not publicly regretted the arrests of the students from my campus?

In fact, have I not actually gone to the extent of asking if just raising slogans constitutes sedition prima facie?

In offering me teach-in lessons, Professor Kidwai seems to have forgotten my unequivocal condemning during the Q&A of multiple incidents of violence against individuals or groups for political ends.

If she doesn't remember, let me quote from the transcript: 'Do I condemn those things. Of course, I condemn those things. Please do not bracket me. There is no defending the indefensible.'[113]

I am, therefore, all the more concerned about how Professor Kidwai has misrepresented my 'teach-in' and what followed. Let's understand what actually transpired.

The lecture series was organized by the JNUTA. Indeed, I had been invited by my own colleagues to be a speaker. When

---

[113] "'Did you check your facts?'": Makarand Paranjape Has Some Questions for Kanhaiya, Leftists and JNU', *Scroll.in*, 8 March 2016, https://scroll.in/article/804802/did-you-check-your-facts-makarand-paranjape-has-some-questions-for-kanhaiya-leftists-and-jnu. Accessed on 27 August 2021; Readers are invited to see a video of the Q&A where I clearly condemn threats and violence against ideological opponents: Q&A Session, YouTube, https://www.youtube.com/watch?v=V7vLpSZ05sk. Accessed on 27 August 2021.

I reached the administration building, however, I found that the JNUSU president, Kanhaiya Kumar, mic in hand, already stood centre stage, loudly cheered by the partisan audience.

When I asked Professor Janaki Nair, one of the organizers, 'Isn't this JNUTA activity?' She replied, 'Yes, but today's lecture is merged with some student events.'

What she meant is that Kanhaiya Kumar had already seized control of the proceedings—possibly with the connivance of the teachers. Kumar thereupon informed me that he would 'chair' my session.

Why should a public 'teach-in' by a professor of long-standing be 'chaired' by the leader of the students' union was baffling. But given how JNU comrades orchestrate their attacks on their 'internal enemies', I need not have been surprised, let alone upset.

Mind you, I had not been forewarned, let alone consulted about the altered arrangements. I had literally been upstaged. I had been set up.

Another surprise awaited me. A few minutes into my lecture, Kumar escorted another speaker to the centre, seating her next to me. He said, 'She will also speak.' I asked, 'Okay. Do you want me to stop?' But of those gathered many said, 'No, no, you must carry on.'

Kumar then said, rather brusquely, '*Achha, jaldi* finish *kar deejiye, aap ke baad doosare bhi karyekram hai* [All right. Finish quickly. After yours there are other programmes too].' In fact, even before I had reached, a Hindi pamphlet, with derogatory remarks against me, had been circulated.

It claimed that I had signed a Hindi petition of some sort, which I do not recall signing.

After I started, several students moved about in front of me with anti-Manuvadi placards, clearly part of the pre-planned 'welcome' arranged for me. Later, I was also jeered a few times. This stopped only when student leader, Shehla

Rashid Shora, stood up to hush the hecklers. My talk was also interrupted several times by heckling, booing and other distractions.

During the Q&A afterwards, a couple of respondents made lengthy comments, without raising questions. Kumar allowed them all to say what they liked. A Chinese student defended his country and its government for five minutes without responding to my question as to why no support had come in from Chinese universities to the JNU student protests.

All this happened with the blessings of the 'chair', Kanhaiya Kumar.

Then, Kumar himself took to interrogating me. He tried to corner me several times, saying I wouldn't be let off that easily, that I would be held accountable. Where, under which convention, does a self-appointed chair of a meeting, subject the invited speaker to such an inquisition?

Yet, I decided to answer the questions. But, when I got my turn, he didn't let me answer properly, saying that I had to finish in a line with 'yes' or 'no'. I protested. All this can be seen on the YouTube video.[114] I am, therefore, not sure that 'great attention and patience', as Kidwai puts it, describes Kumar's or the audience's behaviour.

Let me now come to the more substantive parts of Professor Kidwai's attack. She begins with egregious condescension: 'The invitation to Paranjape was issued precisely because his is an oppositional voice within the teaching community at JNU.' Really? 'Oppositional' according to whom? Those who have constituted themselves as the self-appointed spokespersons of the entire JNU community?

If these same custodians of JNU really cared about 'oppositional voices', why was I the first and the last of the so-called internal opposition? Was a great favour done by

---

[114]Ibid.

inviting or allowing me to speak? Do folk of her ideological ilk own JNU so that the rest of us must subsist upon their largesse and sufferance? Tell me, Professor Kidwai, is the JNU campus really so united behind you and your cohorts?

What about the JNU Staff Association, representing hundreds of karamcharis and non-teaching staff? Didn't they pass a resolution clearly condemning the pro-Afzal event and the stance of the student union? What about the dozens of JNU teachers who also wanted a clearer censure of that same event and who do not approve of the manner in which their association has been bamboozled to make common cause with the students' union, possibly flouting the JNUTA constitution in the process?

Left-hegemony, Professor Kidwai, is not the same as Left majority. Perhaps, the real majority in the country, which you chose to ignore, does not approve the glorification of the likes of Afzal Guru.[115] Similarly, the anti-India sloganeering and, indeed, the generally anti-establishment, anti-state and anti-government rhetoric that emanates out of JNU does not meet with the approval of the outside world.

Indeed, sections of the JNU community, the students, teachers, non-teaching staff, the daily wage earners and the dependents of all of the former who also live on campus, who may not agree with you, have never been given a chance to speak out. Sure, the Left dominates the campus, but do they actually represent it?

Now let me refer to your remarks on Professor Chaman Lal.

I don't believe Professor Lal asked me to check my facts. Instead, he cast doubts on the veracity of the Soviet archives, asking me to check *their* facts, from which the figures of

---

[115] '78% People Say Parliament Attack Mastermind Afzal Guru Be Hanged: Poll', *India Today*, October 30, 2006, https://www.indiatoday.in/magazine/exclusive/story/20061030-parliament-attack-mastermind-afzal-guru-be-hanged-782092-2006-10-30. Accessed on 27 August 2021.

the millions of Soviet citizens who were sent to the Gulags, perished there or were executed by the State. Therefore, her comment is contrafactual and misplaced.

Actually, there are several different studies and accounts of these numbers, which even if they vary, generally establish the terrible atrocities and misdeeds carried out by the Soviet State against its own citizens.

This is also true of communist China under Mao and of Cambodia under Pol Pot. Thus, the outrageous record of communist regimes in torturing, executing, repressing and imprisoning their own citizens was not disputed by Professor Lal.

I would also like to ask Professor Kidwai how she concluded that I signed a petition for the dismissal of Professor Sheldon Pollock from the directorship of the Murty Library 'because of his endorsement of the JNU resistance'.

On what evidence did she make such an assertion? How did she come up with such casuistry? She stoops to ascribing a base and retaliatory motive to me, which I totally reject.[116]

I published my reservations over Pollock's style of scholarship in a leading newspaper on 21 March 2016.[117] In an article titled 'The Problem with Pollock', I clearly spelt out why I asked for his removal as the mentor and general editor of the Murty Library. The project would be much more cost effective to do in India:

> Handing USD5.6 million to elite US universities reverses the very logic that made Infosys rich. If

---

[116]From here until, 'My article did not mention JNU at all', was not in the original rejoinder. In the original, I only had one line, 'But there will, I hope, be another occasion for me to explain my position on the Murty Library.' One might say that I have exercised that option here.

[117]Paranjape, Makarand R. 'The Problem with Pollock', *The Indian Express*, 21 March 2016, https://indianexpress.com/article/opinion/columns/the-problem-with-pollock/. Accessed on 17 September 2021.

brainpower, not to mention manpower, is at least five times cheaper in India, wouldn't we get more bang for the buck here?

Secondly,

[t]he West's study of the rest was not always benevolent nor impartial. Instead, it was involved in the West's agenda to conquer, subdue, exploit, and even exterminate several nations, societies, and cultures. We Indians need to remember, as Bernard Cohn famously put it, that 'The conquest of India was a conquest of knowledge'.[118]

Finally, Pollock, in his 1985 essay, 'The Theory of Practice and the Practice of Theory in Indian Intellectual History', damned 'the entire *shastric* tradition, which he considers co-extensive with Sanskritic culture, as authoritarian'.[119]

Should such an ideologically motivated US professor, who had signed several petitions against Prime Minister Narendra Modi, be the best head of such a large project on Indology? To say the least, Pollock's motivations and academic politics were not to be trusted:

> Pollock has increasingly identified himself with Left-Liberal, even Hindu-phobic causes, signing various petitions, working to nix positions in Indic studies that diaspora philanthropists wished to endow in the United States, in addition to advising the Government of India reportedly to end 'its authoritarian menace' on Indian campuses.[120]

I asked if such 'politically motivated hegemonic practices, which are ideological rather than academic'

---

[118]Ibid.
[119]Ibid.
[120]Ibid.

wouldn't 'influence the content, translations, and outputs of the Murty Library'.¹²¹

My article did not mention JNU at all.

Another example of Kidwai's motivated causistry is her astounding assertion that I had 'traced the crackdown on JNU to … the absence of compulsory attendance in classes'.

Professor Kidwai was not present at my Sahitya Akademi paper, the date of which she erroneously cites as 16 February instead of 19 February. She does not reveal the source of the claim, which could only be the PTI story, which reported just a small section of my paper. But even in that report, the state crackdown and the lack of compulsory attendance were not connected. I had mentioned the latter only to show the prevailing culture of academic unaccountability in JNU. As a matter of fact, I do not endorse 'compulsory attendance' as much as oppose demand of non-attendance as a right. I hope she understands the difference.

Likewise, what are the 'epistolary proclivities' that she accuses me of? She claims in her 'open letter' that I 'have for some time now endorsed a pro-government, pro-Hindutva position'.¹²²

---

[121] Pollock has numerous powerful students, colleagues and defenders all over the world. Rohan Murty, his patron, also continues to support him. His critics, on the other hand, are comparatively very few and not at all as well-regarded. Many are not even academics, let alone from his discipline. Here is a rare statement of why his scholarship and politics are so troubling to a section of Indians, both in India and overseas: 'Twenty Statements from Sheldon Pollock on India, Hinduism and Sanskrit', *IndiaFacts*, 26 January 2015, http://indiafacts.org/twenty-statements-sheldon-pollock-india-hinduism-sanskrit/. Accessed on 17 September 2021.

[122] 'Here's How Not to Teach a Class: JNU's Ayesha Kidwai Responds to Her Colleague Makarand Paranjape', *Scroll.in*, 10 March 2016, https://scroll.in/article/804879/heres-how-not-to-teach-a-class-jnus-ayesha-kidwai-responds-to-her-colleague-makarand-paranjape. Accessed on 25 August 2021.

Apart from the earlier mentioned petition on the Murty Library, I joined a group of academics voicing concern over how universities in India had become war zones of a very dangerous and divisive caste politics, and lent my name to a statement on 'Hypocrisy and Indian History'.[123] How is this a pro-government or pro-Hindutva position? Why, moreover, should every such position be necessarily or automatically damned?

Shouldn't each of us be free to take positions on individual matters and issues according to our own critical assessments? Isn't this the freedom that I was trying to champion in my talk? Why should we be held to ransom by the Left or have to justify our ideas in accordance to their standards? Who are they to sit in judgement, dismissing, condemning the rest of us?

As if name-calling in itself was sufficient grounds of censure and dismissal? Is there no need to critique the actual content of a statement? Isn't this what constitutes bad politics, bad academics and bad pedagogy? Is the Left so short on substance that it has nothing more than tired and repetitive ad hominem attacks?

Despite her hectoring, superior tone, it is Professor Kidwai who has shown herself deficient in thinking clearly and making rational arguments. Where I differ from Professor Kidwai—and this is where I reassert the space of the hermeneutics of mediality which I never vacated—is that I do not believe that the present situation forces us to take sides for or against the government. Instead, I believe that one can take positions based on the merits of each case, without

---

[123] The petition is worth reading as a critique of the dominant, Leftist historiography of India: 'Hypocrisy and Indian History', *Change.org*, 17 November 2015, https://www.change.org/p/concerned-indians-statement-on-hypocrisy-and-indian-history. Accessed on 25 August 2021.

throwing one's lot with one ideological grouping or the other.

That is how I understand a truly independent, critical and interrogative politics, which does not allow the voice of the awakened citizenry to be instrumentalized for any one political cause.

To me, the fight is not only between opposing ideologies, but between ideology and integrity. I respect the Left when it shows integrity, but not when it cynically distorts, misrepresents and targets its ideological 'Others'.

Finally, to an intriguing passage in Professor Kidwai's criticism, which I had almost overlooked, until a friend pointed out how sinister it was:

[T]he enthusiastic questioning cannot get Paranjape to completely disassociate himself from the promise being aired on social media that Umar Khalid, another student accused of sedition, will be delivered the same *azadi* as the one that was given to 2001 Parliament attack convict Afzal Guru and Jammu and Kashmir Liberation Front founder Maqbool Bhat—both of whom have been hanged. Rather, Paranjape says, he cannot 'understand what this slogan means'.[124]

It is only with a slow and growing horror that the sinister implications of Professor Kidwai's insinuation became clear.

Which slogan did I not understand, Professor Kidwai? By 'cannot get to dissociate' did you mean that I have already associated myself with calls on social media for the hanging of Umar Khalid? But here's the problem with such innuendos: Professor Kidwai, you will never be able to show one instance of such an association, even one occasion where I said that due process should be denied to someone. You will never be able to show me saying that Umar Khalid or

---

[124]"Here's How Not to Teach a Class: JNU's Ayesha Kidwai Responds to Her Colleague Makarand Paranjape", *Scroll.in*, 10 March 2016, https://scroll.in/article/804879/heres-how-not-to-teach-a-class-jnus-ayesha-kidwai-responds-to-her-colleague-makarand-paranjape. Accessed on 25 August 2021.

his likes ought to be summarily executed or lynched. That is because I have never endorsed such things.

What other options would anyone setting out to slander me thus have except hints, nudges and jibes of this sort? Not only does Professor Kidwai totally distort what I stand for, but also seems to deny me the basic courtesies due to another human being, let alone a fellow-academic and colleague.

I see little generosity in her, only misunderstanding and prejudice. Why has she stooped so low as to malign me through insinuation and innuendo?

Could it be that she is genuinely confused, anxious and fearful that people like me have suddenly turned viciously homicidal? Or is it that that her ideological certitudes have so completely and utterly blunted her from perceiving, let alone appreciating, that those who do not subscribe to her politics are also capable of caring for humanity, justice, equality and truth?

If so, ideology destroys humanity. Isn't that what we learn from George Orwell, Arthur Koestler, André Gide, David Caute and a host of others?

What happened, Professor Kidwai, to the responsibility of purvapaksha? Did you absolve yourself of your own pedagogical imperative after enjoining it upon me?

At least in the above-cited passage, far from representing my position to *'the best of your ability'*, you have failed to accord it even the slightest benefit of doubt.

Instead, you have superimposed a monster of your own making on me, projecting your own paranoiac fantasy of horror and intolerance. Worse than a straw man, you have turned me into an effigy of murderous bigotry and hatred, which even those who largely profess ahimsa might not hesitate to set on fire.

Tell us, Professor Kidwai, you, who so readily denounce

and brand others, where do you stand? Do you glorify and commemorate the Afzal Gurus and Maqbool Bhats of our times, or merely support those who glorify and commemorate them under false pretexts?

Do you support Hindu-bashing and Hinduphobia, the burning of smritis such as Manu's, organizing beef festivals and calling the Hindu goddess Durga a 'sex worker' as a poster promoting the worship of Mahishasura in JNU did?[125]

Have you spoken out against such divisive and hate-mongering politics so virulent on our campuses? Did you take a stand against our own JNU campus being turned into a site of pitched battles between feuding political factions? Let me assure you that if you did, I would applaud your mediality and stand with you.

Unfortunately, you are used to seeing or imagining others as if they are just like you, liable to distort, misrepresent, bully, accuse or evade reality—all for a cause, of course. Sorry. Some of us are neither as ideological nor ideologized. On the contrary, recalling Hamlet, we think that there are more things in heaven and earth than are dreamt of in your ideology. Or, to invoke, Rohith, we are truly magnificent beings, made of stardust, capable of helping and transforming each other.

But as long as Left patricians and partisans selectively attack, condemn and conspire, all the while arrogating to themselves the moral superiority of 'objectivity', 'history' or even 'science', they will continue to be critiqued and questioned.

---

[125]Basu, Saurav. 'Manu Smriti: Locating Dharma and Adharma in the Light of Modernity,' *India Facts*, 7 February 2016, http://indiafacts.org/manu-smriti-locating-dharma-adharma-light-modernity/. Accessed on 16 September 2021; Jahnavi Sen, 'Mahishasura and the Minister,' *The Wire*, 27 February 2016, https://thewire.in/politics/mahishasura-and-the-minister. Accessed on 16 September 2021.

> Evidently, such lessons don't please you. Is that why you resort to falling out and crying foul, 'here's not how to teach ... this is not a good class'?
>
> Makarand R. Paranjape

In her bio-line, Professor Kidwai, with typical virtue-signalling, had made much of her PhD: 'Ayesha Kidwai got her PhD at age 28 because she comes from a family where women were educated for five generations before her.'

I didn't want, but was perhaps forced, to respond in kind:

> Makarand R. Paranjape, submitted his PhD at the University of Illinois at Urbana-Champaign at 24, has authored or edited over forty books, published more than 150 academic papers, and been Professor of English at JNU for 15 years.

Of course, those publication figures have only increased since then. I have now over 50 books and 180 papers to my credit, in addition to thousands of periodical or popular essays, op-eds and columns.

One aspect of Kidwai's 'open letter' which I did not react to was the veiled reference to Rohith Vemula, a research scholar in the University of Hyderabad, who had died by suicide on 17 January 2016. His suicide had been turned into a national cause célèbre by the Leftists, who argued that it was the brutal murder of a Dalit.

However, there was considerable confusion over Vemula's caste. Though he had claimed benefits of reservation due to scheduled castes, his father did not belong to such a community. His mother too had been adopted by an OBC family. Though Vemula was projected as a Dalit who had been driven to his death by caste discrimination, a state enquiry committee revealed that neither his mother nor him were actually Dalits. This meant that he had availed of scholarship benefits, probably, by falsifying his caste.¹²⁶

This was tragically ironic because Vemula was considered to be at the forefront of a group of Dalit students, who were, in my view, being used as a shield and front by various activist groups spearheading a nationwide movement against the Modi sarkar.¹²⁷ In fact, as his suicide note shows, Vemula was disillusioned by campus politics.¹²⁸ Arguably, their associates in JNU included Umar Khalid and Anirban Bhattacharya, because as per intelligence reports, it was allegedly they who conceived the idea of organizing a cultural evening to mark the so-called 'judicial murder' of Afzal Guru, a known separatist.¹²⁹

Vemula had penned a moving suicide note, which many have appreciated and glorified:

> The value of a man was reduced to his immediate identity and nearest possibility. To a vote. To a number. To a thing. Never was a man treated as a mind. As a glorious thing

---

¹²⁶'Rohith Vemula and Mother Radhika Are OBCs, Not Dalits, Says Andhra Pradesh Government', *Firstpost*, 14 February 2017, https://www.firstpost.com/india/rohith-vemula-and-mother-radhika-are-obcs-not-dalits-says-andhra-pradesh-government-3282654.html. Accessed on 4 October 2021. I cover this issue at greater length in a chapter to come.

¹²⁷'Arun Jaitley's Full Speech in RS in JNU and Rohith Vemula Suicide', 26 February 2016, *The Indian Express*, https://indianexpress.com/article/business/budget/arun-jaitleys-full-speech-in-rajya-sabha-on-situation-arising-in-central-institutions-of-higer-education-with-specific-reference-to-jnu-and-university-od-hyderabad/. Accessed on 4 October 2021.

¹²⁸Henry, Nikhila. 'Away from the Red Dye Towards a Blue Sky: Rohith Vemula's Scathing Attack on Indian Left', *The News Minute*, 10 August 2016, https://www.thenewsminute.com/article/away-red-dye-towards-blue-sky-rohith-vemulas-scathing-attack-indian-left-47958. Accessed on 4 October 2021.

¹²⁹Bhalla, Abhishek. 'JNU's Umar Khalid Had Planned Afzal Guru Show Across India: Intel Reports', *India Today*, 18 February 2016, https://www.indiatoday.in/mail-today/story/umar-khalid-had-planned-afzal-show-across-india-report-309266-2016-02-18. Accessed 28 September 2021.

made up of stardust. In very field, in studies, in streets, in politics, and in dying and living.... If there is anything at all I believe, I believe that I can travel to the stars. And know about the other worlds.[130]

I too was deeply touched by it, by the loss of a young, talented man, a member of our society. But the politics around his death was rather sordid and unscrupulous.

At the end of her letter, Professor Kidwai, tried to extract political capital from Vemula's suicide:

> This assault is on the very idea of the university because it seeks to produce a (self-)censorship that limits what we students and teachers may be allowed to say. How in the panopticon envisioned for us as the new university, can a student ever be 'treated as a mind', as 'a glorious thing made up of stardust'?[131]

I deliberately refrained from responding to this portion of her letter. I didn't want to add fuel to the fire that had turned Vemula's body to ashes just a couple of months ago.

But I would have liked to ask Professor Kidwai: who is it that had turned our universities into factories to produce radicals? Who had destroyed the idea of a university as a place of learning and scholarship? The new BJP government? Or the Leftists, who over the decades had turned JNU into a den of self-serving, hatred-spewing, near-hysterical ideologues, not to mention parasitical hypocrites and free-loaders? Did Professor Kidwai or others of her

---

[130]'Dalit Scholar Rohith Vemula's Suicide Note', *The Times of India*, 19 January 2017, https://timesofindia.indiatimes.com/city/hyderabad/Full-text-Dalit-scholar-Rohith-Vemulas-suicide-note/articleshow/50634646.cms. Accessed on 27 August 2021.

[131]'Here's How Not to Teach a Class: JNU's Ayesha Kidwai Responds to Her Colleague Makarand Paranjape', *Scroll.in*, 10 March 2016, https://scroll.in/article/804879/heres-how-not-to-teach-a-class-jnus-ayesha-kidwai-responds-to-her-colleague-makarand-paranjape. Accessed on 25 August 2021.

ilk treat their students, let alone political colleagues or adversaries, as glorious minds, made up of stardust?

Epistle IV: Cows, Castes and Classes: Maitreyee Shukla's Misguided Meanderings

On 14 March 2016, the very same day as Ayesha Kidwai's diatribe, I was assaulted by another 'open letter'. This one was from Maitreyee Shukla, an MPhil student of Sociology at JNU. Titled 'Dear Prof. Paranjape, We Are Not "Manufacturing Discontent"', it was published on *India Resists*, the same Left-wing portal that had earlier published Professor Rajat Datta's letter.[132] Despite promises that they would publish my response on their portal, they did not do so. Perhaps, their intolerance had finally caught up with them? *Swarajya* came to the rescue by publishing my rejoinder on 31 March 2016.[133]

To,
Maitreyee Shukla,
MPhil Scholar,
Centre for the Study of Social Systems, JNU

25 March 2016

Maitreyee-ji,

I hesitated to respond to your 'open letter', one more in a series of many, this time from a student of JNU. Especially

---

[132] Shukla, Maitreyee, 'Dear Prof. Paranjape, We Are Not "Manufacturing Discontent"': A JNU Student's Open Letter', *India Resists*, 14 March 2016. Now archived on: https://web.archive.org/web/20210507004835/https://www.indiaresists.com/discontent-not-sedition-open-letter-prof-paranjape-jnu-student/. Accessed on 8 December 2021.
[133] Paranjpe, Makarand R. 'Prof Makarand Paranjape Responds to Maitreyee Shukla's Open Letter', *Swarajya*, 31 March 2016, https://swarajyamag.com/politics/prof-makarand-paranjape-responds-to-maitreyee-shuklas-open-letter. Accessed on 27 August 2021. Khalid and Bhattacharya were released from Tihar jail on 17 March 2016.

when two of our students were still in custody. I didn't want to further escalate the war of words or, indeed, to be more misunderstood in my own village.

Also, I wasn't sure that it behoved me to joust with you verbally. After all, it is the privilege of the young to rebel, misunderstand, even to reject what their parents or teachers stand for. Each generation, moreover, has a right to discover its own values and beliefs. Why should you be denied yours?

But now both your comrades are out on bail, thanks to the very same judicial system that they so vociferously condemned.[134] Writing back to you might therefore be less unbecoming.

Frankly, I still might have refrained from responding to you, had it not been for the ominous warning at the end of your letter: 'History will not forget that at this critical moment, you chose not to stand with it.' I wonder if you noticed how the dire threat of Judgement Day of the Semitic faiths now reappears in your missive in the garb of damnation at the dread hand of History.

---

[134]Interestingly, the following evening, on 18 March 2016, there was an unprecedented congregation for what came to be called the 'Vande Mataram' screening of Vivek Agnihotri's film, *Buddha in a Traffic Jam*. Anupam Kher, the world-famous thespian and star of the movie, was also present. After the Dean, Professor Ira Bhaskar, withdrew permission to screen the movie at the Arts and Aesthetics auditorium, student groups who had invited Agnihotri to our campus arranged an outdoor showing in the very 'Freedom Square', next to the admin building, where the 'tukde-tukde' slogans had been shouted. It was a tremendous show of strength. The crowd was so massive that I was unable to get anywhere close to the screen and had to watch the movie later at a private screening. Agnihotri has written about his experience in detail in his bestseller book *Urban Naxals: The Making of Buddha in a Traffic Jam* (2018), for which I ended up writing the 'Foreword'. Agnihotri, it must be remembered, was no stranger to JNU, having studied at the Indian Institute of Mass Communication (IIMC), on the JNU campus.

But what makes you believe that a call to arms, or failing which, punishment in the form of some version of eternal damnation, in the name of history is any less dubious than in the name of a jealous and unforgiving God? To continue in the same theological idiom, do you not remember the admonition, 'She that is without sin among you, let her first cast a stone at him'?[135]

Do you consider yourself so perfectly guilt-free ideologically, not just to cast the first stone, but also to be judge, jury and executioner? I don't think 'History', in whose name you pretend to speak, gives you quite so much authority nor, I am sure, would you consider yourself as its Messiah.

Naiveté, yes! That you may be entitled to being young and idealistic, but omniscience and omnipotence, no! For that is reserved only for the Deity of History, authorized in the name of some other 'father', whether he be Father Marx, Father Lenin or Father Mao.

That is why you need seriously to consider whom you mean when you say, 'Not one of your arguments hold ground when tested logically and factually'. Perhaps, your remark is far more autobiographical, if not self-referential, than you think or realize.

Passion, political romanticism, even commitment and fellow-feeling do not necessarily in themselves make for good arguments, nor do letting off steam, espousing 'worthy' causes, and shooting off indignant 'open letters' without thinking through your positions clearly or carefully.

Being a sociology student you, I am sure, are familiar with Durkheim's idea of the malaise of modernity, which produces free-floating and rootless individuals consequent

---

[135] A slight and deliberate, gender updated version of the famous line from the Gospel according to John (8.7), King James' Bible (1611).

on the breakdown of social and religious norms. Hannah Arendt, another well-known European thinker, argues that without a sense of belonging and purpose, such individuals become vulnerable to manipulation by ideologies because these give them a 'spurious sense of meaning'.

I am concerned about how vulnerable young women and men are being used by political parties for their own purposes. That, Maitreyee-ji, is what I meant when I cautioned against the over-politicization of our campuses. Tell me, is this logically fallacious or without foundation?

Similarly, when you accused me of reducing 'the entire student movement across India to an attempt to "manufacture discontent"', you are obviously wrong. I said no such thing.

In fact, when asked by *FirstPost,* 'Who is manufacturing this discontent?' I replied, 'One shouldn't pinpoint anyone without concrete evidence'.[136] So when you say that I brand the entire student movement as manufacturers of discontent, surely you have misunderstood and misquoted me. The manufacturers of discontent may be far more sinister, using gullible, idealistic and impressionable students for their own purposes. In fact, the labelling of scattered and instigated protests as a country-wide 'student movement' is itself a part of this conspiracy of 'breaking-India' forces.[137]

---

[136] Tripathi, Shishir. 'JNU Is Like a Land of Lotus-Eaters, Where We Haven't Emerged from the Cold War: Makarand Paranjape', *FirstPost*, 10 March 2016, https://www.firstpost.com/india/jnu-is-like-a-land-of-lotus-eaters-where-we-have-not-emerged-from-the-cold-war-makarand-paranjape-2666738.html. Accessed on 27 August 2021.

[137] Indeed, five years later, one might ask: where is this so-called 'student movement'? A popular youth movement was attempted to be kick-started against the Modi sarkar, but it failed to take off. In fact, Modi was re-elected as prime minister in 2019, with an even more convincing majority, with the support of many young people and first time voters.

Now let me come to some of your other strictures. You say pork is not banned, while beef is. This is not, strictly speaking, true. Even if not officially banned, is pork served in JNU hostels? Or for that matter in any university mess in India?

Isn't this tantamount to a shadow ban, even if not a legal prohibition?

But what about Kashmir? Is pork sold or served there? Muhammad Zahid writing in *Greater Kashmir* as far back as 29 December 2009 observes, 'The recent move by Srinagar Municipal Committee regarding ban on products having suspicion that pig fat [lard] might have been used in their processing was welcome indeed. The intention was purely religious that could safely be extended into the realms of spirituality.'[138]

Notice the word 'suspected.' Even products that are suspected, not necessarily proven, to have pig products in them are prohibited. Then what to speak of pork in all its various forms? Isn't pork also a poor person's meat in India, consumed by castes and communities now called 'Dalit'? Isn't this unfair and discriminatory to them, not to speak of other who may enjoy ham, sausage or pork chops?

Note also how the author makes no bones about how this ban is religious. No need for pretentious secularism when it comes to Islamo-fascism? But does this mean you should organize pork parties in Srinagar or even in JNU hostels? No.

If you heard my interview properly, I clearly said that we should *not* do so because it offends the sensibilities of some of our fellow-citizens. My argument against 'beef festivals' is similar. The intent behind them appears to be mischievous

---

[138]Zahid, Muhammad. 'Pig Fat Banned', *Greater Kashmir*, 13 March 2015, https://www.greaterkashmir.com/opinion/pig-fat-banned. Accessed on 8 December 2021.

and provocative, given that this is an intensely divisive issue, not only in today's India, but for hundreds of years.

From the Buddha to Gandhi, several great Indians have taken a stand against the slaughter of animals. Guess who wrote the following words to whom:

> The realm of Hindustan is full of diverse creeds. Praise be to God, the Righteous, the Glorious, the Highest, that He had granted unto you the Empire of it. It is but proper that you, with heart cleansed of all religious bigotry, should dispense justice according to the tenets of each community. And in particular refrain from the sacrifice of cow, for that way lies the conquest of the hearts of the people of Hindustan; and the subjects of the realm will, through royal favour, be devoted to you.[139]

This was not some Hindutvavadi, but none other than Babur, India's first Moghul emperor, writing his secret *vasiyat nama* to his son, Humayun in 1529. He had already issued a decree against cow slaughter in 1526.[140] Even if this so-called will is forged, as has been claimed, it does indicate a move, post-facto, to make the emperors of Hindustan more sensitive to Hindu sentiments.

In independent India, from the directive principles of the Constitution right up to recent legislations, the State

---

[139] This supposed 'Will' of the first Moghul emperor, Babur, and addressed to his son Humayun, can be found here: Jaffar, J.M. *The Mughal Empire: From Babar to Aurangzeb*, S. Muhammad Sadiq Khan, 1936, pp. 23–24. Jaffar says, 'The original document is in Persian and is treasured in the Hamida Library at Bhopal as one of its heirlooms'.

[140] Some, including the translator of *Babur Nama*, Annette S. Beveridge, doubt the authenticity of this *vasiyat-nama* (will), considering it to be spurious and of later manufacture. See 'Further Notes on Baburiana', *The Journal of the Royal Asiatic Society of Great Britain and Ireland*, January, 1923, pp. 75–82. Certainly, the *Babur Nama* itself shows no such sympathy towards Hindus or their beliefs.

has discouraged the slaughter of cows. In all but eight states of the Indian Union, it is a cognisable offence. Yet, as I understand it, the law does not criminalize the consumption of beef by individuals. This is a humane provision that protects eating preferences. I agree, however, that there seems to be an inherent contradiction. You can eat beef but not slaughter cows. In fact, our Constitution is full of similar dodges on 'sensitive issues.' That should give you some idea of how our nation is constituted, by balancing different and contending stake-holders.

Therefore, I say to those for whom cow slaughter and beef-eating are so important, try to change the law. Lobby legislators, conduct public campaigns to convince Indians that beef-eating is desirable and, eventually, you might succeed. Or, more likely, you will fail.

But instead of going about this constitutionally, what do they do? They create friction and foment conflict. They deliberately offend the sensibilities of those who find cow slaughter and beef-eating abhorrent. My objection is to such politics, targeted at certain sections of the populace, with the view to fragment and divide society.

If beef-campaigners respect the Constitution of India and the law of the land, not to mention Hindu sentiments, then they would not try to hold beef festivals, regardless of their private beliefs on the matter. Instead, their aim seems to offend, provoke and attack those who are against cow slaughter.

Now who are their targets? Only Hindus. So the object is to offend Hindus. Why? To hatred and unrest? This is what I object to. Aren't Hindu-phobia and Hindu-bashing also undesirable, even if camouflaged behind politically correct jargon?

The issue of the worship of Mahishasur is similar. As long as such worship is not intended to give offence but expresses alternate traditions, it is not objectionable. But when it is combined with the abuse of Goddess Durga, then it is bound to create hatred and divide society.

I agree that sex workers should be treated with dignity, but what is the evidence that the Goddess was one? Aren't epithets such as 'prostitute' or 'sex worker' used to abuse and defame women? Don't we stand up against such insults? Don't we consider them examples of the indignities that women suffer?

Wouldn't you be hurt and offended if members of your own family, let alone yourself, were so labelled? Wouldn't you consider that to be in extremely poor taste, if not outright offensive? If so, would you blame devotees of Goddess Durga for being outraged at her being tagged with such a marker?

Political correctness, I am afraid, cannot mask wicked and harmful intent. It is the latter which is objectionable, not the former.

Let me come next to the similarly contentious issue of caste. I don't believe that I have analysed or commented on the saddening suicide of Rohith Vemula. So why have you dragged me into a controversy, imputing all kinds of motives to me? The suicide of any young person in this country is a cause of great concern and introspection, but what we have here is an attempt to capitalize on it.

Again, I was referring primarily to political parties and leaders, who scrambled to take advantage of the situation. Instead of dousing the flames, several interested parties added fuel to the fire of caste hatred. That is what I find appalling.

The crisis in Hyderabad was many years in the making, with earlier flare-ups. I taught at the University of Hyderabad (HCU), so can speak from personal experience. In the decade of the 1980s, the dominant line of 'negative' politics was of local, which then meant Telugu, not just *mulki* or

Telangana, versus non-local.

I joined the HCU straight after my PhD in the US, committed to serving my own country and society. But what did I find? Bullies made up of so-called 'local' groups trying to influence decision making at every level, including recruitment, promotions and important appointments.

They had many ways of browbeating and neutralizing their perceived opponents, the 'outsiders', who were to be put in their place. Such was the politics at a 'Central' university. I remember a senior professor taunting me, 'I have served at BHU and know how it is to be treated as an outsider. This is Telugu country. If you don't behave here, you'll be driven out.' I replied, 'Sir, we due respect, I thought we are all Indians here.'

But soon there was another, even more dangerous caste politics that overran regional parochialism.

Unlike JNU, there was no minimum cut-off for most subjects in the HCU entrance exams. The result was that in some disciplines, a person could get single-digit marks, even theoretically a zero, but still be admitted, if a seat in a particular category remained vacant. I remember the university sending an officer in a car going to the homes of some of these low-scoring entrance-examinees to persuade them to join, just so that the reservation categories were filled.

Once admitted, however, these educationally as well as socially disadvantaged students found themselves adrift. The institutional mechanisms to bring them up to par were inadequate. I have myself guided and trained some of them, so I know how hard both the teacher and the student had to work.

Oftentimes that hard work was simply not put in. Instead, some of these students joined radical groups, which claimed to champion their rights. They also ended up targeting those who didn't want to 'cooperate' with their demands. Imagine that you were a teacher at such an institution with a name such as 'Shukla'.

You might find yourself triply vulnerable as an outsider, a savarna with a hated Brahmin surname, in addition to being a woman. You might be accused of being casteist if you didn't pass a student whose performance on your exam was dismal. You might be accused of ruining his or her career if you refused to ensure that the student got the grade or the percentage of marks considered the minimum eligibility requirement to appear for the MPhil or NET exam.

To my recollection, none of these radical groups organized teach-ins or coaching classes for their juniors, nor did they ever emphasize the intense hard work and wide reading required to do well in academics. Think of the message being sent out: to do well, you don't have to study hard or learn real skills. Instead, you need to belong to a particular community or caste, then join groups that would protect or promote your interests.

Even if things had stopped there, many would have considered it merely business as usual. But, no, the campus soon became a battleground of vicious and divisive caste hatred, with socially disadvantaged students being mobilized for other causes than social justice.

You may recall that before the tragic incident that you referred to, an event commemorating 'martyred' Kashmiri separatists was organized, which brought HCU to a standstill. It is this kind of divisive and destructive politics that I have spoken out against. Only to attack the government is to turn a blind eye to what is happening in our own backyards.

Now to your last point about taxes, middle classes and the 'laughable' comparison of JNU to IITs and IIMs. Once again, you have failed to go beyond your prejudices, which makes you unable to understand my point. I merely said that middle-class, taxpaying citizens have the right to ask why they should subsidize 'anti-nationalism'. I didn't say they were right or wrong, only that you can't blame them for thinking this way.

After all, less than 3 per cent of the population pays income taxes in India as opposed to about 45 per cent in a country like the US. Now, why should these Indians face only ridicule and demonisation in return? Shouldn't their concerns be respected? Along with income tax, an education cess is also levied. Why is it ridiculous to ask if that cess goes to paying for education or politicking and sloganeering at publicly funded campuses where academic standards are dubious, if not declining?

I did not mean or suggest that middle-class tax-payers had special claims on the State. On the contrary, India belongs to all of us. Anyone who participates in the organized economy does, as you rightly pointed out, contribute to the state exchequer. But does this mean that you castigate the middle classes for their values when they resist doling out, along with all their taxes, unconditional support to causes that seem invalid to them?

That is why to offer dissent in the name of the poorest of the poor is bad logic, even worse ethics, for middle-class students, such as yourself. This is merely to appropriate someone else's victimhood for your own, some would say parasitical, privileges. These poorest of the poor, if you care to ask them, would be the first to urge you not to squander the opportunities of higher education, to study first and do politics later.

I have myself heard so many daily-wage earners, domestic help and other marginal members of the JNU community complain, '*In logon ko padhayi chhod kar aur sab karne hai. Unke maa-baap par kay beetati hogi? Bachhon ko itni door padhane ke liye bhej rahen hain ki hangama karne ke liye?* [These students are up to all kinds of activities other than studying; what would their parents be going through? Have they been sent here so far away from home to study or to create a ruckus?]'

It is not that I agree entirely with such a view, but please don't be under the illusion that the real subalterns of our society consider you either their representatives or champions. To that extent, the comparison with IITs or IIMs is also not laughable.[141]

These institutions also give research degrees, such as PhDs, even in Humanities and Social Sciences. Do you know that more often than not, their theses are far better than ours? That is because IITs/IIMs are run more professionally, with greater academic accountability, and better work culture than our universities.

In fact, the world over no university is respected or renowned without high academic standards, regardless of its degree of political engagement. The latter is in addition to, not a substitute for, the former.

As to what you call 'non-NET fellowships', may I ask why you call them 'fellowships' when they are given automatically to all students admitted to MPhil and PhD in central universities? And fees? Why call them *fees* when they seem to have no correlation to any economic factor, let alone the actual costs of education, seemingly frozen forever, neither going up with inflation or expenses to keep the university going? These are not 'fellowships' but subsidies; not 'fees' but disguises for free education.

Why not just make JNU free, scrapping 'fees' altogether, doing away with this pretence? Best not to discuss these issues here, lest we are accused of betraying the 'poorest of

---

[141]The comparison is no longer 'laughable' because JNU also started Engineering and Management faculties in 2019.

the poor'. After all, many are deprived even of an opportunity to go to college or university? Don't they need 'fellowships' much more than most of us?

What happened to Louis Blanc's famous slogan '*De chacun selon ses facultés, à chacun selon ses besoins*', popularized by Marx as 'From each according to his ability, to each according to his needs'? Isn't that one reason that the middle classes pay income taxes in the first place?

Surely, by the same logic, many JNU students can afford to pay much more. Indeed they have paid 10 times as much each month not only in school and college fees, but also in coaching classes to clear the JNU entrance tests. These same JNU students spend more for a single dinner at our own local 24x7 eatery than their monthly fees or hostel dues.

So why should one size fit all when it comes to JNU? Let the rich pay more and the poor less. Wouldn't that be more 'socialistic'? Why doesn't any comrade say so? Why doesn't any student group, regardless of political affiliation, ask such questions?

Let me end by referring to your postscript, in which you clarify that your 'open letter' is not meant to bully me. I agree. I don't feel bullied by you. Don't worry. What I do feel is 'othered', misunderstood, slandered.

You address me as an individual, but refer to yourself as 'we'. I take it that it's not the royal pronoun, but the presumed unity of purpose and ideology among those you stand with. You consider me ranged against this collective as this single individual, alone, isolated and worthy of being chastised in your 'open letter'.

Lest you persist in thinking so, let me remind you that in my very first intervention on the JNU crisis at the Sahitya Akademi on 19 February 2016, I clearly regretted the arrest of our students. In my Nationalism teach-in I started by saying that I stood for the autonomy of educational institutions and statutory institutions in the country. In all my statements since, I have always spoken for due process, democratic norms, and the rule of law.

When a well-known TV anchor asked why an 'antinational colleague' shouldn't be arrested, I stated that I would never support such witch hunts, least of all against my own colleagues, even if I believed them to be wrong and disagreed with them. I am quite opposed to authoritarian and totalitarian ideologies, whatever their political colour, as I am to a democratic state repressing its own citizens.

Don't you think we need to redraw the boundaries of 'we'? Tell me who is the real 'enemy' of JNU and India and who the real 'friend'?

The path of the unthinking rabble-rousers in JNU will lead to our ruin unless, of course, you believe it is only pretend-politics. In contrast, my path will, I am convinced, improve, if not save JNU, by reducing divisiveness, discovering a new political idiom and reinvigorating our academic ecosystem.

In this regard, I am glad you mentioned Mahatma Gandhi, because he is at the very centre or heart of the 'we' of the nation and society that we are trying to build, foster, nurture and protect. He said, 'it will be your duty to tell the revolutionaries and everybody else that the freedom they want, or they think they want, is not to be obtained by killing people or doing violence, but by setting themselves right, and by becoming and remaining truly Indian.' Don't you think this applies as much to all of us as to the so-called revolutionaries in our midst? Why not try to set ourselves right before attacking others?

There are millions in India who work harder than most of us in JNU. They do so, moreover, with fewer rewards or benefits. It is such people who make this country viable, not the agitators and nay-sayers, who sow division and discord amongst us for their own selfish and cynical political and pecuniary interests. Maitreyee-ji, don't you think it is the latter that history will not forgive?

I do hope you choose wisely, so as not to belong to the latter.

Makarand R. Paranjape

Epistle V: Fifty Shades of Grey without the Thrills (or Frills)

The last of these targeted 'open letters' which I include here was by Shourjendra Nath Mukherjee, a doctoral student in History at Delhi University. His missive of 5 April 2016 was posted by J. Devika on *Kafila*, a Leftist portal.[142]

At first Devika refused to publish my rejoinder. I wrote to the editorial committee, who finally nudged her, it would seem, to carry it. Hilariously, among other hashtags, my response was also tagged as 'Hindutva Terror'.[143] I pointed this out, once again practically forcing Devika to remove it, but that tag has been retained on Mukherjee's original letter.

Here is my response, which was published on 13 April 2016. Subsequently, *Swarajya* also carried it on 17 April 2016.[144]

---

[142]Mukherjee, Shourjendra Nath. 'An Open Letter to Prof Makarand Paranjape', *Kafila*, 5 April 2016, https://kafila.online/2016/04/05/an-open-letter-to-prof-makarand-paranjape/. Accessed on 27 August 2021.

[143]@Makarandparanspe, Twitter, 15 May 2019, https://twitter.com/makrandparanspe/status/1128459273527185408?lang=en. Accessed on 16 September 2021.

[144]This is the response, originally published in *Kafila* on 13 April 2016: https://kafila.online/2016/04/13/fifty-shades-of-grey-without-the-thrills/. Accessed on 27 August 2021. It has also been carried in *Swarajya* on 17 April 2016: https://swarajyamag.com/politics/fifty-shades-of-grey-without-the-thrills. Accessed on 27 August 2021. *Kafila* continued to post attacks on me as this one the following year on 8 March 2017 by JNU activist, Anirban Bhattacharya, of Bhagat Singh-Ambedkar Student Organization (BASO) shows: 'Looking "Right", Talking

Mr Shourjendra Nath Mukherjee's 'open letter' of 5 April 2016 makes only one substantive point, concerning the *agency* of students, which needs attention.

The rest of it, as the Dormouse said to Alice, is, 'much of a muchness'—confusion, rigmarole and thumb-twiddling over precious little, which scarcely need be dignified by serious refutation.

But because Mr Mukherjee has just joined the *Kafila,* the caravan of my detractors, I have drawn inspiration at least for my title from one of its distinguished leaders, who is 'in search of a new, multi-coloured Left, Red having become monochromatic grey.'[145]

Actually, grey is not monochromatic; it has the proverbial fifty shades. Yet, its dominant constituents, even if not easily visible, remain, on either side of its spectrum of shades, black and white. What is the 'white'—or should I say 'right' side of Mr Mukherjee's grey?

It is the delusion that there is some sort of unified student movement across India spontaneously rising against the Modi *sarkar*'s 'fascism'.

Ranged against this, on the other ideologically 'right' but so 'wrong' to Mukherjee's brand of the 'Left', are Hindutva, neo-liberalism, taxpaying middle classes and so on, and of course, I.

We are 'black' to his 'white.' Such simple and stark binaries,

---

"Liberal"—The Twists and Turns of Makarand Paranjape: Anirban Bhattacharya', 8 March 2017, https://kafila.online/2017/03/08/looking-right-talking-liberal-the-twists-and-turns-of-makarand-paranjape-anirban-bhattacharya/. Accessed on 27 August 2021

[145]I've added 'or frills' to the subtitle. 'In search of a new, multi-coloured Left, Red having become monochromatic grey' is part of the self-descriptive tagline of Aditya Nigam, one of the founding editors of *Kafila,* and senior fellow at the Centre for the Study of Developing Societies, Delhi. Of course, the already intended allusion is to E.L. James's erotic thriller and international bestseller, *Fifty Shades of Grey* (2011).

Mr Mukherjee, for someone who professes to stand against them?

But why should we be surprised? Mr. Mukherjee, given his leanings, seems constitutively incapable of transcending black-and-white oppositions. Ironically, one of his favourite terms is 'binary', which he liberally sprinkles across his text, but is unable to free himself from, let alone deploy accurately.

Mr Mukherjee's simplistic view of the world, thus, comes with a thick overlay of regressive caste and communal politics, entitlement to unearned privileges and, evidently, attempts to insert himself in the network of Left-cronyism by attacking its perceived enemies.

No wonder, on closer examination, Mr. Mukherjee's shades of grey are mostly dull, duller and dullest.

When it comes to his own 'grey matter', three monotones persist: a) factual inaccuracy, b) muddled thinking and c) questionable integrity. A quick run-down of this alphabet of grey is offered in the hope that Mr. Mukherjee may still learn the 'a-b-c' of critical thinking. I am afraid, however, that it may [be] too little, too late, the damage of years of confused thinking being difficult to rectify.

Let me quote a few examples from his text to illustrate.

a) Factual Inaccuracy

Mr Mukherjee: 'Did anyone hear of beef parties, two or three years back? The first party was organized only after the Dadri Lynchings.' *Wrong.*

The first beef party was organized long before Dadri. As far back as 2012 in Hyderabad, radical groups threw a well-publicized beef party in which beef biryani was served and shared.[146]

---

[146]'Violence Breaks Out at Indian Beef-Eating Festival', *BBC News*, 16 April 2012, https://www.bbc.com/news/world-asia-india-17727379. Accessed on 27 August 2021.

b) Muddled Thinking

Notice how illogical Mr Mukherjee's very first paragraph is:

'Your open letter was not addressed to me and therefore you can feel free to not reply to my letter.'

First of all I wrote no 'open letter'. I only responded to the one posted against me by Maitreyee Shukla. It is not clear why Mr Mukherjee took upon himself the burden of taking up cudgels, so to speak, on her behalf. Surely, I cannot ascribe to him a motive as pure—or out of fashion—as unadulterated chivalry.

The truth is that the attack against me was coordinated. When I responded to Shukla, someone else took up the gauntlet to carry on the assault against me.

Why, then, does Mr Mukherjee say that I need not answer him?

It is, rather, for me to ask, why is *he* responding to a letter not addressed to him? The word 'therefore' in his sentence signals nothing but a non sequitur. If he had followed his own advice by keeping quiet, surely I would not have cause to respond. But for him to write against me, then absolve me from responding, as if he is conferring a privilege upon me, is little more than a misdirection.

Having addressed his 'open letter' directly to me, isn't it strange that [he] advises me to feel free not to return the compliment? Mr Mukherjee bravely persists, 'Since, your statements are mostly uncritical appreciation and endorsement of these ideas, I would regard your statements as statements made by an academician who has paused to think academically.'

What does the above sentence, with tautological phrases such 'statements as statements' and 'academician who has paused to think academically' actually mean? The word, 'statements', incidentally recurs thrice in that one muddled sentence. 'Paused to think academically'? Does Mr Mukherjee imply that academicians do not normally think academically but only do so when they pause from academics?

I do hope he is speaking only of himself!

One more gem: 'Every individual has to necessarily participate in this, and these types of histories form popular histories.'

More tautology, with confusing pronoun references, 'this' and 'these'!

Mr Mukherjee, you are a research scholar in History in one of our finest universities. You are, moreover, paid to do research! As a would-be historian, not to speak of teacher, your disciplinary confusions and inabilities leave one worrying about the plight of your future students.

Shouldn't you be studying harder, improving your basic skills as a historian rather than wasting your time writing 'open letters' of this sort? Would you blame the public, at whose expense you are being educated, if it asks you to render a better account of yourself?

I don't wish to nit-pick or be unkind. I have myself spent years teaching students far more ill-equipped, untrained or socially disadvantaged than yourself. But many who really wanted to learn improved themselves to the extent that they are honourable members of the profession today.

What about you?

Suppose you spent most of your time politicking, sloganeering, not attending classes, not bothering about your thesis, moreover showing contempt towards those who were genuinely trying to study? Wouldn't that be perturbing?

Unfortunately, the academic attainments of many students in the Social Sciences and Humanities in JNU, DU, HCU, and so on, are even shoddier than Mr Mukherjee's. I therefore hope that my observation regarding the higher quality of student papers and theses in IITs and IIMs now makes more sense.

c) Questionable Integrity

This brings me to the third problem. Much of Mr Mukherjee's muddle-headedness comes from what was colloquially termed *Aunt Sally* in England, but is more commonly known as the straw man fallacy. Its classic, representational form is false attribution.

The first speaker makes a claim. In order to counter him, the second speaker argues against something similar-sounding, but actually quite insubstantial (hence 'straw man'). Now the modified claim is easy to demolish, giving the impression that the second person has won the argument, when he has not even engaged properly with the original proposition.

Take this very point about IITs and IIMs. Notice the straw man fallacy here. Mr Mukherjee says, 'Most importantly, various departments, in universities like JNU and DU have contributed immensely towards the development of the respective disciplines.' But did I deny that? I only said that the quality of the student papers and theses from most Indian universities was not up to the mark.

Similarly, I never created a *binary*, as Mr Mukherjee puts it, between professional institutions such as IITs and IIMs and mainstream universities. The binary was created by Ms Maitreyee Shukla, who said that the two were totally different and that comparing them was 'laughable'. I only pointed out how they actually could be compared as interconnected parts of Indian higher education, but that the IITs and IIMs were better managed, with a superior work ethic and greater academic accountability.

A couple of instances of false ascription are understandable in the heat of argument. But what can one say of someone who makes not even a *single* correct attribution? From top to bottom, Mr Mukherjee's text is little other than an example of the straw man fallacy. That is because he has, either deliberately or unwittingly, misrepresented each of my ideas. Doesn't his integrity come into question?

One final example. Mukherjee accuses me of 'the elevation of Durga into an image of national mother.' He says, 'You are supporting this wholeheartedly. What you are actually doing is taking the space to contest caste oppression from the Dalits. You are taking away discursive spaces of contestations in the construction of your own narrative.'

Mr Mukherjee, *how* and *when* did I make the case for the elevation of Durga into the national mother? When did I support it 'wholeheartedly'? Where and when did I take away the space to contest caste oppression from Dalits?

How can you make a series of such flagrantly unsubstantiated claims? Isn't this simply false attribution and misstatement of facts? Aren't you aware that it was Bankim who, in *Anandamath* (1882), conceptualized the idea of Mother India as a Goddess?

By that token how come you don't criticize the *fatwa* against 'Bharat Mata ki jai' by the mullas, when the slogan implies respect, not necessarily worship of an icon? Isn't that taking away space from those who want to respect Mother India?

Didn't a professed Muslim, A.R. Rahman, popularize '*Maa tujhe salaam*' in his rendering of *Vande Mataram*? Did that make him a bad Muslim? Aren't sacred symbols in that religion, including their prophets and holy books, accorded veneration? Then why not the motherland? Why is your criticism of religious reverence so selective, Mr Mukherjee? Isn't that in itself a form of communalism if not Hindu-bashing?

Now let me come to your most interesting observation.

Unfortunately, false attribution, operates here as well. I refer to your remark concerning the agency of students. Mr Mukherjee, you claim that I denied agency to students: 'your argument doesn't allow the space to the students to have any agency of their own' and 'When you say "they are being used", you erase the space for any kind of agency....' But, in fact, a few lines later you contradict yourself to say that I 'inadvertently give the students their agency back'.

Mr Mukherjee, please make up your mind. Do I deny or don't I deny agency to students?

You won't be able to answer that clearly because you don't seem to know what you mean by 'agency'. Unfortunately, the cause of the conundrum seems to be your own faulty notion of agency.

The way you describe it, agency can be taken away and restored so facilely. That is what makes it so defective. For surely, I never said any such thing as even remotely denying students of agency. I was, on the contrary, critiquing the *kind* and *quality* of agency that students demonstrate when they were in the grip of certain ideologies.

'Jihadi' suicide bombers also have agency. How else would they choose to blow up so many people along with themselves? But what type of agency is it? Is it sanctioned by the very religion in whose name it is being exercised? Is it ethical or responsible agency? Such are the questions I was raising. Is it 'true' agency at all if they are brainwashed and programmed to carry out such heinous crimes against themselves and humanity?

When crimes against humanity on a gargantuan scale are legitimated then we are in deep trouble. We find ourselves facing pathologies on a scale that is so hard to counter.

Long ago, Michael Polanyi dubbed this phenomenon the 'moral force of immorality' and 'the moral appeal of [the] declared resolve to act unscrupulously'. What was Polanyi unmasking? Not 'Jihadism', since it had not emerged then, but a form of totalitarian Marxism that had created havoc across the world. It was 'a prophetic idealism spurning all references to ideals' so as to become a 'fanatical cult of power'.[147]

Closer home, when students allow themselves to be instrumentalized by ideologies and political parties even to the point of being brainwashed, it is not that they do not have agency. But the kind of agency that they develop and display is counterproductive to society to the point of being really dangerous. This was my point.

As a student of literature, I realized long ago that a human being embodies a potential too immense, too awesome, too precious and too unique to be harnessed to any ideology or political programme.

Isn't this what Rohith Vemula meant when in his suicide letter he lamented: 'The value of a man was reduced to his immediate identity and nearest possibility. To a vote. To a number. To a thing. Never was a man treated as a mind. As a glorious thing made up of stardust.'

Wasn't he protesting against such cynical instrumentalization of precious human lives? And yet you and your ilk will not cease from instrumentalizing even his suicide for your own political purposes. Ironically, you have turned Rohith's suicide into a modern version of *Brahmanvadh*, for which you wish to extract a heavy toll from your targeted political opponents.

Mr Mukherjee, giving oneself over to an ideology, to be used by it and to misuse others in its name, is also the problematic in the great novels of Dostoevsky and Tagore, as I tried to argue in my 'Nationalism' lecture. To

---

[147] Polanyi, Michael. *Personal Knowledge: Towards a Post-Critical Philosophy*, Routledge, 1998, pp. 241–245.

preserve one's creative capacities against the temptations and compulsions of ideologies that destroy our humanity and pit us against one another—isn't this the real meaning of azadi?

Isn't it a matter of great concern when beautiful, original, young minds are yoked to negative and violent political causes? How much might they have achieved, how might they have flowered and contributed to the world!

But instead, how great the loss, the waste of human potential!

When, as a teacher, I see this happening all around me, shouldn't I raise my voice? This is a voice, I believe, of sanity, caution, moderation, a voice against extremes of fanaticism, whether of the Left or the Right. I am not partial to Dadri lynchings, looking the other way when another young RSS worker, Sujith, is murdered in Kerala.

Caravan to Nowhere

Mr Mukherjee, at the start of your 'open letter', you did the honour of calling me 'one of most eminent academicians' [sic] to have engaged in this debate. You also said, 'I very strongly appreciate you for this.' As you warmed up you continued by calling me 'a scholar of ... stature' making 'yet another serious argument', linking it 'quite intelligently' with what follows. But towards the end, you suddenly lost the plot, completely flipped, or should I say *flopped* over.

You were 'appalled' by my response, crying out against my 'logical inconsistency' and 'failure of logic' (as if the two mean substantially different things). You concluded, as if convinced by your own specious rhetoric: 'Most of your arguments are reductionist and flawed. But it is the irresponsibility with which they are made that disturbs me.' Really? Then why have you bothered to refute me at such length? If there is nothing worthwhile in what I say, why take the trouble? Mr Mukherjee, isn't it counter-intuitive that such a sustained, hydra-headed campaign be carried out against someone who is illogical, reductionist, flawed and whose failures are so glaring as to be almost self-evident?

Two esteemed and senior professors have written 'open letters' against me, followed by two more by research scholars from JNU and DU. Why? And besides the one I actually took pains to respond to, there have been others.

Is it because what I say might be true, reasonable, logical and disturbing, precisely because it exposes the delusions, myths and chicanery of certain established ideological positions and practices?

Underlying your name-calling at the end is the mandatory defamation and denunciation practised by the Left, derived, no doubt, from older Church inquisitions and crusades against heretics, apostates, renegades and blasphemers, as the prelude to their liquidation.

In our more sober post-communist times, all that is left of this diabolical institution is the rather tiresome charade of naming and shaming carried out through repetitive, shrill, silly or clumsily crafted 'open letters'. Fortunately, the latter only serve to expose the poverty of thought of their own authors and ideologies.

Speaking of the bankruptcy of ideas, did you know, Mr Mukherjee, that one of the hashtags to your 'open letter' is 'Hindutva terror'? Someone certainly got carried away. Who is the 'terrorist' here? You, me or the one who posted your 'open letter'?

Never mind the stated principles of the portal's comments policy that 'Personal attacks are not okay.' Isn't this a way to character assassinate someone you disagree with? Wouldn't you call this 'intellectual terrorism', except that in this case the charge is so laughable as to be absurd? *Reductio ad absurdum!* With friends, or should I say comrades, like this why would you (or the Left) need enemies?

Before ending, let me remind you what you said at the outset, 'My open letter to you is as much an academic exercise for me as it is political' and at the conclusion, the 'one thing the discipline teaches all its students, is to ask questions'.

Let me, therefore, ask you: have you considered how your 'open letter' may have failed both as an academic *and* a political exercise? If so, the reason is simple: the latter does not substitute or make up for the former. You are left with 'bad' academics as well as 'bad' politics.

You end up empty-handed. What a waste of time, energy and human capacity!

Isn't it sad, pathetic, comic and sometimes, truly tragic? Unfortunately, Mr Mukherjee, there seems to be a huge problem when it comes to students in higher education in India. But are we ever going to address it directly?

We are in denial. We simply cannot admit it, but the world has truly passed some of these ideologies by. Wouldn't we all benefit from some creative destruction?

Since you seem so keen to be, or already are, a fellow traveller, let me offer, with due apologies to Majrooh, my own weak tweak of his famous lines to warn you where you might end up:

Main bhed-chaal hi chalaa tha jaanib-e-manzil magar
Log bichhadte gaye ... karavaan ghat ta gaya

In a herd was I when I started towards my destination but People kept dropping out, the caravan kept dwindling.

So, instead of Majrooh, if you find yourself singing Tagore's '*ekla cholo re*' of Tagore, I hope, you won't complain that you were not forewarned.

But it may well be the best thing that could happen to you, both politically and academically.

Makarand R. Paranjape

At this point, I believe that my ideological opponents, the Leftists in JNU, DU and elsewhere, must have lost interest in me or run out of steam. Did they give up trying to harangue or harass me because I was replying so diligently to most of their diatribes? Did they feel thwarted by my counter-eloquence if not counter-intelligence? Or did they run out of foot soldiers to do their bidding?

After all, sustaining such an attack against an individual required marshalling of considerable intellectual and practical resources. Following each fusillade, did they feel just slightly pushed back?

Whatever be the reason, the Leftist tirade against me, with its attempt to neutralize, silence, shame or defame me, soon came to a close. After a few more such 'open letters' or attacks, things quietened down.

I returned to my own work, which was primarily reading, writing and teaching. But JNU continued to witness interesting, even intensely fractious, times.

As we will see in the next chapters.

6

JNU AND THE STATE OF STRIFE

The Strange Case of Najeeb Ahmed

As if the tukde tukde occurrence, arrests of students and a university shutdown were not bad enough. In that same year, another terrible incident, possibly even more dreadful in its eventual unfolding, occurred. On 15 October 2016, Najeeb Ahmed, a 27-year-old MSc Biotechnology student, went missing.[148]

Went missing—what does that mean? At that time it meant that his family and friends lost all contact with him. But, in fact, to this day, no one knows where Najeeb is. Or what happened to him. Whether he is in India or has left for some unknown destination. Nobody even knows whether he is alive or dead.

Najeeb had just enrolled in JNU in 2016. Perhaps, he wasn't familiar with its highly charged student politics. Or, more likely, perhaps he was part of a political group himself. But on 14 October 2016, some students entered Najeeb's room in the Mahi-Mandavi Hostel and an altercation ensued. In the scuffle that followed, it seems that Najeeb beat up one of the unwelcome

---

[148]'JNU student Najeeb Ahmed Case: The Story Till Now,' *Hindustan Times*, 17 May 2017, https://www.thehindu.com/news/cities/Delhi/in-depth-look-at-the-jnu-student-najeeb-ahmed-case/article18474400.ece. Accessed on 16 September 2021.

guests.¹⁴⁹ Afterwards, another group descended on Najeeb and thrashed him. He was last seen entering an autorickshaw and leaving the JNU campus through the main gate the following afternoon.¹⁵⁰

Immediately, a group of students blamed the administration for what had happened. In fact, they claimed that the VC, Professor M. Jagadesh Kumar, was personally responsible for not doing enough to bring him back to JNU.¹⁵¹

On 23 October 2016, the VC and some of his staff were illegally detained in the administration building for around 20 hours.¹⁵² During the gherao, the administration building was cordoned off, with the VC and some members of his team, confined inside it.

When he was let out, the VC appeared on national television. He told reporters of the harrowing night that he and the top JNU administrators spent confined inside the administration building. A mob of slogan-shouting students surrounded them. Some of

---

[149] Paranjape, Makarand R. 'JNU and the State of Strife: Mindless Protests against the Admin Won't Bring Najeeb Ahmed Back,' *FirstPost*, 21 October 2016, https://www.firstpost.com/india/jnu-and-the-state-of-strife-mindless-protests-against-the-admin-wont-bring-najeeb-ahmed-back-3064200.html. Accessed on 16 September 2021.

[150] Ananya Bharadwaj and Kritika Sharma, 'Inside Story of the Hunt for Najeeb Ahmed, the JNU Student Who Disappeared into Thin Air,' *ThePrint*, 13 October 2018, https://theprint.in/india/governance/inside-story-of-the-hunt-for-najeeb-ahmed-the-jnu-student-who-disappeared-into-thin-air/133628/. Accessed on 16 September 2021

[151] Paranjape, Makarand R. 'JNU and the State of Strife: Mindless Protests against the Admin Won't Bring Najeeb Ahmed Back,' *FirstPost*, 21 October 2016, https://www.firstpost.com/india/jnu-and-the-state-of-strife-mindless-protests-against-the-admin-wont-bring-najeeb-ahmed-back-3064200.html. Accessed on 16 September 2021.

[152] 'JNU VC Jagadesh Kumar Breaks His Silence over Violence', India Today, YouTube, https://www.youtube.com/watch?v=LMzwBAN_j6Q. Accessed on 16 September 2021.

the staff members so corralled had medical ailments. They were denied medicines.[153]

Reflecting over the incident, it appears the actions of the students defy both common sense and logic. It is true that Najeeb was missing, but how was the university administration to be held responsible? Moreover, how could illegally imprisoning the VC and top officials of the university help find Najeeb? Especially when the university authorities had issued directives to the security, the wardens and all concerned staff to try and find Najeeb.

According to this directive, the JNU security forces were seen stopping incoming and outgoing autorickshaws, showing them a picture of Najeeb and inquiring if they had seen him. In fact, a case of kidnapping had already been filed in the Vasant Kunj Police Station. His mother, Fatima Nafees, had also filed a habeas corpus petition on 25 November 2016 in the Delhi High Court. Although it is understandable for a mother to use all possible means to find her son, since Najeeb was missing and not under arrest, the courts couldn't be of much help. Soon after, the Delhi Police also posted a reward of ₹50,000 for information leading to his recovery. In addition, a Special Investigation Team (SIT) was formed to look for him.[154]

Post-Disappearance Politics

To understand the harrowing gherao of the JNU VC and his staff, we must go back to the JNUSU elections.

Earlier that year, after the term of Kanhaiya Kumar had ended, elections to JNUSU were held again on 10 September 2016. The

---

[153]Ibid.
[154]'Special Police Team Formed to Trace JNU Student,' *The Hindu*, 20 October 2016, https://www.thehindu.com/news/cities/Delhi/Special-police-team-formed-to-trace-JNU-student/article16076750.ece. Accessed on 16 September 2021.

Left-wing SFI-AISA combine won all four seats: president, vice president, secretary and joint secretary.

Kumar, the more prominent former president, was a member of AISF, affiliated to the CPI. If anything, the SFI-AISA combine was more Leftist than AISF. JNU observers, therefore, expected a continuous clash with the administration.

The first flashpoint was the sleep-in organized in front of the administration building, demanding immediate hostel accommodation for all students. Few universities anywhere in the world promise hostel accommodation along with admission. In the city of Delhi itself, whether it is in the older Delhi University and Jamia Millia Islamia or the newer Ambedkar University, a vast number of the students, both undergraduate and graduate, must make their own arrangements.

In JNU, however, accommodation is demanded as a right. It was alleged that the administration diverted money allocated to the building of hostels.[155] This story was circulated to make students out to be victims of a callous and villainous administration. It is hardly surprising, therefore, that JNUSU would use every opportunity to keep the pot boiling at JNU. Targeting the administration and, whenever possible, the Modi sarkar, was only to be expected. Najeeb, we must not forget, was also identified, as mentioned earlier, as an AISA activist.[156]

What was nefarious, both in JNU and HCU, is how Dalit and Muslim students had been used by the Left and ultra-Left

---

[155] Paranjape, Makarand R. 'JNU and the State of Strife: Mindless Protests against the Admin Won't Bring Najeeb Ahmed Back,' *FirstPost*, 21 October 2016, https://www.firstpost.com/india/jnu-and-the-state-of-strife-mindless-protests-against-the-admin-wont-bring-najeeb-ahmed-back-3064200.html. Accessed on 16 September 2021.

[156] PTI. 'JNU Student Goes Missing Allegedly after Altercation with ABVP Activists,' NDTV, 17 October 2017, https://www.ndtv.com/delhi-news/jnu-student-goes-missing-allegedly-after-altercation-with-abvp-activists-1475057. Accessed on 16 September 2021

to try to show the present government as anti-Dalit and anti-minority.[157]

Was the fact that Najeeb was from Badaiyun, UP, with its high Muslim concentration, also something that might be used against the BJP in the forthcoming state elections? What was the truth behind the Najeeb incident? From eye-witness reports, it was learnt that the flashpoint occurred on the previous evening, 14 October 2016.

Najeeb reportedly slapped an ABVP student who had come to his door to campaign for a post on the hostel's mess committee. After this confrontation, an on-the-spot inquiry held by the hostel administration found Najeeb guilty of misdemeanour. Even his roommate reportedly testified against him.[158] During these proceedings the warden and the JNUSU president, Mohit Pandey, were present. Afterwards, it was claimed that the ABVP group came back to beat him.[159]

But who knows the exact truth or how credible these allegations are? Especially given the charged and divisive atmosphere on campus? That he was brutally beaten till he was bleeding and unconscious, as the Leftist students claimed, seems somewhat

---

[157] Paranjape, Makarand R. 'JNU and the State of Strife: Mindless Protests against the Admin Won't Bring Najeeb Ahmed Back,' *FirstPost*, 21 October 2016, https://www.firstpost.com/india/jnu-and-the-state-of-strife-mindless-protests-against-the-admin-wont-bring-najeeb-ahmed-back-3064200.html. Accessed on 16 September 2021.

[158] 'JNU Student Najeeb Ahmed Missing Case: When and How Did He Disappear? Why Is ABVP Being Blamed?' 7 November 2016, *India.com,* https://www.india.com/news/india/jnu-student-najeeb-ahmed-missing-case-when-and-how-did-he-disappear-why-is-abvp-being-blamed-1632389/. Accessed on 21 September 2021.

[159] PTI. 'Probe Finds ABVP Member Guilty of Assaulting Najeeb', *The Hindu*, 21 November 2016, https://www.thehindu.com/news/cities/Delhi/Probe-finds-ABVP-member-guilty-of-assaulting-Najeeb/article16661795.ece. Accessed on 17 September 2021.

exaggerated if not blatantly untrue.[160]

After all, he was seen walking out to an autorickshaw on his own, escorted by one of the wardens. He had been asked to leave for a few days because of his misconduct and for his own future safety. Had he been grievously injured, wouldn't he have needed hospitalization? What is more, where is the smartphone footage of his 'lynching' so crucial in such cases?

Does this mean that the attack on him must be denied, ignored or whitewashed? Not at all. A proper inquiry should have been held and the guilty punished. By the same token, he should also have been penalized for slapping a fellow student.[161] In Najeeb's case, none of this proctorial process or disciplinary inquiry happened. He disappeared and, sadly, has not yet been found.

I felt so unhappy and depressed during this entire episode. A university is no place for violence. Ideally, dissent should not only be permitted but welcomed. If owing to an ongoing battle between opposing groups, this is not easy to ensure, even so students with differing views must learn to respect one another. They cannot resort to fisticuffs to sort out their problems.

A university is also not a place where a mob of students hijacks the administration building, imprisoning their own faculty to retaliate against a student who may have voluntarily left campus.[162]

---

[160] Paranjape, Makarand R. 'JNU and the State of Strife: Mindless Protests against the Admin Won't Bring Najeeb Ahmed Back,' *FirstPost*, 21 October 2016, https://www.firstpost.com/india/jnu-and-the-state-of-strife-mindless-protests-against-the-admin-wont-bring-najeeb-ahmed-back-3064200.html. Accessed on 16 September 2021.

[161] Shankar, Aranya. 'JNUSU Calls for Strike after University Calls "Missing" Student an "Accused"', *The Indian Express*, 20 October 2016, https://indianexpress.com/article/india/india-news-india/jnu-student-missing-jnusu-strike-accused-shutdown-najeeb-ahmad-3088827/. Accessed on 27 August 2021.

[162] Paranjape, Makarand R. 'JNU and the State of Strife: Mindless Protests against the Admin Won't Bring Najeeb Ahmed Back,' *FirstPost*, 21 October 2016, https://www.firstpost.com/india/jnu-and-the-state-of-strife-mindless-protests-against-the-admin-wont-bring-najeeb-ahmed-back-3064200.html. Accessed on 16 September 2021.

Least of all should JNU, I felt, be such a university.

But that is exactly what we had been reduced to.

It is not that such gheraos have never happened in the past, but the university community usually condemned them. The anti-administration tactics of the students' union were deplorable, as was their generally negative approach to everything that didn't conform to their narrow ideological credo. Much of the propaganda that they dished out, including their pamphlets and posters, were sheer fabrications. Spewing ideological bilge was their standard practice. Almost a knee-jerk reaction.

On the other side, the ABVP also needed to rein in its cadres, especially in matters of orderly conduct. It helped no one to react violently, whether in word or action, in matters of political conflict, especially at a university. I was not in favour of giving them the licence to straighten the other side out. It was the job of the administration to maintain order. Students' taking matters into their own hands signalled the failure of the administration.

As a long-standing faculty member of this university of national importance, I was deeply pained over these events. I feared that the worst was yet to come. I was, unfortunately, proven right as the following chapters will demonstrate. We lived in a deeply divided campus, with mutual distrust at an unprecedented high. To varying degrees, both the JNUSU and the JNUTA, on the one hand, and the university administration, on the other, stood discredited. They had been unable to maintain peace and tranquillity, let alone academic integrity of the campus.

But what could the administration, perhaps the most important player in this discordant microcosm, alone do, without the cooperation of all sections of the campus community? Perhaps, they could send out a clear signal by punishing the guilty, acting firmly and fairly and, above all, restoring academics as JNU's top priority.

But they did follow this path or felt that they could not have succeeded even if they had tried.

At any rate, their inability to overcome the crisis cannot be overlooked. I am not speaking of Najeeb's disappearance for which we still don't know who is responsible. But we cannot tide over that and other catastrophes that had engulfed JNU before and after. In each case, I felt that more could have been done, better means of conflict resolution and reconciliation adopted.

Without such a healing touch, in the meanwhile, Najeeb became the focal point not only of the angry students protesting against the administration, but of the whole nation. Photos and videos of his crying mother were flashed all over the country. Where was Najeeb and why had he disappeared? These questions have remained unanswered to this date.

But how can we rule out that he might have left of his own accord? Or even worse, he might have gone missing deliberately as a part of a larger political ploy of bringing discredit to the administration? Far worse is the thought voiced by a student, already so disillusioned by JNU politics, 'Campus politics has hit a new low—how do we know that they will not harm Najeeb themselves for political gains?'

I certainly hoped this was not true. I hoped good sense would prevail. I joined JNU colleagues and students in appealing to Najeeb to return so that normalcy was restored to JNU at the earliest.

Alert! Mounted Police on Campus

That year of interesting times—in the worse sense of the term—came to an end rather unexpectedly, if not dramatically. On Monday, 19 December 2016, around 11.30 in the morning, there was a knock on my door. The university was in winter recess. I was sunning myself on my terrace corner, reading the rather abstruse *Tantrasara* by Abhinavagupta, when the bell to the back entrance of my house suddenly rang.

I peeped down from one of the windows upstairs to see who

it was. To my surprise, a posse of policemen, some in plain clothes but with giveaway khaki trousers and boots, was in my driveway.

'*Jee?*' I asked from above. One of them looked up, smiled, and then said, '*Sir, hum aapke ghar ki taalashi lena chahte hain* [Sir, we want to search your house].'

This was, to the say the least, rather unexpected. I could not remember my home ever being searched. And I had occupied, over the decades, a number of houses in different parts of the world. None of them had been raided by law-enforcement officers. For that matter, no policeman on duty had ever entered any of the spaces I had lived in or occupied.

What was it all about? I wondered. What *were* they looking to find?

I found myself a bit annoyed even as I was bewildered and plagued by improbable options.

After I descended, I opened the backdoor and confronted them: 'Why do you want to search the premises? And why didn't you come to the front door?' The gateway clearly said 'Entrance in the front'. Why had they chosen the service entrance to come in?

'Do you have a warrant?' I persisted. The cops looked abashed. 'We are looking for Najeeb,' he said. The penny suddenly dropped. Najeeb had disappeared on 15 October 2016 and had still not been traced.

I almost laughed out loud, 'What?! You are looking for him in *my* house?' The cop replied, 'No, no, we are searching all the houses in JNU. It's a High Court order.'[163] I found that so bizarre. A house-to-house search for a missing student!

Suppose he was actually on campus and he—or those controlling him—didn't want him to be found. Wouldn't he leave

---

[163]PTI. 'Delhi HC Orders JNU Search by Sniffer Dogs to Find Missing Student Najeeb,' News 18, 14 December 2016, https://www.news18.com/news/india/delhi-hc-orders-jnu-search-by-sniffer-dogs-to-find-missing-student-najeeb-1323091.html. Accessed on 16 September 2021.

before the cops entered the campus or even a single house was searched?

The order simply didn't make sense. Nor did they have a search warrant. I asked for it again. He said, '*Hamare afsar bahar khade hain; woh aap ko samjhayenge* [Our commanding officer is waiting outside, he will explain everything to you].' He was very polite, but the truth was that he had no warrant. Nor did he show me a copy of the High Court order.

I realized that the freedom we take for granted is actually quite fragile. The police can, on reasonable suspicion or with justifiable cause, actually search your home without a warrant. The relevant section of the Criminal Procedure Code is 165, the language of which even if not intent, is ambiguous.

I, however, didn't want to make a fuss. As a law-abiding citizen I had no reason to distrust the police force. I invited the cops in. Why would I want to obstruct justice? Or not cooperate?

The men and women in uniform wandered into the house half-heartedly, looked through all the rooms, even the bathrooms, opened a closet or two, peeked into the storeroom and then a couple of them went up to my terrace. Did they think he'd be hiding in the water tank?!

But soon they were trooping down the stairs again, shrugging their shoulders. One of the officers shook my hand and said, 'Sorry, Sir.' The two lady cops smiled and said, 'Thank you, Sir.'

I asked, 'How about some tea?'

They replied, 'No, no, let us find him first, then we'll have tea.'

The man had a sense of humour, but it was, given the circumstances, only dark humour. For Najeeb was never found. Certainly not that day, and certainly not on campus.

After they left, I realized how vulnerable we were to such an invasion of privacy in India. Thanks to the colonial legacy, when the State regarded each citizen with suspicion—as a potential threat.

But, perhaps, I was wrong. In the US too, law-enforcement officers can enter a home without a search warrant to make an arrest, look for a criminal and investigate suspicious activity. Citizens are advised to cooperate to avoid unpleasantness.

But in this instance, they weren't looking for a suspect or a criminal. Nor was there the slightest suspicion of criminal activity. I wondered whether they had come to my house because I had written an article on Najeeb's disappearance.

To imagine that Najeeb would be hiding in the bush, undergrowth or natural caves on campus, without being seen by anyone was so far-fetched as to be ludicrous. Then the sickening feeling that they might be looking for his body also crossed my mind. But pressing sniffer dogs into the operation more than three months after his disappearance would only lead to a cold trail.

As I told one of the policemen who had come to my house, 'If you really wanted to find out where he is, this should have been a covert operation… There should have been plainclothesmen making discreet inquiries, watching the movements of his friends, monitoring phone calls.'

He gave me a wry smile, 'His mother cried in the High Court, so the judges ordered this. What can we do?' So long after his disappearance, possibly under pressure from the media and the courts, the law-enforcement authorities had swung into action. But it was probably too late.

Then it was reported that the autorickshaw driver who took Najeeb out of JNU had been traced.[164] It seems that he told the police that he had taken Najeeb to Jamia Millia Islamia on that fateful evening. The report seemed plausible. Jamia, and its

---

[164]Srivastava, Radhika. 'Auto Driver Who Picked Up Najeeb Ahmed Has Been Traced: Reports', *One World News*, 17 November 2016, https://www.oneworldnews.com/auto-driver-picked-najeeb-ahmed-traced-reports/. Accessed on 26 August 2021.

surrounding Zakir Nagar, remained a hotbed of minority-led political activism.[165]

This phenomenon can be largely traced back to the Batla House encounter that took place on 19 September 2008 in the same area. Two Indian Mujahideen terrorists holed up inside the building, Atif Ameen and Mohammad Sajid, were gunned down. Two others, Mohammad Saif and Zeeshan, were arrested, while one, Ariz Khan, slipped out of the dragnet. Inspector Mohan Chand Sharma of the Delhi Police, who had led the ambush, was shot dead by the terrorists. Nikkhil Advani's movie *Batla House* (2019), is based on this event.[166]

More recently, the anti-Citizenship (Amendment) Act violence and protests also occurred inside the Jamia Millia campus as well as the Jamia neighbourhood, culminating in the Shaheen Bagh sit-in.[167] It continued for weeks in a time of the novel coronavirus pandemic and despite the Delhi chief minister announcing a ban on gatherings in public places.[168]

Why, then, didn't the investigating agencies search where Najeeb might have gone thereafter? From Jamia where did he

---

[165] Jean-Thomas Martelli and Kristina Garalytė, 'How Campuses Mediate a Nationwide Upsurge against India's Communalization. An Account from Jamia Millia Islamia and Shaheen Bagh in New Delhi', *OpenEdition Journals*, 2019, https://journals.openedition.org/samaj/6516. Accessed on 17 September 2021.

[166] Ahmad, Kabool. '11 Years on, Memories of Encounter Haunt Bylanes of Batla House', *India Today*, 19 September 2019, https://www.indiatoday.in/india/story/batla-house-visit-encounter-present-deserted-1600900-2019-09-19. Accessed on 26 August 2021.

[167] 'What Is Shaheen Bagh Protest', *Business Standard*, https://www.business-standard.com/about/what-is-shaheen-bagh-protest. Accessed on 16 September 2021.

[168] 'Shaheen Bagh Protesters Will Have to Follow Ban on Gathering over Coronavirus: Kejriwal', *Hindustan Times*, 16 March 2020, https://www.hindustantimes.com/india-news/shaheen-bagh-protesters-will-have-to-follow-ban-on-gathering-over-coronavirus-kejriwal/story-CYhB1EkHCAknZI7Wddg8VP.html. Accessed on 26 August 2021.

go? Why didn't they contact his friends and acquaintances in Jamia to find out? Without contacts and support, he would not be in Jamia in the first place.

But then we were told that the auto driver story was fake.[169]

It was impossible to tell what was true anymore.

How did we even know if Najeeb was in India any longer? The name, Najeeb Ahmed, is fairly common. Might he not have slipped through Indian Immigration undetected or even crossed the border overland, say, to Nepal?

One thing was certain, though. Not only his distraught mother and family members, but all of us at JNU were deeply concerned. We wanted him back, alive and well. Unfortunately, the whole incident had acquired deeply political overtones. This was bound to affect the quality of the investigations.

My fears were confirmed when I saw mounted policemen strutting about the campus in the afternoon as I walked home from my office. A force of over 500 police personnel had descended on the 1,000-acre JNU campus. The scale of the operation was as mind-boggling as it was baffling. To say the least, the sight, far from prepossessing, was disconcerting. The massive police presence was a huge display.

Of what, though? The resolve to find Najeeb or the appearance of looking for him?

In the meanwhile, Najeeb remains missing.

'Rajini' Gone: Another Precious Life Lost

The fateful year of 2016 passed. But more was in store for JNU, which made me wonder if we had failed our youth. What was

---

[169] PTI. 'Cops Forced Auto Driver to Say He Dropped JNU Student Najeeb Ahmed at Jamia: CBI in High Court', *The Indian Express*, 27 February 2018, https://indianexpress.com/article/cities/delhi/cops-forced-auto-driver-to-say-he-dropped-jnu-student-najeeb-ahmed-at-jamia-cbi-in-high-court-4937722/. Accessed on 26 August 2021.

really in store for them?

Another tragic incident happened right in the middle of Holi celebrations the following year. Holi in JNU is always raucous, raunchy, boisterous, joyous and bordering on the wild. With intoxicants available in the hostel messes and large crowds of people flocking to the campus, things can get a bit chaotic. Drumming, dancing, chanting and crazy, indiscriminate colouring games and frolic are all part of the masti.[170]

But the celebrations in 2017 were marred and turned into mourning instead. By the evening of Monday, 13 March 2017, the heartbreaking suicide of J. Muthukrishnan broke everyone's spirit. His death cast a pall of gloom on the campus.

'Rajini Krish', as Muthukrishnan had fashioned himself, was a 28-year-old PhD student enrolled in the Centre for Historical Studies, School of Social Sciences. Rajini came to JNU after his MPhil at the University of Hyderabad, the same university where Rohith Vemula had died by suicide the previous year on 17 January.

Rajini had finally made it to JNU after trying several times to gain admission. Admitted to JNU at last, he was known to have been ecstatic. His friends and teachers at the Centre for Historical Studies said he was a hard-working and pleasant young man.

On Monday afternoon, 13 March, Muthukrishnan went to Munirka Vihar, outside the JNU campus, to meet some friends and have lunch. Hostel messes remain closed in JNU for Holi. So, most students had to go out to eat.

Some who knew Rajini reported that he appeared depressed, but was unable to properly to explain why. One friend said it might have been a relationship issue. At any rate, he asked to lie down. His host, a South Korean national, kindly arranged for him

---

[170]Kunju S., Shihabudeen. 'Holi 2017: How JNU Celebrated the Festival,' NDTV, 13 March 2017, https://www.ndtv.com/education/holi-2017-how-jnu-celebrated-the-festival-1669089. Accessed on 16 September 2021.

to do so. Muthukrishnan went inside the room and locked the door. When lunch was served a little after 2.00 p.m., his friends knocked to invite him to join them. There was no response.

Thinking that he was resting, they let him be. But after another couple of hours, they felt uneasy. Was he all right? This time they knocked much louder. When they heard nothing, the host pushed the door back forcibly, only to see that he was hanging from the ceiling. The police were informed immediately. They arrived a little after 5.00 p.m. to find Muthukrishnan already dead.

These are the facts as we have them. A five-member team from AIIMS, led by Dr Satish Gupta, head of Forensics, completed the post-mortem examination the following day. The autopsy report put out by them ruled out foul play. There were no marks of injury on Muthukrishnan's body and the contents of his stomach were found to be normal. 'Prima facie it's a case of suicide by hanging,' the report said, 'however, it is a matter of investigation about the circumstances in which the deceased has committed suicide.'[171]

If depression led to Muthukrishnan's suicide, then we must face the bitter fact that it is not all that uncommon in our students. In March 2016, a 26-year-old student had died by suicide in Ber Sarai, near JNU.[172] At first, he was reported to be a PhD scholar at JNU, but later this was denied. He was actually enrolled at a private university.

In July 2013, an undergraduate in Korean Studies, Akash, died by suicide by slashing his wrist after attacking an ex-girlfriend with an axe in Room 203, quite close to my office in the School

---

[171] Fareeha Iftikhar and Sakshi Chand. 'JNU Student Died Due to Hanging: Autopsy', *DNA*, 16 March 2017, https://www.dnaindia.com/delhi/report-jnu-student-died-due-to-hanging-autopsy-2354230. Accessed on 26 August 2021.

[172] Amitabh Sinha and Maneesh Chhibbernew. 'Delhi: Student Found Hanging in Ber Sarai Residence', *The Indian Express*, 11 March 2016, https://indianexpress.com/article/cities/delhi/delhi-student-found-hanging-in-ber-sarai-residence/. Accessed on 10 December 2021.

of Language, Literature and Culture Studies.[173] Akash was obsessed with his classmate, Roshni. In his suicide note, he said that he couldn't bear seeing her with someone else. He prepared to kill her and then himself by arming himself with an axe, a knife, a poisonous pesticide, even a country-made revolver.

Barging inside the ill-fated classroom, he pointed the revolver at the students and the teacher in the class. Roshni and he had a heated argument. He hit her on the head with the axe and stabbed her when she fell to the ground. He then swallowed the poison before slashing his wrist. He collapsed and bled to death. Roshni was admitted to the hospital, critically injured. Thankfully, she recovered completely after a few weeks.

After that shocking and gory calamity, JNU instituted a university-wide process of informal counselling to students. A faculty member was nominated in each centre to be available to students facing difficulties of any kind, whether academic or personal. The university also has counselling and psychiatric services available at its Health Centre. Clearly, however, these mechanisms are insufficient to deal with the volume of mental health-related problems that students face.

In Muthukrishnan's case, that he was a Dalit and Rohith Vemula's friend, lent it an instant caste twist. Unlike Rohith, however, Muthukrishnan did not leave a suicide note. His Facebook posts were used, not only by student groups on campus, but by political parties in Parliament to allege caste discrimination. They called for a CBI inquiry followed by stern action—the question, however, is 'against whom?'

The allegation was that Muthukrishnan was treated badly and denied justice in JNU. That it was the terrible treatment meted

---

[173] Sharma, Kritika. 'Note Recovered from JNU Attacker Reveals Unhealthy Obsession that Ended in Suicide', *India Today*, 2 August 2013, https://www.indiatoday.in/india/north/story/jawaharlal-nehru-university-killing-note-recovered-from-akash-roshni-172485-2013-08-02. Accessed on 26 August 2021.

out to him because of his caste that led to his suicide. But what evidence did we have? How did the narrative of 'institutional murder' begin to gain ground even before the facts were properly known, let alone established?

From reports emanating from the Centre for Historical Studies, Muthukrishnan had requested a change of supervisor. Given that the person he wished to work with, a distinguished member of the faculty, was close to retirement, the Modern Indian History faculty group had yet to decide to whom he was to be reallocated. If there was any other reason for his dissatisfaction or proof of any specific discrimination that he faced in JNU, then it was yet to surface.

Writing about the incident, I had called for everyone to desist from exploiting Muthukrishnan's sad demise for petty political gains.[174] If a gifted young Indian lost his life, it was a loss to the whole nation. We had to work harder to ensure that such mishaps did not recur, rather than immediately launching into a divisive blame game to create further unrest, discontent and anger.

JNU is known for its sensitivity to difference. We have a tradition of inclusiveness, I argued, of reaching out to alienated and marginalized sections of society, coupled with the latter themselves making an effort to integrate with the others. We had to strengthen these traditions to make our campuses more cohesive, compassionate communities rather than hate-mongering, deeply divided spaces.

Muthukrishnan's self-assumed nom de plume, as already mentioned, was Rajini—presumably after the Tamil, or should I say international, superstar Rajnikanth. Unfortunately, this Rajini's life wasn't like the dream run of his idol—from bus conductor, Shivaji Rao, to one of India's greatest actors and icons. Instead, it

---

[174]Paranjape, Makarand R. 'The JNU Suicide: What We Need to Do for Our Young', *News18 India*, 16 March 2017, https://www.news18.com/news/india/the-jnu-suicide-what-we-need-to-do-for-our-young-1360530.html. Accessed on 26 August 2021.

ended in suicide in the room of a hospitable foreigner who gave him shelter and succour during Holi.

Najeeb, Rajini, JNU and National Interest

What is the connection between the still missing Najeeb and Rajini, who hung himself? In my view, it is simply and, quite shockingly, 'national interest'.

At least from the point of view of all of us, who were unable to prevent these two young men from taking the extreme step of ending their own lives. To me, their deaths send a clear signal that Indian higher education, especially in the Humanities and Social Sciences, is in crisis.

It is in the national interest to take remedial action right away. The crisis is such that notifying a new National Educational Policy is far from sufficient. Institutional reform is the need of the hour.

Higher education, or for that matter, the entire education sector in India needs thorough and wide-ranging reform and renovation. As regards Rohith and Rajini, we require better institutional mechanisms to identify those who need special attention or support in our universities.

JNU is yet another site of this confusion and dissatisfaction that our youth experience when it comes to higher education. Especially when it comes to disadvantaged students and identity politics. One of the problems is that many underprivileged students are fed on ideological myths, rather than encouraged to develop actual competence in their chosen fields of study.

When they discover that they are misfits in the real world, which expects from them something other than what their political mentors tutored them to believe, there is a shock of disillusionment, even betrayal. The reasons for student distress run far deeper than caste politics. Perhaps, piecemeal tinkering or insincere political one-upmanship constitutes the cause rather than the cure of the malaise.

In the ongoing war between JNU students and the government, there are no winners. Neither are governments all-powerful and unnecessarily controlling, as their critics complain, nor are students all compromised or corrupted as their detractors cavil.

The real problem is this war of words. Even in peacetime, what constitutes national interest is subject to discussion and difference of opinion. But during war, when propaganda is a serious business, national interest becomes even more challenging and uncertain, fiercely contested and controverted.

Of course, truth is the first casualty. Political parties are quick to cash in on a war. Who really cares for truth, especially when we are at war? The war I am speaking of is not just the one that is waged against our external enemies. It is also our war within, much more a battle of narratives, or who controls the 'India story'.

The latter, incidentally, has been both a native and colonial obsession since the dawn of early transcivilizational encounters. India has been such a powerful territory, both geographically and ideologically, that to gain control over the meaning of India has been an ancient fixation, both Western and Eastern.

During the freedom struggle and well into the early decades of Independence, several competing notions of India struggled for supremacy. Gradually, the Nehruvian socialist secular narrative was overtaken by the rhetoric of liberalization and Hindutva.

This war of words, which is not across our borders, but right within, is the most uncivil of our ongoing clashes for power and supremacy. No quarter is given to the adversary. None is taken either. What complicates matters further is that once we are deeply enmeshed in such a war, it is hard to get out. Even beyond the scramble and scrimmage for votes, or the biggest carnival (or should we say tamasha) on earth—the Indian elections.

The tornado of propaganda unleashed by all sides, even after the elections, is deafening. What happens to truth is the least of anyone's worries. Claims upon claims are plied without any justification or need of verification. In the midst of all this cacophony, the easiest charge to level at one's opponents is that they are unpatriotic. Every question, whether fair or otherwise, becomes a provocation. Every questioner is accused of being a traitor.

However, one might ask in exasperation: doesn't the citizen have a prerogative to question those who rule them? Or are governments beyond questioning? What really happens in any given situation? Don't we have the right to know? Why must every question—or for that matter answer—be instantly politicized? Why are aspersions cast on the character of the one asking the questions? Isn't accurate information available to an informed electorate the best safeguard for democracy? That is why the nation has a right to know what happened to Najeeb.

As to 'Rajini', the matter is closed. It is, supposedly, an open and shut case of suicide. But that shouldn't prevent us from asking what factors led to it? How can we prevent its recurrence? Najeeb's disappearance, on the other hand, is an unsolved case.

To tackle such issues, however, we will have to go beyond the simplistic and divisive narrative wars. Whether of JNU or Indian nationalism. In fact, the entire education system must be reformed. Only that would truly be in national interest. Only that will get us beyond the state of strife in which we are at present entangled.

7

JNU KI AZADI: EK-DO SAAL BAAD

How I Touched My Students' Feet

Well, strictly speaking, it didn't happen quite the way it sounds.

It was purely voluntary. Also pragmatic, rather than reverential. In fact, it was the only way to tunnel through to the entrance of my building past a thick wall of blockading protesters. I was glad to be able to do so and also to tell how it happened.

6 January 2017. Just a couple of days before the first anniversary of the tukde tukde eruptions on JNU.

It was a Monday morning. When I reached the School of Languages building, JNU, where my office is, I saw a crowd of students blocking the entrance. I was gheraoed and prevented from entering.[175] The students' union had called for a strike, picketing the school buildings.

Neither a strike nor blocking entry to buildings is unprecedented in JNU. However, usually, faculty members are not barred from going in. Karamcharis and non-teaching staff also enter. Even students, who don't wish to strike, may be permitted to pass after some negotiations and arguments. What was different

---

[175]Dutta, Nirmalya. 'Watch: JNU Professor Who Opposed Kanhaiya Kumar Prevented from Entering His Class', *DNA*, 6 February 2017, https://www.dnaindia.com/india/report-watch-jnu-professor-who-opposed-kanhaiya-kumar-prevented-from-entering-his-class-2313704. Accessed on 16 September 2021.

this time was that not a single person was allowed inside.

When I reached the building, the dean of the school and her staff were right there. I expected her to get in. I even suggested that we go through the crowd of students together. She gave me a strange, unbelieving look.

'The students have called for a strike,' she said.

'Yes, it seems so,' I replied, 'But that doesn't mean us, I suppose.'

I thought she was following me as I climbed the stairs.

Instead, she had retreated, with her office staff. I couldn't believe it. Instead of admonishing the students, showing her resolve to continue discharging her duties by going to her office, she had caved in.

Was it cowardice, connivance or just convenience?

I was now alone in the face of the blockade. Even the JNU security guards gathered there were ineffectual, if not incompetent, spectators as our building was being taken over right before our eyes.

I asked the guards, 'Why aren't you clearing the way for those who wish to enter? Are we to surrender our university to those who have taken the law into their own hands?'

They shrugged their shoulders and said, '*Order nahin hain* [We have no orders].' Who gave the orders? I asked.

The dean had, by now, left. So there would be no one to answer my question.

I felt let down. Regardless of the provocation, authorities should not break up a peaceful strike or demonstration. But they should also not allow a small section of students to hold the university to ransom.

But the university had done precisely that. At the cost of faculty members. We were left unprotected. Our right to enter our own buildings or offices were not safeguarded.

That day, there were around 30 to 40 protesters at the steps of my building, several not even from my school, let alone JNUSU representatives. How could they enforce a strike, especially given that some, evidently, weren't JNU students at all?

Who gave them that authority? It was obvious that the university administration had decided to look the other way and let them carry on their illegal and anti-academic agitation.

Looking at their age and demeanour, it seemed like a planned lockdown, with a larger political network behind it. When I moved resolutely towards the door, a group of them advanced towards me menacingly, trying to cow me down.

'You cannot go in,' a couple of them said threateningly.

'Why?' I asked.

They said loudly, in a chorus, 'No one will be allowed in today. We are on strike.'

'But I am not on strike,' I countered. I paused for a while, then continued, 'How can you stop me for discharging my duty?'

'What is your duty?' a bearded man mocked derisively.

'To teach, read and write,' I said quietly. Then raising my voice a bit, 'I thought you knew that already.'

They changed their tactic. Two others came forward, 'We are fighting for social justice.'

I said, 'I support social justice too. But how is your cause served by debarring me from going to my office?'

'We are opposed to the UGC [University Grants Commission] notifications.'

'I may or may not agree with you on that, but that does not mean that you can prevent me from going to my office.'

They looked at me, not knowing how to react.

'I am not a student. This may be your strike, but it is not mine. You cannot use force. That is against the ethos of JNU and the ethics of a strike.'

'We are not using force,' they said.

'Okay, then let me go in.'

'No,' they shouted, barring my way.

'Is this not using force?'

Again, they tried to change the topic, 'You gave a lecture on nationalism, now give one on social justice.'

'Sure.'

'*Right now!*'

'Yes, I will do so, but no zabardasti please. Right now I want to go to my office, which is inside this building. And you are blocking me.'

They started shouted slogans, resorted to name-calling.

I said, 'Now that you're done shouting, let's talk.' I approached one of them and said, 'Tell me, what is your name? Which centre are you from?'

Immediately, I found that student backing off. My suspicions were confirmed. Many of these people were not from my school; some were not even from JNU.

Their cynicism and evasiveness were evidenced by the fact that not one of them divulged their identity, let alone academic programme or year of study.

'How can we have a dialogue if you don't tell me your name?' I said, pointing to the student backing off.

They countered with a rather effective barb, 'We are Najeeb,' after the still missing Biotech student.

I returned, 'I am Najeeb too, but you can't stop me from entering my office.'

Looking at them more carefully, I realized that several of them were probably too old to be actively enrolled in a programme at JNU. The whole protest, I surmised, was orchestrated with outside collusion.

The aim was to bring the university to a standstill. We were just three days away from the first anniversary of the 'azadi' protests. On 9 February 2017, I wasn't going to be surprised if there was more trouble on campus.

That is exactly what transpired. And it was the institution and its ordinary students who suffered the most. That is what I deeply regret. If I, an ordinary member of the faculty, was able to figure out what was in the offing, how come the university administration did nothing about it?

Including clearing this cordoned-off building?

While all these thoughts were going through my head, our altercation continued.

The older outsiders tried to scare me with veiled threats, 'We are 30, you are only one.'

'Yes, you may even be chhapan or sava lakh [56 or a lakh-and-a-quarter]. You can't impose your views on me.'

'We have the right to dissent.'

'Of course; but I have a right to dissent to your mode of dissent.'

'You are not supporting the JNU culture.'

'If dissent is part of the JNU culture, why can't I dissent against you? Or is yours an enforced dissent, which is only a form of coerced consent?'

They had no answer. They stared at me. Some made taunting gestures. Others began whispering amongst themselves about what to do with me.

'Don't tell me about JNU culture; I have been teaching since before some of you were even born. I have been a professor in JNU alone for more than 16 years.'

Our parley had reached a dead end.

They had nothing sensible to say really. On not a single issue could they offer a logical, reasonable argument. The stand-off continued for nearly a quarter of an hour.

There was one other faculty member who wanted to go inside. I held his hand and said, 'Let's protest against these anti-democratic students.' But he extricated himself and fled.

Even if five teachers had stood up to them, this motley crowd of protesters would surely have failed.

But I was all alone.

Finally, I said, 'I myself will offer satyagraha.' I sat down with them.

They thought they had won and began to clap. They were

under the impression that I was joining their protest.

Just then, I held the feet of two of the ringleaders and pushed them away from the door.

'What are you doing, Sir?!' the students exclaimed. They had not expected me to move them aside in this manner.

At that point, a couple of the seniors stepped in: '*Usko jaane do* [let him go].'

The students barring the entrance stepped back a bit.

I said, 'Move aside; let me enter with dignity.' As I stood up, they seemed to be taken aback.

I turned around to face them.

'This is my building. I come here to work practically every day. Even on Sundays. You cannot stop me from entering it during working hours. That too on a Monday morning!

'No one, certainly none of you, is going to stop me. Understood?'

It felt good to get into my own building, to walk up the stairs to my office on the second floor like a free man.

I realized that I was shaking after that confrontation. Not from fear but from some sort of prehensile, nervous response to an unprecedented situation.

Fight, flight or freeze? I'd opted for the first. When I reached the second floor, the shivering was gone. Instead, there was a swag and bounce in my step.

The next day, the video of what had happened was posted on my public Facebook page.

It has been viewed over a hundred thousand times. Unfortunately, someone hacked my page and I have not yet been able to gain control of it again. Perhaps, I have not tried hard enough.

Azadi: One Year After

It was 9 February 2017, one year after the tukde tukde rally.

Walking to my office, past the administration building,

dubbed Freedom Square, I was startled to see a female student with a bandaged eye, with blood marks on the white gauze.

Her wound looked really bad. My heart skipped a beat. I stopped her to ask, 'Are you okay? What happened?' She just ignored me, giving me a strange look, and rushed on.

Then I saw another, with an equally bad head wound, similarly bandaged in white gauze, also blood-stained. He scurried on too, rather vigorously, for one with so grievous a lesion and apparently injured badly.

What was going on?!

When I saw dozens of such bandaged students scuttling about, the penny dropped. These were not injured students. They were protesters, commemorating last year's incident, with dressed-up wounds and bandages.

'*Bharat tere tukde honge, Inshallah, Inshallah,*' I remembered.[176] The slogan-shouting Kashmiri separatists and their supporters, who under the false pretext of a cultural programme, had staged the rally that triggered off the JNU crisis.[177]

The bandaging of eyes, faux blood and red marks were meant to signify pellet wounds. Injuries suffered by stone pelters in the Valley. This was part of the performative of sympathy and solidarity of JNU-ites with stone-throwing activists in Kashmir.

Last year, there were clashes between two groups of students, the police entered the campus and student leaders were charged with sedition and arrested. JNU had become the focus not just of national, but international attention. Naturally, on the first

---

[176]'EXPLOSIVE: These are the "Tukde Tukde" Slogans Raised in the Explosive JNU Chargesheet Tapes Accessed by Republic', Republic World, 22 January 2019, https://www.republicworld.com/india-news/general-news/explosive-these-are-the-tukde-tukde-slogans-raised-in-the-explosive-jnu-chargesheet-tapes-accessed-by-republic.html. Accessed on 16 September 2021.

[177]Dasgupta, Surajot. 'What Actually Happened in NIT Srinagar', *Swarajya*, 7 April 2016, https://swarajyamag.com/politics/what-actually-happened-in-nit-srinagar. Accessed on 16 September 2021.

anniversary of our troubles, I was apprehensive.

Just a couple of days before, on 6 February, the students' union had called for a strike, cordoning off university buildings, denying entry even to teachers and the non-teaching staff. As narrated above, I myself was subjected to a gherao and blockade, replete with slogan shouting, name-calling and intimidation. It is another matter that I was one of the fortunate few who managed to defy such coercive tactics, enter my building and even see some of my PhD students later in the day.[178]

Now, after seeing these bandaged protesters, I knew we had to expect something unpleasant if not untoward. Even though the last thing we needed in JNU was another flare-up of hostilities in an already embattled campus.

The day seemed to pass quickly. There were student morchas, the usual tramp from building to building, shouting slogans and making lots of noise. But things quietened down around 1.45 p.m., before the close of lunch in the hostels. No shouting, no drum-beating, no raucous protests in the afternoon, just students lounging about, having tea, smoking and chatting loudly. It looked as if hardly any classes had been held, at least in the Languages and Social Studies.

Business as usual?

In the evening, walking back from the office, I saw more agitators, some donning red-and-white Arab keffiyeh. One of them, sporting a beard and wearing a skullcap, recognized me as I passed the library.

'Sir, Sir, I know who you are!' he said in Hindi.

'*Jee*?' I turned around.

'You're one of *them* that writes, haan?'

---

[178] Mehta, Nirwa. 'A Year after Students Gheraoed JNU VC, JNU Teachers' Association Holds Kangaroo Court against Him', *OpIndia*, 23 October 2017, https://www.opindia.com/2017/10/a-year-after-students-gheraoed-jnu-vc-jnu-teachers-association-holds-kangaroo-court-against-him/. Accessed on 16 September 2021.

'*Jee*,' I sighed grudgingly, as if admitting to some misdemeanour. Then I countered, 'What have you read?'

That stumped him. 'I don't know... something, *yeh-woh*,' he stuttered.

Laughable, I thought. Just like a normal JNU student. Ill-read.

I smiled, 'Well, as a scholar, shouldn't you know your sources?'

He grinned, then retorted, 'But, Sir, you only give your point of view.'

I chuckled, 'Naturally. You don't expect me to give *your* point of view.'

He was taken aback. To encourage him, I added, 'Why don't you write something?'

Now, he looked crestfallen. 'But *hum ko space nahin milta* [No one gives us space]'.

I said, 'You're right. Not everyone gets space in the media.'

That seemed to rile him. He flared up and raised his voice, 'Ah, do you mean to say only those with merit can write?'

'No, no', I tried to soothe his hurt pride, 'The media is biased. In fact, I get rejected all the time.'

He looked at me, surprised. In wonder, he exclaimed, '*Sach*? Really?'

'*Ji. Sach mein* [Yes. It is true.] I get rejected all the time.' He looked at me wonderingly, almost gratefully. My failures seemed to soothe him.

'You must not give up,' I said. 'Keep writing. Keep expressing yourself.' I assured him, 'I have been kept out many times from many forums. In fact, you have a better chance. Much of the media is so Left-Liberal.' I even mentioned the names of some newspapers and periodicals. 'As a Muslim, they may even give you a special place.'

He paused, with a sad, somewhat mysterious air, 'No more, Sir, no more...'

He rushed away. I was a bit perplexed, even concerned. So many of our youth were being indoctrinated and alienated. Used, then discarded. When would this stop? When would academics be JNU's top priority again? Soon I reached home. The day had passed without major mishaps.

Or so I thought.

When I turned the TV on, I saw something quite contrary. The administration building had been completely cordoned off. Students had gheraoed it, stopping the staff and workers from going in. The VC was nowhere to be seen.

So the 'anniversary' had not passed unmarked after all.

I also learnt that an anonymous student was fasting today to protest against the treatment meted out to her teacher. That teacher, whom they had tried to prevent from entering my building, was none other than me.

Students blockading the building and the lone student fasting against such a practice. Didn't they constitute a perfect allegory of the two faces of JNU?

We Don't Need a Tank to Win the Battle for JNU

A few months later, I was to appear on a TV debate on a leading channel. At the studio, a well-known journalist asked me, 'Do you have a nice office in JNU?'

'Not bad,' I said. The story of my unusual office would be too long to narrate, I thought to myself with a smile.

'Tank view or lake view?' he persisted, with a smile.

I was quite foxed and said nothing. We had no lakes in JNU—as to tanks...?

But when I returned to my shabby genteel JNU campus after the debate, the question suddenly made sense.

At the gate, I saw a large signboard of what was called the 'Tiranga March' on Sunday, 23 July. It was the pre-celebration of Kargil Vijay Diwas to be observed on 26 July.

Among the VIPs at the function were Union ministers Dharmendra Pradhan and V.K. Singh, the latter a decorated soldier and former chief of army staff. Also present were retired Major General G.D. Bakshi, a familiar face on TV, NRI civilian crusader Rajiv Malhotra and cricketing legend, Gautam Gambhir. The family members of the 23 Kargil martyrs were also brought in to heighten the element of pathos to the poignancy of patriotism.

Earlier, on 16 May 2017, the university authorities had inaugurated a 'Wall of Heroes' with framed photos of 21 Param Vir Chakra awardees.[179] Honouring war heroes makes sense because JNU is the degree-awarding university for the following Defence institutions: Army Cadet College, Dehradun; College of Military Engineering, Pune; Military College of Electronics and Mechanical Engineering, Secunderabad; Military College of Telecommunication Engineering, Mhow; National Defence Academy, Pune; and Indian Naval Academy, Ezhimala. With these innovative and unprecedented moves, the JNU administration was striving to change the dominant Leftist, some would even say 'anti-national' narrative of the university.

But what really made the news was the VC Jagadesh Kumar's request to the ministers present to help JNU procure an army tank.[180]

A tank! What for?

No, it was not to scare students or bring the armed forces directly on campus. I had to tell my utterly perplexed and nonplussed friends abroad that it was not a live tank that he wanted. After all, in some, less fortunate, more authoritarian, parts

---

[179] PTI. 'JNU Turns "Nationalist" with "Wall Of Heroes"', *Outlook*, 16 May 2017, https://www.outlookindia.com/newsscroll/jnu-turns-nationalist-with-wall-of-heroes/1052599. Accessed on 16 September 2021.

[180] Bhardwaj, Ananya. 'JNU VC Wants Tank on Campus to Remind Students of Army's Sacrifices', *Hindustan Times*, 24 July 2017, https://www.hindustantimes.com/delhi-news/tiranga-march-a-message-for-anti-nationals-v-c-wants-army-tank-in-jnu/story-kTO0q2kglet2wnQbgULtyO.html. Accessed on 16 September 2021.

of the world, actual tanks had rolled into university campuses to contain unrest.

Jagadesh Kumar had asked for a tank only for 'display purposes'. To remind the students 'of the sacrifices and valour of the soldiers'.[181]

Rajiv Malhotra, like a warrior, declared, 'This is not only a victory of taking over Kargil in the external war, but also the victory of taking over JNU in the internal war.'[182] Imagine comparing JNU to Kargil! Did that mean that our own students were being likened to enemy soldiers who crossed the border and infiltrated into Indian territory? Surely, such needless exaggeration even of patriotism was unwarranted.

General Bakshi added that other *gadh*s or fortresses of the Left, such as Jadavpur University and the University of Hyderabad, also needed to be captured. With interested commentators criticizing such goings-on and the JNU VC, perhaps it might have been worthwhile to ask whether this is a case of 'tanking up' or 'tanking out' as far as the patriotism overdrive on campus is concerned.[183]

Let us not forget that 'tank' was itself the secret code word in 1915 for the British project to create an armoured land ship. It was meant to confuse the Germans. The British Army had wanted their enemy to think that they were building a water carrier instead of a land-cruising battleship. But the short form of 'water carrier' would be 'WC', the polite word for toilet. So they used the word 'tank' instead, which was universally adopted, for an armoured land vehicle. That is why the battle tank of today is not mistaken for a water carrier. The point is that the idea of a tank need not be taken literally.

---

[181]Bhardwaj, Ananya. 'JNU Vice Chancellor Wants Tank on Campus to Remind Students of Army's Sacrifices', NDTV, YouTube, https://www.youtube.com/watch?v=GPoCg2qYB1Y. Accessed on 25 August 2021.
[182]Ibid.
[183]Ibid.

Would the ideological metaphor be a Trojan horse? The Trojan horse was a gift that turned too costly because it contained soldiers who took the Athenians by surprise. Would a battle tank, even an obsolete one which was a war trophy, serve a similar purpose in JNU? Would it stoke patriotic rather than warlike fervour? Would it help to turn the tide of JNU's student unrest? Would putting a tank on campus make all of us staunch nationalists?

Perhaps, the humbler talwar might serve better? How about adorning our major buildings, particularly the 'Pink Palace', with various displays of arms and battle gear? Or were we, to change metaphors, barking up the wrong tree?

Patriotism cannot be instilled merely by very tall flag poles or very large flags on campuses. Similarly, to put it rather bluntly, we don't need a tank to recapture JNU. Just the existing rules and regulations, if properly applied, might be sufficient.

Wouldn't denying registration to several miscreants, rusticating rule-breakers and bringing strong disciplinary action on habitual troublemakers do the trick? Isn't that what duly appointed proctoral committees are for?

To strike at the root of the JNU problem, we must understand the system of patronage and propaganda that nurtured it. Their formula is simple—keep fees ridiculously low, next to nil, in fact; remove attendance requirements; subsidize all or as many students as possible; ensure inadequate hostel spaces so that seniors accommodate and indoctrinate juniors; create a self-perpetuating system of state-funded dissent; use state money to produce anti-state cadres. Along with this, ensure that the 'true' history of communism is never taught. The idealism of the youth to work for the less privileged must be continuously harnessed—for an anti-bourgeoisie, anti-state and, ultimately, anti-national opposition.

Since capitalism is a known 'evil' and communism largely an unknown 'good', such indoctrination would continue to attract the innocent year after year. Once indoctrinated, the innocent would become not-so-innocent. They, in turn, would attract the innocent. Let the vicious cycle flourish.

Fundamental to its continuation, however, was the system of backing and patronage. The spigot of incentives should never be turned off. The rewards on offer—admissions, degrees, fellowships, admissions to foreign universities, eventually jobs and promotions—all for toeing the Leftist line—must continue.

What better way to join the comfortable bourgeoisie than by making a career of criticizing them?

With students staying on, the near-gratis hostel space would always be inadequate, giving the agitationists a permanent cause to fight for. Plus, a never-ending catchment area of new recruits from socially disadvantaged, 'backward' classes and areas. In grateful repayment of guest accommodation by seniors.

Furthermore, the subtle understanding was that as long as certain lines were not crossed, student leaders would eventually be protected and bailed out. No one was really at risk of being thrown out, rusticated or sent out of JNU sans a degree. Several teachers, themselves student leaders once, supported by Left-sympathetic parliamentarians, a few from JNU itself, would ensure that this convenient arrangement was sustained. The Left-Liberal press, of course, also played its part in promoting this parasitism in the guise of protest.

Obviously, to change such an incentivized and well-supported ecosystem, just a heavy dose of patriotism is not enough. Academic excellence had to be restored as the top priority. The nexus between recompense in the real world and ideological affiliation had to be broken. At the same time, the dilapidated campus, overrun by stray dogs, also needed to be cleaned up.

The southeastern wall, where the campus abuts Vasant Kunj, was broken for years. Anyone could come in or go out unchecked. It needed urgent repair. The apparently heavy checking at the main gate is laughable, when one realizes that streams of people can enter and leave the campus at will. The trail behind the Sanskrit Centre, leading to the garbage-sorting area, is a perennially littered health and eco-hazard. I wondered if the VC or JNU authorities knew about these things. If they did, why weren't they rectifying these problems and loopholes?

Apart from the main roads, many pathways and lanes are in utter disrepair. Several houses, including mine, haven't been painted or repaired for dozens of years. The day-to-day functioning of the administration, including support to the faculty in executing projects, is severely stressed. JNU is now almost a dysfunctional system, with contract workers in the administration who do not know the rules or the intricacies of the e-governance system.

In other words, the infighting in JNU has well-nigh destroyed the normal functioning of this once-great university. Unless that is restored, how can the university be saved? If the entire energy of the administration and its backers is devoted to winning ideological battles, what of the more crucial struggle to ensure academic excellence, administrative efficiency and high-quality infrastructure? Even if we attain a symbolic victory, the real battle for JNU will be lost.

Having at least understood my journalist friend's jest—'lake view or tank view?—I messaged back. 'No lakes in JNU. Hopefully no battle tanks either. The view remains drab—just facades of red-brick buildings, surrounded by an overgrowth of thorn and scrub.'

We don't need a panzer to win JNU. We have to fix the more important things first.

JNU's Attendance Row: What's Really at Stake

On 10 September 2017, Leftists captured JNUSU again on a united 'Left Front' comprising AISA, SFI and DSF. Geeta Kumari of AISA was elected president and Simone Zoya Khan, also of AISA, the vice president. Duggirala Srikrishna of SFI became the general secretary, while Shubhanshu Singh of DSF, won the joint secretary's post.

Before the year ended, on 22 December, the university

administration issued a circular to make 75 per cent attendance compulsory for students. Else they would not be permitted to take end-semester exams. The administration claimed that the decision had been taken at the Academic Council (AC) meeting held on 1 December. But this was denied by several members of the AC. Both JNUSU and JNUTA disputed this.

Simone told the press, 'Attendance was not discussed at the academic council meeting with students or teachers.' She claimed, 'It was not even on the agenda. The VC had mentioned something about this, saying they would do it, but no decision was made.'[184]

Professor Ayesha Kidwai, JNUTA president, called the move 'unnecessary' and 'ridiculous'. She told a newspaper, 'This is not the way we do things in JNU, and we don't think establishing a police culture is the way to ensure academic excellence'.[185]

The JNU ABVP wing, affiliated to the ruling BJP, also opposed it. They dubbed it a 'regressive *Tughlaqi farmaan*' referring to the eccentric, mad to some, medieval despot, Muḥammad bin Tughluq.[186]

Geeta Kumari said, 'JNU's academic excellence achieved till date has rested on the philosophy of freedom of debate and discussion, inclusion and equality. The move to impose compulsory attendance is highly absurd.'[187]

After a short period of relative stability and slightly less

---

[184] Alavi, A. Mariyam. 'JNU Makes Attendance Mandatory from Jan, Students Say It's Against "Tradition"', *Hindustan Times*, 27 December 2017, https://www.hindustantimes.com/delhi-news/jnu-makes-attendance-mandatory-from-jan-students-say-it-s-against-tradition/story-q9RAdGS99M6kQYPXj6yOgL.html. Accessed on 27 August 2021.
[185] Ibid.
[186] 'Students, Teachers Call JNU's Decision to Make Attendance Compulsory for All Courses Absurd', *Scroll.in*, https://scroll.in/latest/863029/students-teachers-call-jnus-decision-to-make-attendance-compulsory-for-all-courses-absurd. Accessed on 27 August 2021.
[187] Ibid.

conflict, the university was thrown out of gear again. It was just when matters seemed to be on the mend and the administration was gradually getting a grip on the situation.

An emboldened VC took the decision in the 146th AC meeting on Friday, 13 July 2018, to make daily attendance mandatory for the faculty as well. At the same AC meeting, it was also decided to make entrance examinations to JNU completely online from the next session.

Though a member of the AC, I was loath to jump into JNU's latest fracas, the attendance imbroglio. The reasons for my reluctance were both personal and pedagogic.

The personal first. Taking contrarian positions in the very place where one lives and works makes one unnecessarily disliked. Just as cheap popularity is undesirable so is gratuitous disapproval. It interferes with one's primary job, which is to learn and to teach.

Students, moreover, are young, impressionable, passionate and often unreasonable. They can form extremely strong, even uninformed, views about their teachers. Constantly going against the tide in JNU only gives a handle and fillip to those who wish to misunderstand and misrepresent what one stands for or believes. The fallout is an attenuation of one's ability to contribute one's vocation, if not a shrinking of one's sphere of positive influence.

The fact was that I too loved the many freedoms of JNU. These freedoms, if used responsibly, added greatly not only to formal learning outcomes but the development of personality. One of the most important functions of a truly nurturing academic environment is to facilitate independent-minded, unafraid, self-regulating, highly responsible, fair and deeply compassionate human beings. For this, liberty is absolutely vital.

Now to the pedagogic argument. There are essentially two views on how students learn best. The first is epitomized by the age-old and well-known maxim: 'spare the rod and spoil the child.' As opposed to this, consider, 'The mind has to be consulted in its own growth.' This injunction of Sri Aurobindo I found not just useful, but accurate, especially as we get into the subtler dimensions of transformative learning.

Does this mean that the first principle, that discipline is necessary to acquiring knowledge, is untrue? No. For much of what is basic, from mastering the alphabet, cramming tables or grasping the 'fundas' of any subject, repetition, regulation and revision are indispensable. What this means is that the best pedagogical scheme requires a combination of the two—discipline and liberty, instruction and freedom, structure and autonomy.

But here comes the moot question: is JNU such an ideal environment in the first place where new, some would say coercive, rules are unnecessary? Instead, it would perhaps be more accurate to call JNU a place where academic and institutional laxity, bordering on indiscipline and irresponsibility, prevails.

This does not mean that a university where both teachers and students enjoy a huge degree of autonomy and emancipation should be turned into a boot-camp, with army-style discipline or a super-efficient corporate organization, with soul-crushing deliverables. Again, the answer, is no.

Neither zero answerability nor rigid control would be conducive to the ends of higher education. What needs to be done? Intermedial hermeneutics demands mediation between contending extreme positions, both of which, on closer examination, are shown up as inadequate and not in the interests of the greater common good.

The answer is balance, respecting freedom and autonomy, and also ensuring academic excellence and accountability. That is the demand of intermediality, the methodology of steering between extremes, which I pursued and promoted.

Unfortunately, in JNU, like many of our other universities, liberty has often turned into licence. In their anti-attendance agitation, students blocked roads and buildings, demanding the 'right' not to attend classes. How 'no-attendance' can be a 'right' or a 'demand' is difficult to understand.

How can the main purpose of securing the extremely difficult admission into JNU be reduced to the right not to attend classes? Isn't blocking buildings and disrupting the academic calendar unfair to the majority of students who wish to attend classes? The fact is that having no-attendance requirements at all in JNU has led to many distortions of our cherished academic freedoms and principles.

In a worst-case scenario, a student can get a degree without attending a single class or draw scholarships worth thousands of rupees a month without doing any work or even coming to the university, except occasionally, having some papers signed by their supervisor. Imposing minimum attendance would certainly plug some of these loopholes in the system. But doing so in a harsh, punitive, mechanical manner would also be counterproductive.

Once again, when it comes to JNU, the core issue is not attendance, but what the very purpose of the university is. Is its primary purpose to bankroll agitational politics, with near-zero tuition and hostel fees and subsidized food? Or is it to offer high-quality higher education aiming for greater excellence?

Who runs the university? Who controls its functioning? Protestors and activists or administrators and academics? Given how the latter have had a free run of the place for decades, isn't an overcorrection unavoidable? Can deeply entrenched vested interests be dislodged so easily, without bitter resistance on their part? Will they give up their unearned privileges and advantages so easily?

Cleaning up JNU's Augean stables was, therefore, long overdue. That is what VC Jagadesh Kumar was trying to do. It was a difficult, disliked, even detested job, but necessary.

Yet, I felt that he was overdoing it, almost with a vengeance. Some sort of minimum attendance requirement for students was fine. But daily, biometric attendance for the faculty too? Wasn't that going too far?

The JNU administration seemed punitive, rather than remedial. Filled with a strange sort of vindictive anger and hatred for its own faculty, staff and students. It was as if they were hell-bent on disciplining all of us and teaching us a lesson we would remember for the rest of our days.

JNU's Ongoing Turmoil

Two years after the February 2016 uprising in JNU, one thing was abundantly clear in all the ongoing confusion and turbulence—the gradual but sure marginalization and isolation of the radical and extreme elements.

True, the organized Left still controlled both the students' and teachers' unions. But their hold and sway were considerably dented, at least when it came to the JNUTA. As to the latter, one might have asked if its so-called elections were really elections at all. That's because the top positions were occupied by walkovers, without any voting.

Designated by the oxymoronic term, 'elected unopposed', dummy candidates were put up who withdrew their names at the last moment. Then these 'unopposed' JNUTA office-bearers would escalate matters, especially after the JNUSU once again occupied the administration building. Far from halcyon days, I saw more trouble in the days ahead. But the big change was that neither union enjoyed unconditional support or legitimacy on campus.

Outside the campus, in the larger world that is India, what the JNU potboiler has invoked is nothing short of the derision and rage of both the masses and classes. This is quite contrary to wish-fulfilling fantasies, fomented by media notables colluding with sections of the Opposition, of a mass movement against the Modi sarkar, during the heyday of the agitation in 2016.

Instead, two years later, most responsible, taxpaying citizens ran out of patience. They'd rather the university close down than put up with any more dharnas, illegal blockades of buildings and never-ending shenanigans of the Lefties.

Not surprisingly, on campus too, most students and teachers dreaded and detested the prospect of the crisis worsening. Unfortunately, however, as we approached 2019, an election year, we were staring at delayed or cancelled admissions even if not an indefinite shutdown. Not to speak of bitter confrontations between the students' and teachers' unions on the one hand and the university administration on the other.

This brings me to the second realization. Despite their best efforts, the well-meaning JNU VC Jagadesh Kumar and his team had still not managed to bring the situation under control.

In my own way, I was relieved not to be invited on any of the committees. I didn't want to be closely identified with the JNU administration or the small coterie that ran the university. I preferred to maintain my intellectual integrity and professional independence. The VC, of course, was headed for greater things. As this book goes to press, Professor Kumar has been named as the new UGC Chairman. But questionable practices brought disrepute to the university and demoralized those who wanted to serve it sincerely and diligently.[188]

The VC himself became less and less accessible. Why would he want to expose himself to rabble-rousers, who were only

---

[188] See: 'HC Sets Aside JNU's Appointment of Centre Chairperson, Says Not Done As Per Statutes', *Hindustan Times*, 29 September 2021, https://www.hindustantimes.com/cities/delhi-news/hc-sets-aside-jnu-s-appointment-of-centre-chairperson-says-not-done-as-per-statutes-101632939803057.html. Accessed on 24 December 2021; 'Delhi HC Quashes Advertisements Issued by JNU for Appointments for Two Posts', *The Indian Express*, 6 December 2020, https://indianexpress.com/article/jobs/hc-quashes-parts-of-jnu-adverts-for-appointment-to-posts-of-prof-associate-prof-7093013/. Accessed on 24 December 2021; 'Appointment of Nine JNU Centre Heads by VC without Authority: Delhi HC', *The Hindu*, 4 November 2021, https://www.thehindu.com/news/cities/Delhi/appointment-of-nine-jnu-centre-heads-by-vc-without-authority-delhi-hc/article37332349.ece. Accessed on 24 December 2021.

campaigning for his ouster? I sympathized with him, but his aloofness did not endear him to the faculty or students.

What was more depressing was that JNU's logjam actually appeared to suit some. Why? This was the last-ditch stand of the Left. If they were routed in JNU, losing whatever little prestige or credibility they had left, they would be utterly dispossessed. They would have nowhere to go, which is all the more why the times were dangerous. If they couldn't be winners, our JNU radicals would yet be spoilers. If JNU couldn't be theirs, they wouldn't let it be anyone else's either.

I wondered if the mandarins in charge were fully cognisant of the situation. As adversaries, the organized Left could not be taken lightly, at least in JNU. Beyond their usual nuisance value, they also had real gifts, not just intellectual and artistic, but also strategic. They are not lacking in courage, even if they might be in conviction. What is more, they had a proven track record of persistence, determination and unscrupulousness.

They could not be simply brushed aside; having captured the Pink Palace they would not vacate it peacefully. Their occupation of the administration building actually reminded me, in some respects, of the endgame in Rakeysh Omprakash Mehra's *Rang De Basanti*. Superimposing their fight against the state with that of revolutionaries like Bhagat Singh, Chandrashekhar Azad and Ramprasad Bismil, the youthful rebels in the film occupy the All India Radio (AIR) building. Finally, in a bloody stand-off with the authorities, the misguided but innocent rebels are gunned down by commandos.

While matters were nowhere as dire in JNU, we ought not to have underestimated how, being thus cornered and provoked, the romantic dreams of the student leaders of courting real or symbolic martyrdom may be stoked.

Was it also convenient for the JNU administration to let matters slide awhile? After last year's miscalculations, they wouldn't have wanted to use the iron fist, lest it provoke a backlash, especially during the run-up to the upcoming 2019 elections. No point giving the Opposition such wished-for traction.

As to the protesters, some would continue being anti-establishment no matter how many demands, justified or otherwise, are met. Besides, all discerning parties know that there are unresolved, even controversial, issues in the JNU notifications. To build a university-wide consensus on them would take a long and demanding multilevel consultative process, for which there was simply no time now, with the new admissions about to be announced.

The implications go farther than compulsory attendance or rationalizing the number or allocation of PhD candidates. At the least, JNU MPhil/PhD admissions would change from a two-step (written+oral) to a three-step (qualifying, written+oral) process. The cut-offs of the qualifying, it was alleged, would dilute statutory reservations. If they were not intended to, why have a qualifying exam when the written test at present served that function? In addition, the AC meeting accepting the UGC communication was disputed as already indicated.

Fundamental to ongoing academic regulations controversy in JNU was something deeper than the issue of university autonomy. Was JNU bound by whatever the UGC dictated? The simple answer would be yes. He who pays the piper calls the tune, is the ancient adage. The government pays, so in this case, its arm, the UGC, calls the tune.

But JNU saw itself as a leader, not a follower. The UGC, on the other hand, has hardly been the source of good, let alone game-changing or cutting-edge, ideas. Underlying the ongoing struggle, thus, were not just two ideologies, but also two ideas of what JNU was.

The first attitude I would call JNU exceptionalism. JNU was a unique institution, extraordinary, distinctive and, therefore, not only worth preserving, but irreplaceable. The mirror opposite of such inflated self-exaltation was the notion gaining ground that

JNU is exceptionally degenerate, a den of shiftless bloodsuckers and anti-national vipers, fit only to be purged, cleansed or bulldozed. Less harsh but ultimately similar is the argument that JNU is not just commonplace or ordinary, but utterly underserving of any special treatment. It should be straightened out, if not mercilessly levelled. That seemed to be the ruling party's and the JNU administration's approach.

The truth, as usual, lay in between. Of course, JNU had to measure up, not just to fair, but the best practices implemented elsewhere. On the other hand, like many institutions of national importance, JNU had its own distinctive character and contribution, not reducible just to its ideological or political hues.

How do we safeguard, even enhance, its real capacities and achievements while reducing its drawbacks and problems? That, in brief, was the real challenge. If faced squarely and sincerely, it may lead to the transformation of JNU, saving it from being destroyed before our very eyes, as many institutions of excellence have been over the years in India.

But was anyone paying attention? Most of all, was the JNU administration and the government bureaucracy capable of the visionary leadership, dynamism and will to transform our beleaguered university? To save it, in fact, from certain doom?

8

A NATION UNITED, A UNIVERSITY DIVIDED

JNU and Modi's Re-election

Soon, three years passed since JNU's turmoil of February 2016.

The hectic countrywide general election campaign started in 2019 had its ups and downs. Pulwama and Balakot, for instance. Such events of national, even subcontinental dimensions, eclipsed JNU, if momentarily.

In May 2019, Narendra Modi won the battle for Raisina Hill. He returned to power to head a 303 BJP majority in Parliament. It was an astonishing and convincing victory, far outstripping the predicted margins or numbers. It was a triumph that demonstrated that Modi had united the nation. Modi had succeeded in integrating the country as no leader since Jawaharlal Nehru had.

But the university named after the latter was more divided than ever before. While Modi won two mandates at the hustings—first in 2014 and again in 2019. JNU was not only as anti-Modi as before, but with a pro-government administration in place, also in the throes of internecine conflict.

How to explain and understand this paradox? How, above all, to reform, even save JNU? Trying to puzzle out answers to such questions became an additional reason to write this book.

I started working on it in earnest from October 2019. That was because I thought that there was perhaps no better way to start writing about JNU than bring into focus two opposing trends highlighted in those weeks. Nothing illustrated the divided legacy and contradictory public perception of JNU as graphically as those events.

It is another matter that the passage of the book seemed to catch the JNU virus after it was finished. Though commissioned by a leading international publishing house, it got so entangled in what was evidently a conspiracy to block its publication that I had to withdraw it and seek another publisher.

Back in those days, when I was working on the manuscript, the situation remained fluid, even volatile.

On 29 October 2019, when I opened the newspapers, I found myself staring at yet another business-as-usual morning in JNU— the 'high drama' of yet another protest-cum-gherao.

During an inter-hostel committee meeting, agitating students forced their way into the dean of students' office. They barricaded the wardens and the dean. The latter reportedly fell ill; his blood pressure shot up. An ambulance was called to take him to the hospital, but the students directed or diverted it to the campus Health Centre.[189]

There, his wife pleaded with the students to let her husband be taken to a hospital. Instead, both the dean and his wife were blockaded for several hours inside the Health Centre. Late in the evening, the dean was allowed to be hospitalized. After a check-up and tests, he was declared out of danger and permitted to return home.[190]

As usual, tempers rose and voices were raised in the public sphere. Fuelled, expectedly, by outrage in the social media about

---

[189]PTI. 'JNU Students Block Ambulance for Ailing Professor During Protest,' *Financial Express,* 28 October 2019, https://www.financialexpress.com/india-news/jnu-students-block-ambulance-for-ailing-professor-during-protest/1747974/. Accessed on 16 September 2021.

[190]'High Drama at JNU Hostel Committee Meeting', *Hindustan Times,* 28 October 2019, https://www.hindustantimes.com/cities/high-drama-at-jnu-hostel-committee-meeting/story-ANgIaR4vVrnrICOaTc2peI.html. Accessed on 16 September 2021.

how wicked and fallen this government-funded university was! Why shouldn't its callous and unruly students be dismissed or even jailed?

I was then in Shimla, at the Indian Institute of Advanced Study (IIAS), when the fracas unfolded. So I did not, as it were, have had a ringside view to the proceedings. But the fact is that this premier Indian university, consistently rated among the best in the country, had been on the boil for the last several years. Indeed, in its short, chequered history, since its founding by an Act of Parliament in 1969, JNU was often in turmoil.

This time, too, any curious, let alone halfway intelligent observer, might rightfully ask, 'But why are the students protesting?' A better way to frame the question might have been with the suffix *again*. What were they protesting against *again*? For it does not take much for students of this university to break into a demonstration, hunger strike, gherao or boycott classes.

However, to be fair to them, this time the students probably had some cause to come out and display their displeasure, if not alarm, to the university administration. A whole set of new hostel regulations was to be discussed in that meeting of the inter-hostel administration, which the students had crashed. These included newly proposed curfew timings, restricting entry to women into boys' hostels, appropriate dress codes in the dining rooms and so on.

Many, if not most, students must have perceived these as a huge encroachment on their freedom. Yet another of the draconian, anti-student measures by the administration aimed at changing the fundamental character and ethos of the university known the world over for its unencumbered liberty, not to mention sexual liberalism.

According to VC Mamidala Jagadesh Kumar,

> The committee members requested the agitating students to go out and let the meeting continue. However, due to their unruly behaviour and sloganeering, the Dean of Students

Umesh Kadam fell sick with high blood pressure. This kind of behaviour by a section of JNU students is highly condemnable and outrageous.[191]

On the other hand, Aishe Ghosh, the new JNUSU president, offered a different version of what transpired. She asserted that:

> The administration did not invite the student body to the crucial meeting. When the students reached there to submit JNUSU's letter against the hostel rules draft, the meeting was abruptly adjourned by the Dean of Students. We did not hold anyone captive and the students were peacefully protesting. In fact, two of the JNUSU members accompanied him to the health centre.[192]

It is not a question of whether the JNU administration was right or the students. Matters are always more complicated than they seem. But in the commotion that unfolded on campus that day, the administration had found a way to manage, if not the protests of the students, at least the narrative surrounding it.

The students were portrayed as lawbreakers in addition to being heartless. After all, they had resorted to blockading their own teachers. They had been so mean even to the dean, who had taken ill. Not allowing the ambulance to take him to the hospital—wasn't that utterly unconscionable in addition to inconsiderate? Heartless ruffians, JNU-haters screamed!

If the administration wanted to paint our Leftist agitators in such lurid colours, they actually succeeded. The attention of the media and concerned citizenry was, once again, diverted from the core issue to sensational and often absurd theatrics. The university lurched, yet another time, from the Left to the Right. From one emergency to another. Indeed, if I had not highlighted it, even

---

[191]Ibid.
[192]Ibid.

this particular eruption is likely to have been long forgotten by the time readers laid their hands on this book.

What was going on? In simple terms, it was the shifting of the JNU problem from a real issue to a sort of public show trial. Events inimical to the university were allowed to be staged after which the narrative was sought to be managed. But was there sufficient effort or attention to addressing the actual challenges that the university faced?

Sadly and evidently not.

Wow! JNU Alum and Nobel Laureate on Campus

The gherao of the dean was one side of the JNU story that October. But there was another side to JNU's legacy, which was also showcased just 10 days prior.

On Saturday, 19 October 2019, just a few days before the barricading of the dean of students, JNU received a very distinguished visitor—the 2019 Nobel laureate in Economics, Abhijit Vinayak Banerjee.

Banerjee and his wife Esther Duflo, along with Harvard's Michael Kramer, were awarded the Sveriges Riksbank Prize in Economic Sciences in Memory of Alfred Nobel. More commonly called the Nobel Prize in Economics, this is the most prestigious international recognition in the field of Economics.

Not only was Banerjee the first Indian to win this prize, but he had also earned his master's degree in Economics (1981–1983) from the Centre for Economic Studies and Planning, JNU.

So, on one hand, the university was in an almost unworkable situation owing to the constant conflict between its administration and students. On the other hand, it could boast a Nobel Prize winner among its alumni.

What is fascinating to recall when it comes to this Nobel laureate was that though a consistently good student, Banerjee himself had spent 10 days in Tihar jail for gheraoing, along with a bunch of other students, the then VC P.N. Srivastava. What was the reason for that protest? Srivastava had dismissed, at the behest of the then prime minister Indira Gandhi, the JNUSU president. A move considered grossly undemocratic by the students.

The protesters, according to Banerjee, were put in jail. As Banerjee recalled, 'We were beaten and thrown into Tihar jail, charged not quite with sedition, but attempt to murder and the rest. The charges were eventually dropped—thank god—but not before we spent 10 days or so in Tihar.'[193]

A more detailed account of those momentous happenings is offered by Dr Sanjeev Chopra, director (retd), Lal Bahadur Shastri National Academy of Administration (LBSNAA), in a personal note.[194] Chopra, who was then the vice president of JNUSU, was also jailed:

> That fateful evening, when the police came to the campus, I was in the JNUSU office. They picked up all of us, physically. There was use of force. After our arrest, there was mayhem on the campus for any arrest on a campus always has a violent aftermath. Later that evening, in one of the police stations, where we had been taken initially, there were many busloads of students who joined us.
>
> As all the other office-bearers refused to negotiate with the government, I took up the gauntlet, and a compromise was struck at the behest of Arun Singh, who would later become minister of State for Defence. Government appointed the Prithvi Raj commission of inquiry which concluded that students had courted arrest in a fit of youthful passion and had solemnly affirmed that were going to be law-abiding citizens. Note that the term was 'courted arrest', instead of 'arrested'.

---

[193]Joy, Shemin. 'When Abhijit Banerjee Was Thrown into Tihar Jail', *Deccan Herald*, 14 October 2019, https://www.deccanherald.com/national/when-abhijit-banerjee-was-thrown-into-tihar-jail-768374.html. Accessed on 29 August 2021..
[194]Personal communication via email received on 10 May 2020.

We can be sure that the JNU administration would scarcely have imagined what Banerjee's subsequent advancement would be like. Not just from Tihar to Harvard for his PhD and thence to a prestigious professorship at the Massachusetts Institute of Technology (MIT), but to the very pinnacle of global renown and recognition—the Nobel Prize in Economics.

As of now at least, Banerjee's journey is certainly more noteworthy and momentous than what is described in *Bihar to Tihar*, the title of Kanhaiya Kumar's book.[195] Kumar, the JNUSU president in 2016, who was charged with sedition and also thrown into Tihar jail. He contested the Lok Sabha elections from Begusarai, Bihar, on a CPI ticket, but lost to the BJP candidate. Who knows—Kumar may yet become even more famous than Banerjee?

But in October 2019, when Banerjee visited JNU accompanied by India Today News Director Rahul Kanwal, one might justifiably have called him our most distinguished alumnus. This blast from the past was filmed and broadcast in the show 'Jab We Met [When We Met]'.[196]

Banerjee freely reminisced about his time at the university. Notably, he said he clearly remembered our current finance minister, Nirmala Sitharaman. She was a friend, a year senior. Sitharaman 'was a very pleasant person and intelligent. Her political views were not dramatically different than mine,' Banerjee recalled.[197]

---

[195] Kumar, Kanhaiya. *Bihar to Tihar: My Political Journey*, Juggernaut, 2016.
[196] 'Abhijit Banerjee, Nobel Laureate in Conversation with Rahul Kanwal', India Today, YouTube, https://www.youtube.com/watch?v=gyAnlaCxUiw. Accessed on 10 December 2021.
[197] 'Nirmala Sitharaman Was a Friend in JNU, Our Views Were Not Very Different: Abhijit Banerjee', *India Today*, 20 October 2019, https://www.indiatoday.in/india/story/nirmala-sitharaman-abhijit-banerjee-1611171-2019-10-20. Accessed on 26 August 2021. Sitharaman's husband, the distinguished political economist and commentator, Parakala Prabhakar, also studied in JNU. He got an MA and MPhil there before proceeding to the London School of Economics for his PhD.

In addition to Sitharaman, JNU boasts another member of the Union Cabinet of India, holding as important a portfolio, Dr S. Jaishankar. Yes, India's External Affairs minister, is also a JNU alum. Jaishankar not only earned a master's degree and MPhil from JNU, but also a PhD in 1981. The latter, four years after he had joined the Indian Foreign Service in 1977. As it happened, both Sitharaman and Jaishankar were 'Free Thinkers' (FT), a non-Left political party, which was not Right wing either.

Jaishankar, who joined JNU in 1973, was an active debater in addition to being a topper. In an interview, Jaishankar described his years at the university as 'the most impactful of my life'. According to him, JNU 'shaped my intellectual outlook and brought out an abiding interest in international politics'.[198]

Like Sitharaman, who met her would-be husband, Parakala Prabhakar in JNU, Jaishankar made many friends in the university, including his first wife. JNU was also a place for 'great ideological debates', he said, for it teaches 'you to think and to talk'.[199]

On 31 October 2019, the hundred and forty-fourth birth anniversary of Sardar Patel, the prime minister was addressing the young civil servants at Kevadia, at the footsteps of the Statue of Unity. Some 425 of them from 22 services had come together for 'Aarambh', the first-ever common foundation course. I was privileged to be invited to this important programme. An unexpected insight was just how significant JNU's contribution had been to the Indian republic.

I noticed that the four most powerful senior civil servants in the front row, seated adjacent to each other, Dr C. Chandramouli, secretary of the Department of Personnel and Training; Dr J.N.

---

[198] Kritika Sharma and Sunanda Ranjan. 'Free Thought, Politics & Love: Charting Nirmala Sitharaman & S Jaishankar's JNU Days', *The Print*, 17 June 2019, https://theprint.in/india/freethought-politics-love-charting-nirmala-sitharaman-s-jaishankars-jnu-days/249641/. Accessed on 26 August 2021.
[199] Ibid.

Singh, former chief secretary, Gujarat, Dr Sanjeev Chopra, director of LBSNAA; and B.B. Acharya, director general of the Dr Marri Channa Reddy, Human Resource Development, Institute of Telangana, were in JNU, all at the same time. Two of them also coincided with the Nobel laureate, Abhijit Banerjee, in Tihar! That was what JNU was once. Who could doubt its contribution to the nation? And now? JNU was notorious for its 'anti-nationalism'. What a fall!

But let's return to Banerjee's visit. He called on VC Kumar and also went to Brahmaputra Hostel, where he had resided. He visited the library too, where he used to spend long hours studying. During his JNU days, he often took a break at the library canteen, where he drank endless cups of bad tea.

But that day, he did something totally unexpected. He not only descended to this humble canteen, but actually cooked up a storm. Banerjee, evidently, is much more than a very smart economist. He is also a great cook.

In that very humble canteen, the Nobel laureate proceeded to chop onions in the most natural and unaffected manner, then whip up some eggs. A nobel, or should I say Noble, omelette indeed! Fit to be shared with the TV anchor interviewing him. Banerjee, who is a legendary cook, said, rather modestly, that he has no expectations of winning another Nobel Prize for cooking!

Instead, he proceeded to play ping-pong (table tennis) with his host, Kanwal. During the course of the interview, Banerjee discussed a variety of topics and, not surprisingly, the state of the Indian economy. We might pass over some of those remarks to focus more specifically on JNU.

In 2016, Banerjee had criticized the government for charging Kanhaiya Kumar and two other JNU students, Umar Khalid and Anirban Bhattacharya, with sedition and sending them to jail. Returning to that theme, Banerjee said, 'One of the jobs of an academic and intellectual is to be critical of the authority. I have no particular brief for bad policies. It is extremely important and it is our right to articulate constructive criticism. I think to be constructive you need to be allowed to be critical.'[200]

Banerjee, a few days earlier, had met Prime Minister Modi. However, when speaking to Kanwal, he refused to criticize Modi personally: 'I would value the country doing well over particular political biases of mine getting favoured.'[201] But the Nobel laureate emphasized just how valuable a culture of dissent was for a university in a democratic country. Clearly, it is not a matter of ideological Left versus the Right, but of values far more important, such as the democratic right to dissent.

A defining moment occurred during Banerjee's visit to his erstwhile Centre for Economic Studies and Planning at the School of Social Sciences. Kanwal, waving the Nobel laureate's latest book, *Good Economics for Hard Times* (2019), asked the students gathered how many had read it. Not one hand went up. Neither did they have a clue as to who its author was.

But, soon after, when they realized that their distinguished visitor really was the global celebrity and Nobel Prize winner, several students scrambled around Banerjee for selfies.

Selfies over books: this sums up the deterioration of JNU.

The Decline and Fall of JNU

The contrasting stories about JNU that I have just recounted encapsulate the calamity that has overtaken it.

On the one hand, it is soiled by unsavoury controversy and what seems like never-ending student unrest. On the other hand, no other university in India can boast two senior serving Cabinet ministers, a Nobel laureate, besides a host of secretaries,

---

[200]'Abhijit Banerjee, Nobel Laureate In Conversation With Rahul Kanwal', India Today, YouTube, https://www.youtube.com/watch?v=gyAnlaCxUiw. Accessed on 10 December 2021.
[201]Ibid.

ambassadors, Director Generals of Police and so on, as its distinguished alumni.

Between these two poles is the sad truth of nosediving academic standards.

Given its current sorry state, it is difficult to imagine the university attracting the likes of Sitharaman, Jaishankar or Banerjee in the near future. Especially in the disciplines of humanities, social studies and international relations that the university was once famous for. Parents, on the contrary, would be loath to send their children to an institution where studies are so uncertain and politics so rampant.

Sitharaman was the first woman to serve as defence minister and then finance minister of India. Both she and Jaishankar received the university's first-ever 'Distinguished Alumni' awards in 2019. Similarly, Banerjee's JNU connection came in for its just share of celebration, with the laureate himself contributing to it by writing about his student days here. It was in JNU that he learned so much about India, coming as he did from a much more limited and homogenous caste, class and linguistic cohort at Presidency, his undergraduate college, in Kolkata.

But no amount of tom-toming or trumpeting its past glory is going to save JNU. In 2016, following the tukde tukde—break India into pieces—episode, JNU has been under severe attack, from within, by the Leftist students and teachers, and from outside by irate and outraged citizens who are still calling for its closure.

As this book has already recounted, I was very much a part of that history-in-the-making as a beleaguered insider. For years, I had been at odds with the Left-dominated culture of JNU. I had faced repeated barrages of the five Bs—as I called them—or pancha b-kar. Brainwash, bully, brand, browbeat, boycott—and if all these five fail—bullshit.

Looking back, I reflected on the events of the last 21 years since I had joined JNU in 1999. Especially what had transpired in the last five years since February 2016.

I realized that I did not hate JNU. It was a place of possibilities. Even if you were in a minority of one, you had space, especially, if you had academic standing. Since I had joined as a full professor way back in 1999, I did not have to kowtow for my promotions to lobbies and vested interests that ruled JNU.

The Centre for English Studies, where I taught, wasn't as Left-dominated as the other centres either, certainly not as far as the faculty were concerned. Though I wasn't the beneficiary of the JNU gravy train, I hadn't fared badly either. I had managed to write, publishing papers and books, take on visiting assignments abroad and had been able to survive, even thrive through great personal upheavals.

In any case, my world was much larger than JNU.

As an outsider, who had neither studied nor begun my teaching career in JNU, I had always been astonished by the smugness and inbreeding that characterized the university culture. It was a land of lotus eaters where few of those who entered ever wanted to leave. Some, indeed, stayed on forever, either securing employment or never leaving despite having no formal standing.

Many who entered as BA students in the School of Languages went on not only to do their MA, MPhil and PhD in JNU, but also got married to fellow-JNUites. Becoming assistant professors, they stayed on till their retirement at 65. Or even for a few years more on re-employment. It seemed like a cradle-to-grave deal. Almost too good to be true.

Yet, there was so much that was so clearly wrong, so crying for reform, apart from the fact that most of the faculty, probably over 75 per cent in many schools and centres, were JNU products. In addition, especially in certain disciplines, all that the students seemed to do was agitate. Politics trumped academics. Standards were so low in some centres that one wondered why certain programmes were permitted to continue.

In the School of Languages, I often found students copying in tests. They didn't even bother to hide their cheat sheets too carefully. I would find them strewn in the gents' toilets during exams. The contents or script in the chits gave away the course and exam in which the malpractice was going on. Once or twice, I tried to point this out to the teachers concerned or the invigilators. After the customary and perfunctory noises of righteous regret, they would lose interest.

In my own classes, I found rampant plagiarism. Failing students, however, was almost impossible. To my surprise, quite often, my own colleagues didn't support severe penalties for copying. Almost each semester I found students cheating. Almost each semester they were allowed to get off scot-free or with minor penalties such as grade cuts. It was I who got a bad name for catching them, not them for plagiarising.

I taught 'Research Methodology', the only compulsory MPhil-level course in my centre, for over 15 years. One semester, I caught most of the class copying or cheating in their assignments. I down-marked them all and was boycotted. For a couple of years, no one wanted me as a PhD supervisor. Instead of feeling hurt or rejected, I embraced the proscription. I wrote and travelled, both within and outside India. While no one in JNU seemed interested in me or my work, I found an ever-willing and widening audience outside.

After I started speaking out against the 'anti-national' students and teachers in 2016, I became even more unpopular on campus. The attendance in my MA classes shrunk, for the first time in my career, to single digits. I didn't even need a classroom. My students sat in my office, across my table. When scholars from the Centre for English Studies stopped coming, I got, to my surprise, out-centre sign-ups and attendees.

The atmosphere inside the campus became both suffocating and explosive. The new punitive measures imposed by the administration, including 75 per cent mandatory attendance, biometric attendance marking by teachers, controversial and ideologically motivated recruitment, frequent fining of students and so on, bred greater resentment.

In 2016, students had 'permanently' occupied the 'Pink Palace', as the administration building was called. They camped there, even sleeping nights. The space around the administration building came to be known as 'Freedom Square' after the 'azadi' slogan-shouting.

Clearly, things had gone too far. One could say that the university was being used as a platform to attack a legitimately elected government. There was something sinister brewing, a plot to unseat the government. At the very least, an attempt to stoke a nationwide youth movement against the Modi sarkar.

That is when, as seen earlier, by a series of accidents, I was interpellated into the centre of the vortex. The trigger was my speaking out against both the JNUSU and the JNUTA in the 'nationalism debates'.

I realized that even after teaching diligently, faithfully, one might even say inspiringly, for over twenty years, I found no recognition, let alone affirmation in JNU. I was the first serving JNU professor to be called up as the director, Indian Institute of Advanced Study, Shimla. There were no congratulations, no notice of this achievement in *JNU News* or elsewhere. When my book publications crossed half-a-century, no one noticed, whether in JNU or outside. In other systems, each book would have attracted an incentive. Here, being the most published professor didn't count for anything at all. Later, in a TV interview, Bibek Debroy, the most prolific translator of classical Indian texts of our times, asked me, 'How is it that we fail to recognize those who excel until they are first feted and awarded abroad?' The answer was simple. We are not a merit-rewarding or merit-recognizing society. We remain deeply insecure, culturally cringing and somewhat anti-intellectual. Tagore, Aurobindo and hundreds of other contemporary greats faced this neglect, jealousy and hatred. Then what of us?

But, quite significantly, during this transition, so marked by the pandemic, it was as if my peaceful, non-political persona was overtaken by a new engaged, Right-of-centre, pro-Modi avatar. Whether this was true or not, that was the perception. What is, however, true is that I became a public intellectual. I not only began to write columns and make television appearances, I soon discovered a new-found leverage in social media. I began to be invited to fora both in India and abroad as someone who could offer a counter-point to the Left-Liberal position.

The more I was shunned in JNU, the more I found myself admired and supported outside. Wherever I went people recognized me as the lone voice who spoke out against Kanhaiya Kumar and Left-hegemony. Yet, at the height of the JNU crisis in 2016, when the whole nation was baying for its blood, I never hesitated to support the university or its ethos.

Freedom, academic autonomy, social, political and ideological diversity, safety of women, social justice and equal opportunities, levelling of caste-hierarchies and many other things that JNU stood for were, in my view, well worth preserving. I still hold that position.

What is more, no matter how isolated or hated I was among a certain section of the students, I never felt unsafe on campus. I was confident that JNU remained a place of civilized debate and disagreement. No matter how overwhelmingly dominated by the Leftists, if you stood up for yourself, JNU left you alone.

I realized that while it is very hard to build a great university, it is relatively easy to destroy it. What JNU needed was reform, not demolition. But reform needed vision, planning and persistence. Moreover, academic excellence had to take centre stage again.

How was that to happen if we had no reprieve from protests, agitations and politics?

Perhaps, things had gone too far. We needed peace and reconciliation in JNU, not punitive measures and punishments. A velvet glove, rather than an iron fist.

A Convocation Gone Wrong: Fee Hike Protests

About a year later, I was in London, at the Nehru Centre, when yet another ugly incident at JNU erupted.

It was 14 November 2019, the birthday of our first prime minister after whom the centre was named. In dark, dreary, rainy London, the sun sets around 4.00 p.m. in the winters. In addition, it was rather depressing that no one remembered Nehru on that day even at the Nehru Centre.

When it came to JNU, another institution named after Nehru, even in distant London, despite Modi's second term and three-and-a-half years after February 2016, we were still in the news. Totally bizarre. Given that hardly anyone was worrying about India in London. Why, then, was JNU making it to the Beeb, not to mention the British tabloids?

Well, JNU was in the news, as always, for the wrong reasons. It was because water cannons had reportedly been used against students. Why? The students had targeted the university's third convocation on 11 November 2019 using the recently imposed fee hikes as pretext.

They had tried to block and disrupt the vice president of India, M. Venkaiah Naidu, who was to address the convocation. They jammed the roads and prevented Ramesh Pokhriyal 'Nishank', the then minister of Human Resource Development (HRM), from leaving the premises.[202] At some point, the police must have deemed their actions as a bit too much and used water cannons to disperse the crowds.

In London, those who knew I was from JNU asked me what was going on. Is the State using its power to crush legitimate democratic demonstrations? Or should such an

---

[202] PTI. 'Protest by JNU Students Leaves HRD Minister Stranded,' *The New Indian Express*, 11 November 2019, https://www.newindianexpress.com/nation/2019/nov/11/hrd-minister-inside-auditorium-since-morning-as-jnu-students-protests-2060239.html. Accessed on 16 September 2021.

anti-national university, funded by taxpayers, be finally shut down?

I thought I had to write about it all. To dispel the many myths around the JNU fee hikes. Like many other JNU-related matters, the fee issue, too, is highly contentious. In fact, the problem has not yet been fully solved, though the university has partially rolled back the increase.

In those days, however, what was highlighted in the media, both Indian and foreign, was the extent of the increase, not the details of the actual fees. The headlines screamed of the 150 per cent hike, without highlighting that the proposed fees were still just ₹300 for a double-occupancy room and ₹600 for a single room for the whole year.[203] No one said that the present fees were laughably low at ₹150 a year for a double-occupancy room and ₹400 a year for a single-occupancy room. Less than ₹23 and ₹34 per month! Even adding establishment and annual charges, the JNU rates would be ₹7,200 and ₹9,700 for double and single-occupancy rooms, respectively.

Consider the current fee structure, for the academic year 2021–2022.[204] The annual fees for Indian BA(Hons.), MA, MSc and MCA students is a ridiculously low ₹216, which is less than ₹20 a month. Many of the other charges are either voluntary or refundable.

---

[203]Indo Asia News Service. 'Despite Massive Fee Hike, JNU Still Has Cheapest Hostels', *Hindustan Times*, 16 November 2019, https://www.hindustantimes.com/education/despite-massive-fee-hike-jnu-still-has-cheapest-hostels/story-Hc9RXyrOFRRHngUlVguj2O.html. Accessed on 18 September 2021.
[204]Jawaharlal Nehru University, https://jnu.ac.in/content/fee, Accessed 23 December 2021.

Indian Nationals

BA (Hons.), MA, MSc, MCA	In INR
Tuition Fee (Annual)	216.00***
Sports Fee (Annual)	16.50
Literary & Cultural Fee (Annual)	16.50
**Students' Union Fee (Annual)	15.00
Library Fee (Annual)	06.00
Medical Fee (Annual)	09.00
Medical Booklet	12.00
Students Aid Fund (Annual)	04.50
*Admission Fee	05.00
*Enrolment Fee	05.00
*Security Deposit (Refundable)	40.00
Student Hostel and General Information Guide	15.00
Identity Card Folder	10.00
MPhil/PhD, Pre-PhD/PhD, MPH/PhD, MTech/PhD	
Tuition Fee (Annual)	240.00***
Sports Fee (Annual)	16.50
Literary & Cultural Fee (Annual)	16.50
**Students' Union Fee (Annual)	15.00
Library Fee (Annual)	06.00
Medical fee (Annual)	09.00
Medical Booklet	12.00
Students Aid Fund (Annual)	04.50
*Admission Fee	05.00
*Enrolment Fee	05.00
*Security Deposit (Refundable)	40.00
Student Hostel and General Information Guide	15.00
Identity Card Fold	10.00

Would anyone in their right minds agitate against a fee hike? But that is precisely what the JNU students, backed by their political patrons, did.

Our fees are, of course, considerably lower than the comparable government-funded institutions such as Delhi University, Jamia Millia Islamia or Ambedkar University. We will not even mention private universities like Ashoka or Jindal that charge several lakhs a year. A government-funded 'minority' college such as St Stephen's in Delhi charges as much as ₹60,000 per annum. JNU is possibly the cheapest university of national or international repute to live and study in.

Moving from overseas perceptions to those in India, JNU remained in the news constantly, usually for the wrong reasons. Indian media, though more balanced, documenting both sides of the story, remained sympathetic to the students. Among the larger public, however, the image of JNU students as state-sponsored freebooters and 'anti-nationals' remains quite prevalent.

No wonder, all over the country, there was outrage over these protests, with calls for the closing down of the university. In this fight between the authorities and the students, the former seem to have scored some sort of media or narrative advantage, if not victory.

But does that solve the problem? Not really. Winning the narrative war is not as important as saving the university from further damage. Students need to get off the streets and return to their classrooms. Teaching and research need to resume. At least a working relationship between the JNU administration and the demonstrating students is required so that the university returns to being a university, not a battleground of opposing forces and factions. It is crucial, therefore, to get to the root of the present round of disturbances.

I would suggest that the fight between students and JNU administration is really not about fee hikes at all.

True, that was the pretext for the massive mobilization. Even the pro-government BJP-affiliate ABVP joined against the hike.

The cause is so populist that it has united sworn ideological enemies. Unfortunately, what the 'azadi' movement, some would call it the 'tukde tukde' movement, failed to do, the fee hike succeeded in accomplishing. Sit-ins, occupations, gheraos, non-cooperation and whatever else it takes, all with a view to crash the university. And also to catapult JNU and the student movement into national and global limelight.

The students scored some brownie points in targeting the JNU convocation, which was addressed by the vice president of India, with then HRM also present. Though the administration tried to cordon off and sanitize the venue, which was not inside JNU but at the adjacent All India Council for Technical Education (AICTE) auditorium, the students succeeded in gheraoing Pokhriyal. The latter was detained for several hours.

While the earlier attempts to use JNU as a platform against the Modi sarkar failed, this fee-hike protest had more traction, even partial success. After students took over the 'Pink Palace,' they sprayed offensive graffiti right across the doors and corridors of the VC's office.[205]

The fee hike itself, in my view, was not only justified but also necessary. In fact, it was long overdue. But saying so, let alone implementing it, makes the administration seem anti-student and anti-poor. Other issues such as caste and reservations are also thrown in to muddy the waters. An issue like this has, regrettably, managed to focalize and channelize pent-up student anger. The many other, at times less necessary, punitive measures against student or even faculty interests made even legitimate administrative moves take on the appearance of a draconian measure.

What could have been done? First of all, the administration could have de-escalated the tension, negotiated if necessary and

---

[205]Paul, Sudeep. 'Battleground JNU', *Open*, 29 November 2019, https://openthemagazine.com/features/battleground-jnu/. Accessed 13 January 2022. When these were circulated in the public domain, the disgust against the protest only increased.

got the students back to the classes. They could have avoided non-essential or needlessly antagonistic steps, which could give rise to unrest or feed discontent. The facts behind the cost of higher education could have been put out into the public domain so that both prospective students and parents, in addition to taxpaying citizens, knew that the present structure is not sustainable.

A principled stance on fees was necessary, even if an immediate hike not opportune. But even more importantly, JNU should have set its priorities right. The object is not to win a political or ideological battle with the so-called Leftists, but centre-stage and highlight academic excellence as the primary objective of a university. In order to do this, there is no need to stamp out dissent or bring in moral policing or to try to punish a section of the teachers or to fix appointments or even appear to do so.

Containing excessive 'Leftism', cutting the support base of state-funded 'anti-nationals', cleaning up the campus culture, and all the subsidiary goals and objectives, will naturally follow from re-emphasizing academics and de-emphasizing politics. Rather than making JNU a battleground of Left versus Right, it is much better to make it a dialogic space where a certain openness to contrarian, even anti-establishment thinking in a politically awakened space, can flourish alongside excellence in teaching and research.

After being so reviled on campus for being a pro-Right professor, I now found myself on the other side as it were—a critic of the JNU administration and its repeated failures at containing the unrest or restoring normalcy on the campus.

It was as if one of India's best universities was being destroyed before our very eyes with no one raising their voice to stop it. Instead, the powers that were be, it would seem, resolutely turning their face away from JNU.

I kept thinking, *what to do, what can be done?*

9

HOW NOT TO DESTROY JNU

Cry, My Beloved University

The lowest point in JNU's decline in living memory occurred on 5 January 2020.

Sadly—some would say luckily—I was not in JNU on that fateful evening.

Masked hoodlums went on a rampage inside the campus, injuring several students, even a couple of teachers. They roamed the hostels and buildings armed with sticks, hammers, bricks and rocks. Later, the usual narrative war of mutual recriminations and accusations broke out, with both the Left and the Right blaming each other for the violence.

As it happened, I was in Mumbai. It was a Sunday evening. I remember it so clearly. My wife and I had been invited by our friends to the 'Wet Wicket', the watering hole of the Cricket Club of India. We had just finished ordering.

Suddenly, I started getting frantic calls and messages from the US. 'Are you all right? Is everything okay?'

Then came a call from someone very close, 'Where are you? Hope you're not injured.'

I responded, 'We're in Mumbai. We're fine. What happened?'

'Thank God!' I heard after a pause, 'There are rioting mobs in JNU. They've invaded the campus and are beating up students and teachers...'

I felt a sickening sense of pain and alarm. Then anger. I immediately started checking up on my phone. In my 20 years at JNU, such an incident had never happened. Even in the worst of times—hooligans on campus beating up people, wrecking things, breaking into hostels, labs and offices. Worst of all, attacking students and teachers. This was unprecedented and shameful.[206]

Now JNU was just like Delhi University, Jamia Millia Islamia, Aligarh Muslim University (AMU), Banaras Hindu University (BHU), Jadavpur University, University of Hyderabad or Maulana Azad National Urdu University.

What did all these universities have in common? They were reputed central universities, for one. But all of them were also strongholds of recent student agitations against some policy or other of the Modi government. More to the point, all of them witnessed pitched battles between student groups or between students and authorities. They are all sites of a serious and simmering discord and unrest, even violence.

Coming back to my beloved JNU, there was blood on the asphalt.

Horrifying? Certainly. Shocking? Of course. Also, exceptional. Because this had never happened before.

Immediately I thought, was there a pattern? Were these brawls politically instigated or supported? Who were the perpetrators? Who were the beneficiaries? Who were the victims? Who was responsible? Paid hooligans? 'Professional' thugs and rioters? Or student factions?

Why did the university administration fail to act in a timely fashion to prevent and control the outbreak?

Returning to our temporary lodgings in Cuff Parade, we

---

[206]Nanda, Prashant K. 'Masked Mob Enters JNU Campus, Attacks Students and Faculty', *Live Mint*, 6 January 2020, https://www.livemint.com/ education/ news/violence-returns-masked-men-barge-jnu-attack-students-vandalize-hostel-11578242423650.html. Accessed on 19 September 2021.

passed by a protest at the Gateway of India, right opposite the Taj Hotel. It was being led by Umar Khalid, formerly also of JNU. Again, azadi slogans were being shouted: 'NRC *se azadi* [freedom from the National Register of Citizens], CAA *se azadi* [freedom from the Citizenship (Amendment) Act], *jaativad se azadi* [freedom from casteism], *Sanghvaad se azadi* [freedom from the ideology of the 'Sangh'], RSS *se azadi* [freedom from the RSS], Mohan Bhagwat *se azadi* [freedom from Mohan Bhagwat].'

I heard the slogans myself. Later, I saw the video, which corroborated this.[207]

We visited the Gateway of India the following evening to have tea at the Taj Mahal Hotel. The whole place was barricaded. The protests were still going on, right opposite the iconic hotel. We did manage to get in, though.

When we stepped out, I thought of checking out the protestors. Of course, they didn't say '*hijab se azadi* [freedom from the hijab]', '*triple talaq se azadi* [freedom from triple talaq]', '"love jihad" *se azadi* [freedom from "love jihad"]' and so on. As in Shaheen Bagh later, it could be said that there were communal and Islamist elements in constitutionalist and secularist garb at play.

Maharashtra is currently ruled by the strange coalition of the Shiv Sena, the Indian National Congress and the Nationalist Congress Party. No surprise that Umar Khalid was addressing yet another 'azadi' rally here. Nothing in India was untouched by politics. There, in JNU, mobs were running amok on campus, here a former JNU-ite, charged with sedition, was leading an anti-government rally.

Business as usual.

---

[207] 'Midnight Protest at Gateway of India against JNU Students' Attack', Gallinews India, YouTube, https://www.youtube.com/watch?v=SjZeuC9HKvM&t=3173s. Accessed on 19 September 2021.

What Actually Happened?

But I wasn't satisfied. I wanted to get to the bottom of the attack on JNU.

What triggered this round of violence at JNU? What was the truth behind it? As in Najeeb's disappearance or police action in Jamia, we may not fully know. But here is what I found out.

For months on end, during the second half of 2019, JNU had been under a lockdown.

You couldn't enter your office if you were a faculty member. Labs, classrooms and even the administration building were closed. End-semester exams for the monsoon semester 2019 were cancelled or postponed. It was a zero semester for most students. Registration for the winter semester 2020 had just opened.[208]

All this was before the COVID-19 pandemic engulfed India in March 2020.

On 3 January 2020, according to the statement put out by the JNU registrar, masked students entered the Communication and Information Services (CIS) building. They threw out the staff and shut down the servers. The campus Wi-Fi system was crashed, virtually bringing the registration process to a standstill.[209]

Why and how did the administration not forestall this? What was the point of crying victim now, after months of losing control of the campus? After permitting no classes, no exams, no labs, not to mention protests and lockdowns? What was the point of issuing statements and clarifications? JNU's reputation was already down in the dust.

---

[208] Chandra, Neha. 'What Happened in JNU between Jan 3 And Jan 5: A Timeline', *India Today*, 10 January 2020, https://www.indiatoday.in/india/story/jnu-violence-timeline-1635785-2020-01-10. Accessed on 19 September 2021.

[209] Pandey, Munish Chandra. 'Was Attack on JNU a Pre-Planned Conspiracy? Blame Game Continues', *India Today*, 7 January 2020, https:// www.indiatoday.in/india/stor y/was-attack-on-jnu-a-pre-planned- conspiracy-1634548-2020-01-07. Accessed on 19 September 2021.

Now it was the last straw—masked marauders thrashing students and teachers and rampaging through hostels and university buildings. The logical question would be: where were the JNU security guards? Why were they so ineffective? The usual blame game ensued, with the private security agency passing the buck to the Delhi police.[210]

Great. If so, where were the police?

Well, the truth is they were right outside the gates, in good number. They even had plainclothes intelligence personnel who warned of the impending violence. Why didn't they enter the campus when they saw the rampaging thugs? Apparently, they were waiting for written orders from the VC. According to police sources, they had already intimated the university authorities, but heard nothing back for hours. By then most of the damage was done.[211]

It was only around 8.30 p.m. that the police came in and then shut all the gates. By then, politicians, celebrities, social media activists and others had already started intervening. As to the delayed reaction of the police, their Jamia experience, just a few days before, had made them extra-cautious, they said.

Not surprisingly, most of the day after was occupied in a war of words. Or to phrase it one better, a 'war of versions'. An endless blame game of saying the other side did it.

The Left and much of the Opposition accused the ABVP, part of the 'Sangh Parivaar', for perpetrating the violence. Predictably,

---

[210] Hrishikesh, Sharanya. 'Who Failed JNU Students? Ex-Army Org, Cyclops Security Pass the Buck to Delhi Police', *HuffPost*, 20 January 2020, https:// www.huffingtonpost.in/entry/jnu-violence-security-awpo-cyclops-cso in5e21bd2fc5b673621f74a616. Accessed on 19 September 2021. The author is a former student of JNU whom I have taught.

[211] Yamunan, Sruthisagar. 'JNU Violence: Delhi Police Admit They Saw Mob Attacking Students—but Failed to Act', *Scroll.in*, 7 January 2020, https:// scroll.in/article/949047/fir-on-jnu-violence-shows-delhi-police-was-present-on-campus-when-masked-mob-attacked-students. Accessed on 19 September 2021.

the ABVP denied the charge and blamed the Leftist student groups that control the JNUSU for instigating it by shutting down the JNU servers. Both sides marshalled evidence, including video clips and images of those injured.

But what everyone concerned needed to realize was that, when it came to saving JNU, it is not winning the battle of narratives that matters. What's the point of winning the battle of perceptions if you lose the actual war on the ground? It's winning the war at the level of reality that counts much more than scoring points in the skirmish of views and opinions.

What constitutes winning that war? It is saving our universities from dangerous and negative politics. The future of our best educational institutions is at stake and that matters much more than all the ideological and political brinkmanship that we are being subjected to.

Universities such as JNU should be restored to their primary purpose, which is academics and research. Unfortunately, many, if not most, people are only interested in politics right now, whether it is anti-government, anti-state politics or the other way round. Nothing more.

A small group of students holds the rest hostage. Preventing them from going to class, taking exams and, eventually, getting degrees. Fee hikes, CAA, NRC and so on, are merely pretexts. In fact, as far as JNU is concerned, it seemed that the anti-CAA movement did not gather traction.

The immediate spark, this time, was registration for the new semester, which was sought to be prevented through force, coercion and illegal means. What could have been done? First of all, a negotiated settlement. Fee hike could easily be postponed. There is no urgency because JNU is fully funded by the government. Raising the fees as proposed will not make a huge difference to the budgetary outlay.

In fact, fees can even be abolished in JNU as an experiment on the condition that students agree to maintain discipline and devote themselves to studies. But foregrounding academics requires re-emphasizing quality rather than political affiliations. It does not help only to replace the Left with the Right. What really matters is what you know and how you teach. Not which side you support. Depoliticization and reintellectualization, not ideological substitution should be the method.

The administration should not only be fair, but perceived to be such; rather than anti-students and teacher-unfriendly. It should be decisive and consistent, rather than hesitant and confused. It should negotiate with all stakeholders rather than barricading itself and playing victim.

All illegal occupation or blockading of buildings and labs should be cleared forthwith. Principled force should be used to restore normalcy. The guilty, regardless of their political stripes, should be held accountable. To start with, an impartial inquiry into the recent violence on campus should have been conducted. Those responsible should be exposed and punished without fudging or massaging the truth.

That, however, did not happen. Instead, we only got more spin and no action.

2016–2021: The Most Dramatic VC's Term

Mamidala Jagadesh Kumar was appointed VC of JNU in January 2016. He is a professor of electrical engineering at IIT-Delhi, on lien to JNU as the VC. After his ME and PhD from IIT-Madras, he went to the University of Windsor to pursue post-doctoral research. On returning to India, he worked at IIT-Kanpur for a couple of years before moving to IIT-Delhi in 1995 as assistant professor.

I joined IIT-Delhi as an associate professor in the Department of Humanities and Social Sciences, in February 1994. Through some mutual friends, I was introduced to Dr Kumar and his wife. Just a few days after he took over as JNU VC, I went to visit him in the VC's chambers. I wanted to congratulate him and wish him well in what was going to be a very tough job. He remembered our IIT-Delhi connection.

Although cordial, he was somewhat guarded about JNU. I didn't blame him. He was new and simply trying to figure out his way. Unfortunately, within a month of his joining, things went out of control. Not just the tukde tukde assault on the nation's decency, but clashes, gheraos, shutdowns, arrests of students and what not. All outlined in the previous chapters in some detail.

Kumar, an utterly dedicated teacher, continues his lectures at IIT-Delhi, which is practically next door to JNU. He is also, to those who know him, a thorough gentleman—friendly, approachable, reasonable and decent to the core.

He is also a brave, determined and courageous individual. A karate expert and fitness enthusiast, he has withstood the worst protests, agitations, harassment and mental pressure—more than any VC in India that I know of. Yet, his smile, his simplicity, his loyalty to a cause and his personal integrity remain unscathed.

His term, which finished in January 2021, has possibly been the most dramatic, if not turbulent and controversial, of any JNU VC. I believe that it is under his tenure that JNU's fundamental character, from its long-standing Left-orientation, will be permanently changed. He has also introduced new schools such as engineering and management, in addition to new courses, attendance requirements, hostel regulations and, yes, the fee hikes that I have already discussed.

But the real danger is that all the measures taken during his term may not really solve JNU's difficulties. What might actually happen is that the university will slide into further deterioration, no longer being a prestigious or sought-after educational destination for students from all over India and abroad. Moreover, JNU's ethos and culture, at least the best parts, will be gone forever. Including its tremendous freedom, creativity, dissent, debate and intellectual innovation. If that were to happen, it would be a great loss to the nation.

For, as I have shown, JNU is not just the preserve of anti-nationals and freeloaders. It is also a place of possibilities—intellectual, social, political and transformational. It has produced leaders and outstanding change-agents in nearly all walks of national life. Especially in politics, civil services, media and academics. In the latter sphere, JNU PhD scholars are in every major Indian university, especially in the humanities and social sciences departments. They also excel in these disciplines in many parts of the world.

What is to be done? How is this great university to be reformed? This is the question that all Right-thinking people are asking today.

Kumar's role in transforming JNU will go down in history as memorable, even game-changing. It is said that he is destined for even higher posts. I certainly wish him well.

After a delay of over a year, Professor Santishree Dhulipudi Pandit, a JNU alum herself, has been appointed as the new VC. She is the first woman to have assumed this role. I sincerely hope that she succeeds in this sensitive, challenging and unenviable role and will be able to heal our fractured university, eventually restoring it to its former glory, even taking it to greater heights. That, certainly, would be the fervent wish of most JNUites. I worry, though, that it may not be smooth sailing. As soon as she assumes charge, the pitched battles inside the campus may be reignited. The difference? This time around, the Right is in a much stronger position. At the same time, the Left is not entirely defeated yet.

Mishandling Student Protests

The blueprint for the reform of JNU can only emerge if we understand the nature of student protests all over India in recent years.

A good case study, other than JNU, might be the University of Hyderabad, better known as HCU. I have some attachment to this institution. It was here that I began my teaching career in India in February 1986. That was immediately on my return from the US with a PhD. I have already described, earlier in the book, how vicious and deadly caste politics took over the campus.

Going back to 2016, the HCU had been unstable and volatile for several months. Rohith Vemula's suicide on 17 January 2016 was the flashpoint, which brought both the university and its politics into national focus. Several interested parties, mainstream and fringe, tried to exploit this sad loss of a young life, turning it to their own political advantage. Tents were pitched outside the campus to make the protests not just ongoing, but quasi-permanent.

Political parties, it is alleged, funded these. This makes sense, if not for nothing else because food costs money. The protesters had to be fed, watered and supported for months, as is the case with all professional agitators. Besides, prominent opposition leaders, including Rahul Gandhi of the Congress, visited the troubled campus regularly.[212] Ostensibly to show solidarity with the students demanding justice for Rohith.

Soon, however, the epicentre of student agitation moved to JNU, New Delhi, especially, after the tukde tukde slogans and the arrest of Kanhaiya Kumar, the president of the students' union.[213] Again, political parties and their agents jumped into the fray, escalating the uncivil strife. There was unrest on other campuses too, such as BHU, AMU and Jadavpur. The authorities, in the meantime, appeared to be scoring self-goal after self-goal, neither

---

[212]Mrinalini Mariam Fernandez and Uma Sudhir. 'Rahul Gandhi Likens Rohith Vemula to Mahatma Gandhi: 10 Developments,' NDTV, 30 January 2016, https://www.ndtv.com/cheat-sheet/rahul-gandhi-may-join-hunger-strike-for-rohith-vemula-in-hyderabad-10-developments-1271650. Accessed on 19 September 2021.

[213]Singh, Shubham. 'New footage of "Tukde-Tukde Gang" substantiates the Allegation of Seditious Slogans,' *TFI Post*, 23 January 2019, https://tfipost.com/2019/01/tukde-tukde-video-slogans-01/. Accessed on 19 September 2021.

able to restore normalcy on campuses, nor significantly advance their own nationalist agenda in the process.

For radical groups, this seemed like a golden opportunity to widen their urban support base by both creating and capitalizing on dissent and disaffection. An intelligence report submitted to the Home Ministry claimed that as many 128 organizations all over India, linked to ultra-Left and Maoist groups were currently active.[214] Their strategy was to combine radical politics with social justice crusades, thus creating a potent cocktail that appealed to large sections of the populace, but was especially irresistible to students.

Perhaps, these forces outplayed their hand, alienating key elements in mainstream politics and civil society. On the one hand, the strong-arm measures being adopted attracted anger, criticism and protest. Unleashing the repressive power of the state against unarmed citizens, especially students, gives the Opposition and anti-BJP forces much greater leverage. But on other hand, the government also attracted praise and support from those who felt that too much leniency and leeway had been given to 'anti-nationalists' in the past.

Yet, softness, tact and diplomacy—skills that the present regime might have learned from its predecessors—are conspicuous by their absence. Instead, a muscular and masculine nationalism imposed upon largely Left-leaning students has not quite yielded the expected dividents, whether in JNU or elsewhere.

What matters, in the long run, is how Indian democracy has been diminished, power has been centralized and the Indian polity itself moved closer to authoritarianism. It is this that is more worrying. Democracy is not just about holding or winning

---

[214]Malik, Aman. 'Government Identifies 128 Front Organizations for Naxals', *Live Mint*, 7 October 2013, https://www.livemint.com/Politics/B9Pmu3NurDrcRdD9ttb6JP/Government-identifies-128-front-organizations-for-Naxals.html. Accessed on 27 August 2021.

elections. It is also reflected in the quality of daily life of citizens and how open to criticism the state is.

Now, it seems, there is little difference between positive and negative criticism. Both are unwelcome. Many in the government and its wider circle of supporters cry foul over what they see as one-sided and prejudiced reporting. But surely this is not a battle only over media coverage, perception and portrayal. It is not merely an issue of who is winning or losing the broadcasting wars.

Though a firm state needs to stand against certain forms of 'anti-nationalism', can it afford to act in a way that immediately allows its critics to brand it as authoritarian, despotic or undemocratic? Shouldn't we learn from history? For any elected government, using police or troops against its own students is counterproductive to the point of being perilous.

Student protests in May 1968 brought down the French government of Charles de Gaulle. More than 10 million workers joined in the strikes. De Gaulle himself fled from Paris. Through a series of brilliant counter-manoeuvres, however, he managed to reinstate himself after an overwhelming electoral comeback following the dissolution of the national assembly.

In the US, anti-Vietnam protests and the civil rights movement echoed European disaffection with the state of affairs, bringing about long-lasting political and social changes.

In India too, the Naxalbari uprising began around the same time, but a year earlier in May 1967. Six or seven years later, student movements, such as the Navnirman Andolan in Gujarat, brought down the Chimanbhai Patel government. The Bihar movement, led by Jayaprakash Narayan, was one of the triggers for the clamping down of the disastrous Emergency imposed by Indira Gandhi, followed by her subsequent defeat at the hustings.

The present crises across campuses in India is, admittedly, quite different, lacking the scale or support of these earlier revolts. Yet, its mishandling will only bring the government brickbats and flak.

All over the world, the young want change.

In the US, the candidacy of Bernie Sanders, though twice-doomed, has highlighted calls for the 'socialist' reorientation of the US domestic policy. Across the northern border, Justin Trudeau's repeat victory clearly represents the return of Left-Liberal politics at the helm of affairs in Canada. All over Europe, too, students tend to support socialist and Left-leaning causes.

No wonder the Right-centric and conservative Indian government, despite Modi's enormous energy and charisma, gets so much bad press. Add to this the obnoxious intolerance of the fringe elements of the parivaar and voila! Hinduphobic Indian secularists have a field day in maligning the Modi sarkar.

Now midway through its second term, the Modi government seemed to be on the brink of squandering its gains, at least when it comes to managing dissent. The COVID-19 pandemic, paradoxically, gave them a fresh opportunity to regain political advantage. But fundamental questions, which occasion soul searching, still persist.

What were they elected for? The answer is good governance, removal of corruption and economic development. Instead, they are embroiled in so many skirmishes on so many issues, some rather unimportant. Offering battle on multiple and oftentimes frivolous fronts will only weaken even the best of armies. This is reflected in their losing the key states of Delhi and Bengal in the assembly elections.

It is not too late for course correction, at least when it comes to higher education and reform of our universities. While campuses need to be cleansed of divisive and dangerous politics, this is a long-term objective, which is to be carried out with careful planning and determination. The more immediate need of the hour, though, is to restore normalcy and calm. This can be done through restraint, conciliation and tact.

The government and university administrations should use constitutional means at their disposal to settle contentious matters. Clear and transparent procedures to identify violation of rules, responsible and fair procedures by duly constituted disciplinary committees with due process to offenders to present their case and, finally, just and timely penalties—such moves may send the right message. The targeting of entire universities or large groups of students/teachers will only consolidate the opposition and prove counterproductive.

Take the instance of HCU. The crisis over caste has been many years in the making, with earlier flare-ups. Poisonous and divisive campus politics will, without question, take months of corrective action and healing to rectify. Confidence-building measures and active attempts at reconciliation will only be the first steps. Eventually, the entire ecosystem will have to be reoriented away from divisive caste- and ideology-based politics to academic excellence, which HCU has come to be known for.

What is required is firmness coupled with empathy—a loud and clear message that campuses must not be misused for anti-national and unconstitutional activities. Such a message should go hand in hand with the commitment to preserve freedom of expression, even dissent, on campuses. India and the world must hear the message that the autonomy and integrity of universities will not be targeted or threatened, even while unlawful and unauthorized activities are curbed.

State universities are not only national assets, with huge ongoing public investments, they also shape the future of the country. If these universities are allowed to degenerate or collapse, the loss to the nation will be incalculable.

Universities are not merely sources of employment or engagement for cadres of political parties or their sympathizers. They are incubators of competence and excellence in all fields of human endeavour.

Today, even as creeping privatization is taking over the education sphere, our government-funded institutions, barring IITs and IIMs, are declining. How can we harbour dreams of becoming a *visvaguru*—world teacher—under these circumstances?

The Crisis in Higher Education

If we take a bird's-eye view of our higher education system, we quickly discover that it is very complicated. We have close to 40,000 institutions, of which nearly 1,000 are universities of one sort or another. Together, our enrolment in tertiary and post-tertiary education is close to 35 million people—almost the whole population of Canada.

The system can be broadly divided into professional and non-professional colleges, publicly funded, partially funded and fully private institutions. But at the apex of the triangle are what are known as institutes of national importance (INI), as designated by Parliament.

In 2021, there were 161 such institutions. When it comes to professional courses, we have 15 All India Institutes of Medical Sciences (AIIMS), 23 Indian Institutes of Technology (IITs), 20 Indian Institutes of Management (IIMs), 23 Indian Institutes of Information Technology (IIITs), 31 National Institutes of Technology (NITs, formerly Regional Engineering Colleges), five Indian Institutes of Design (NIDs), seven Indian Institutes of Science Education and Research (IISERs), seven National Institutes of Pharmaceutical Education and Research (NIPERs), three Schools of Planning and Architecture and one Indian Institute of Science (IISc).

In the non-professional, that is the arts, sciences, social studies, commerce and so on, we find a similar hierarchical structure. At the top are 54 central universities, and below them a hodgepodge of 438 state, 395 private and 126 deemed-to-be universities, bringing the current total to over 1,000.

Hubs like Bengaluru or the greater Coimbatore region produce lakhs of engineering graduates each year, from the hundreds of engineering colleges that dot their urban sprawls. Some of these colleges had no teachers, classrooms or labs when they started. They only conducted examinations and granted degrees.

Students had to live in rented rooms nearby, get private tuitions or other inputs, and somehow appear for exams on their own. In addition, these establishments collected what were known to be rather exorbitant 'capitation' fees. Of course, gradually, these very colleges have improved, with proper buildings, hostels, labs and competent teachers. Today some of these are leading institutions in their own right.

What is clear, whether in non-technical or technical institutions, is a top-down structure. There are a few institutions of excellence at the top, many mediocre ones in the middle and a vast majority of really useless institutions at the bottom.

Studies comparing India with China have found that India had a much better start around Independence. In 1947, we had many more centres of higher education than China, but now they are far ahead of us. According to some of these studies, hardly 10 per cent of Indian graduates from non-professional institutions are employable because 90 per cent have practically no marketable skills. It is not that these 90 per cent of our graduates remain unemployed, but they must supplement their college degrees with vocational courses. What is more, not a single Higher Education Institute (HEI) in India features in the top 100 worldwide.[215]

To restructure such a complex system is very difficult. Some believe that all that is required is a cultural or nationalist turn to make these institutions and their curricula more responsive to our national needs. They are wrong. This is a crisis of governance, not content.

The National Educational Policy will not be the magic wand or silver bullet to fix all that ails Indian education. Much

---

[215]'Missing Skills: Low Employability Calls for Academia-Industry Link', *The Times of India*, 24 September 2021, https://timesofindia.indiatimes.com/blogs/toi-editorials/missing-skills-low-employability-calls-for-academia-industry-link/. Accessed 23 December 2021.

more is needed, not just radical structural reform or proactive and corrective legislation and policymaking. What we need is nothing short of a major change in the entire system, especially in philosophy and politics of how education is controlled and managed in India.

Social Justice and Identity Politics

The first question to ask in today's embattled context is whether there is a difference between social justice and entitlement. What is it that we are fighting against or disputing? In a fundamental sense, being entitled to rights and privileges by virtue of birth actually militates against the idea of natural, even though it appeals to distributive justice.

In other words, even if were to argue that offering reservations in educational institutions and, subsequently, government jobs on the basis of one's caste or community is an attempt to offset past deprivations, such a claim would still not qualify to be considered under the framework of justice or equality. The right to equality being fundamental in the Indian Constitution, perpetual birth-based quotas may be considered as going against it. At best, such quotas might be termed counter-entitlement compensation or recompense. By its very nature, such redress cannot be extended unto permanency lest it institute another system of hereditary privilege, albeit upside-down.

On closer and dispassionate examination of the claims and counterclaims over reservations, we notice that it is quite different from affirmative action. The latter implies that all other things being equal, the deprived should be preferred over the privileged. But nowhere does affirmative action imply fixed and rigid quotas, without minimum qualifications or competence.

What we have instead in India is differential scales of 'merit' for different castes and communities. In effect, though an internal order of merit is followed within each category, it is abandoned overall. In such instances, the only criterion of suitability is, paradoxically, one's birth. Imagine what it would mean if extended, say, to a Nobel Prize or Olympic Gold Medal, where only those so certified by birth and caste would be considered eligible to participate.

I was confronted with this lesson when a 'category' student told me, 'I am against reservations for my children; I will persuade them not to claim them.' Slightly taken aback, I asked, 'Why?' She replied, 'Because if they get things without struggling for them, they will never learn to better themselves or compete with the rest. In time, the whole community, with free hand-outs, will become thoroughly incompetent if not corrupt.'

This student and several like her have gone on to do extremely well. They used reservations as an entry point, after which they struggled to acquire real skill sets and proficiencies in their chosen fields. What this has taught me is that reservations make no sense without de-reservations. That is, once they serve the purpose for which they were designed, the person ought to exit the advantage conferred by them.

Such an exit has already been legislated in the case of the 'creamy layers' of the OBCs. The principle is that once a just compensation is offered for a disadvantage, it cannot be claimed over and over again. If we do not follow this principle, caste-based reservations will destroy the idea of the annihilation of caste. They will only serve to reify caste, divide society and create resentment.

It is hardly surprising, then, that those screaming the loudest for perpetual reservations are actually disguised supporters of the caste system, only with themselves on top. They are, perhaps, not in the least interested in equality or social justice, let alone competence or merit. Often because they are right at the top of the caste pyramid in their own reserved category, enjoying its benefits generation after generation. Why would they want a change in the system?

Our strategy should be to place the onus of upliftment of

the most excluded upon the most privileged members of their communities, showing how the latter end up blocking the rise of the former. The question to ask is: how many generations of reservation are needed before a person or his progeny can stand on their feet? By claiming reservations for another generation, aren't these privileged 'backward elites' denying benefits to those less privileged than them?

In IITs, for instance, most of the SC, ST students have parents who were IAS officers, senior-level bureaucrats, bank managers or other members of the elite. How long do such already-advantaged need reservation? Till they vacate their seats, how will the more needy get a chance? Surely the daughter of the former president of India cannot be considered a Dalit if the term means someone oppressed and deprived?

We might not be able to scrap reservations altogether, but we must alter their basis, broadening it from caste and community alone to other parameters of dispossession, including plain old poverty, whether rural or urban. Else, in our real or imagined fear of majoritarian consolidation, we will institutionalize the perpetual fragmentation and weakening of Indian society.

Fortunately for India, such views are gradually gaining ground. There is an increasing demand, as a consequence, for a major rethink on caste-based reservations.

Structural and Institutional Reform

When it comes to overhauling Indian higher education, findings of study after study bear out a simple but harsh truth. As Devesh Kapur and Pratap Bhanu Mehta pointed out over 15 years back, the Indian education system can be characterized by Gresham's law of 'the bad drives out the good':

> The prevailing political ideological climate in which elite institutions are seen as being anti-democratic, finds its natural

response in political control to influence admissions policies, internal organization, the structure of courses and funding.

As quality deteriorates, students are less and less willing to pay the very resources without which quality cannot be improved. In India's case, the growth of private sector higher education institutions has been the answer and, increasingly, the consumption of education abroad. However, as our analysis suggests, private sector investment has been confined to professional streams, bypassing the majority of students. Furthermore, it is plagued by severe governance weaknesses, raising doubts as to its ability to address the huge latent demand for quality higher education in the country.[216]

The subtitle of their paper sums it up rather well: 'From Half-Baked Socialism to Half-Baked Capitalism'.

What Kapur and Mehta emphasize is that most Indian institutions of higher education are only placeholders. They keep people out of trouble or away from the streets for a couple of years. But giving them a space to be in and an affiliation to attach themselves to isn't enough. Soon they find themselves jobless, skill-less and clueless in the real world. That makes some of them frustrated and angry.

Over 70 years of confused or dishonest policies have made Indian higher education the playground of a dangerous and dastardly political game. We tinker with higher education to hide or disguise our failure to provide free, high-quality, universal primary education. That, in fact, is the mandated responsibility of the government.

---

[216]Devesh Kapur and Pratap Bhanu Mehta. 'Indian Higher Education Reform: From Half-Baked Socialism to Half-Baked Capitalism', Centre for International Development, Harvard University, Working Paper Series, No. 108, September 2004, https://dash.harvard.edu/bitstream/handle/1/42406326/108.pdf?sequence=1&isAllowed=y. Accessed on 13 September 2021.

Despite huge resources, there is no will to do what is required at the base of the pyramid, where all other social and economic inequalities have their origin. Instead, in token or high visibility gestures, it is higher education that is interfered and tampered with.

This only serves the vociferous elites, 'Dalit Brahmins' as some have dubbed them, while the masses of the truly deprived remain greatly disadvantaged. By over-politicizing higher education, we send out the wrong message that what matters is not competence but entitlement. One progresses not by really learning anything useful or productive, but playing one's caste or community card. The result is that we spend most of our time and energy in identity politics rather than learning and growing intellectually. In the end, agitational identity politics is all that we have learned.

Such dumbing down of Indian higher education has made a mockery of our academic standards. Most bachelor's degrees in the humanities and social studies, not to mention commerce, science and other disciplines, are practically worthless.

No wonder in institutions such as JNU, students never want to leave. Where else will they get nearly free lodging, subsidized board, plus a stipend, that too for doing so little? Unfortunately, these same 'users' and 'losers' end up becoming future teachers, mostly reproducing their own inadequate training or levels of incompetence.

In one of my visits to China, I went out on a tour bus with several Chinese colleagues. All of them had only one child, which is the state policy. The upshot was that the child of the vice president of the university and the child belonging to a driver employed by the university went to the same school. But by the time they were ready for university, they were sorted according to their interests and grades. Only the smart ones made it to the best colleges and universities. Their birth advantages or disadvantages did not matter.

The Chinese, or for that matter American, lesson is simple. If you want an egalitarian system, you need to start at the grassroots.

Every child born in India must have access to affordable, high-quality primary education. The government does not want to take up this challenge in earnest, though they have legislated education as a fundamental right. Instead, they toy, tinker and tamper the higher end of the education spectrum.

Why do they do so? It is because the impact in terms of jobs and status is most visible here. No wonder, a large number of our universities have been started to cater to some political demand or the other. One of the underlying problems is that too much state interference, even dominance, in higher education only ends up undermining if not destroying it.

The government, as Mahatma Gandhi said long back, should not be in the business of education. Society must cater to its own needs, especially when it comes to higher education. Only primary and secondary education should be the government's responsibility. Looking at the end product rather than the foundation has been our mistake.

Instead of allowing society to determine its own needs and fund what is required, the government has imposed what it regarded as right by spending lakhs of crores of the nation's resources. The only 'Nehruvian' exception we might allow is institutes of national importance and excellence, where quality should never be compromised for political considerations.

If we look at the Indian information technology (IT) revolution, especially at its genesis, then it is clear that the large numbers of trained programmers and engineers required did not come from conventional universities or institutes of higher education. Only the higher echelons come from IITs and IIMs, while the hundreds of thousands of programmers, who actually slogged to write code, came from private institutions and coaching classes or were skilled by the companies themselves. The official website of one such service provider claims that they have trained more than five million programmers.

So, our IT revolution was not powered by the official institutions into which the government has sunk in hundreds of crores, but by 'non-state' teaching shops that arose out of the colossal demand while the government and its agencies were napping.

During the colonial period, too, the British tried to block the formation of the IISc in Bangalore. Lord Curzon himself opposed it, even though Jamsetji Tata was paying for it from his own funds. IISc could only be started in 1909 after Curzon left and Tata died. But today, it is one of the premier institutions of higher learning in the country.

Similarly, though we are blocking privatization of higher education, isn't it coming in through the back door in a slew of un- or semi-regulated universities mushrooming all over India, with little standardization or accountability? Some years back, 97 universities ceased to exist in Raipur alone as a consequence of a Supreme Court order.

Losing Our Competitive Edge—if Ever We Had One

As somebody who has spent all his life studying or teaching, I am worried. As a country, we are not only falling behind in the field of education but will soon cease to be competitive if we continue like this. The only reason why we have survived is because of the tremendous creative energies of our people who find informal and unorthodox solutions to extremely complex problems.

The entire future hangs in balance. If we lose what little we have now, it is difficult to imagine how we can remain at the forefront of the new economy, which is a knowledge economy. This neglect of our education system is especially lamentable if we remember that we have been a knowledge society for over 3,000 years. But today, we have fallen into tremendous ignorance and apathy.

Failing to find opportunities in our own country, we witness the phenomenal flight of young Indian people out of India. The estimates are that to the US alone, about half a million students go to study each year. Only about 10 per cent of them are on scholarship. The remaining 90 per cent pay huge fees, often taking massive loans to cover costs.

We not only suffer from brain drain, but also from capital flight. The same is also true of the UK, Canada, Australia, Singapore and so on. Thus, we have created a system in India that encourages the export of both talent and money. We spend an estimated $15 billion on these students each year, enough to fund over 500 JNUs in India.

We can change all this. India can be a profitable hub of education not only in the Global South, but in the wider world. Brands such as IITs and IIMs already have global recognition and bandwidth. In a positive development, the government has finally allowed the former to open campuses abroad. But there are several other Indian universities and institutions that can also be competitive, attractive and affordable if they become true centres of learning and excellence, rather than just of politicking, picketing or picnicking.

If we don't react fast, foreign universities, where our best youth will prefer to study despite charging hefty fees, will overrun our own country. That, unfortunately, will be the prelude to the recolonisation of India.

A lot needs to be done. The question is: do we have the political will to do it?

Winning the Narrative Battle, but Losing the War?

In ongoing discussions on soft power, friends often ask how the dominant, Left-Liberal, Congress-sponsored narrative about India is so durable. They wonder how it continues to rule not only mainstream media, but also academics, diplomacy, culture, arts, literature and other domains of soft power, even when the UPA is out of power at the Centre and the Congress routed in most states in India.

But to understand the persistence of residual Left-Liberal soft power, the explanation that the Congress ruled nearly 60 of the 70 years of post-Independence India, is not entirely adequate. Actually, even after the manifest failures of Congress-style socialism and secularism, their idea of India is prevalent not only in India, but in many parts of the world.

The reason for its depth and tenacity is that it is more insidious than historical. The fact that this idea of India, as a continuation of the older colonial narrative, is easily supported by current Anglophone and Anglocentric, neo-colonial stereotypes, is not understood by many. In this narrative, much of the glory of ancient India is a myth, propped up by the Right-wing, Hindu nationalist fantasies of a lost golden age, which in itself is an orientalist invention.

The neo-Ambedkarite debunking of ancient India as caste-ridden, oppressive and thus fit for rejection is, therefore, one vital plank. This unyielding opposition to any positive reconsideration of classical India is crucial to the modernist-Marxist-secularist agenda. It helps perpetually to divide Hindus between the guilty savarnas and the outraged avarnas, the latter constantly in need of reverse discrimination, if not appeasement.

Then there is the minority constituency to cater to. Here, the argument advances that the Hindu majority is unfit to assume power. That's why Hindu deities, festivals, practices and texts are ridiculed or undermined at every opportunity. Numerically significant Muslims and the theologically well-equipped Christians are discouraged from joining the majoritarian formation led by Modi. Instead, they are constantly provoked and bamboozled to criticize the ruling dispensation.

Minority resentment and insecurity is stoked by highlighting, even fabricating, atrocities against them, thus demonizing the majority as perpetrators of violence and hatred against the weak and defenceless sections of society. Shaheen Bagh is only the latest example of this.

The entire history of India must be seen as one endless series of foreign conquests, with little native resistance or spine, let alone a coherent cultural, social, economic or political order. India is thus projected as a weak state that should not aspire for greatness, either domestically or internationally. It should remain a second-rate power, part of some larger alliance led by one superpower or other. Any assertion or will to power is castigated as jingoistic sabre-rattling, dangerous to national security and threatening to peace in the neighbourhood.

India as a weak, divided country, with a fragmented society, internally contradicted polity, controversial history and confused self-identity, would be easier to rule by people who claim to be its guardians by virtue of not belonging to any group, region, language or community. Essentially outsiders, they gather around them, representatives of various interest groups and powerbrokers, distributing the largesse of office in proportion to their supporters' efficacy or utility. This non-patriotic alliance of opportunists has only one binding glue: their own selfish interest to retain power at all costs.

When we feel badly about ourselves and our past, when we have little hope for the future, our Left-Liberal elites become happy. This is because they can tell us that only they can keep this ragtag, divided nation, with its unwashed, benighted masses, together.

That is why I have been arguing that the battle that we face as a nation is not only between two political formations or ideologies, but between two ideas of India itself. One is informed by idealism, hope and the prospect of greatness. The other stokes our fears, resentments, doubts, confusions and insecurities.

The rise of Narendra Modi is threatening to the Opposition precisely because he has unleashed the power of the people to think, dream and hope to create a better India for themselves and the future generations. Modi is the great disrupter of the dominant narrative of India as a backward, unfortunate, divided, abused and abusive society in need of a motley crew of modernist protectors who have no deep passion or connection with Indian civilization. But even after the BJP, led by a strong, visionary leader like Modi, won another term in 2019, the actual work to reform the country and change the dominant narrative will not be easy.

For better governance with less 'governmentality', steady economic growth, corruption-free systems, real empowerment of the common people, in addition to defence and diplomatic ascendancy are imperative. All these can lead to a true Indian renaissance in which the nation's real soft power, cultural and spiritual, can benignly spread across the world, as in the days of yore.

Soft vs Hard Hindutva?

Another, more important, battle is also in the offing. Its outcome will actually determine the kind of India we will become. It is not a battle between the Left and the Right, the Liberals and the nationalists, with which I started this book. It is a different sort of face-off, consequent on the noticeable shift in the national narrative.

The Right-wing, nationalist, Hindu majoritarian narrative has actually gained ground. But in what manner and to what extent is another matter. In my view, a soft-Hindutva, which doesn't disturb our constitutionally guaranteed secular state, is more suitable to India rather than a hard-Hindutva-driven strident call to make India a Hindu rashtra. In fact, even those advocating the latter would need to ask themselves what kind of state and society it would engender—egalitarian or Hindu supremecist.

Some disagree with this nuancing. They say Hindutva is Hindutva. There's no classifying it as soft or hard. Interestingly, proponents of this view abound on both sides. But the fact remains that hyper-nationalism, even as hyper-Hindutva, will threaten the fabric of our society and the stability of the state.

Too much militarism of the public space, coupled with the polarizing machinations of majoritarianism will not necessarily make for a better future for India even if it wins votes in the short run. Targeting religious or ideological opponents is no substitute for the politics of appeasement and minoritarianism which the BJP was voted in to check.

The anti-Hindutva forces demonize all of it, without regard to distinctions between moderate and extremist versions. They argue that the main fight is between Hinduism and Hindutva. The latter must be defeated. On the other hand, many Hindu nationalists refuse to acknowledge that there are shades of Hindutva, from the political to the spiritual. They say Hindutva is the right word, of Indian provenance, whereas Hinduism is an import. To them, Hindu cannot have an 'ism' attached to it. That makes it alien and alienating. It is a modern, therefore, treacherous neologism.

The locus of India's debate on nationalism has shifted. From being a contest between the Left and the Right or the liberal and the nationalist—as identified at the beginning of the book—the debate has shifted to a tussle between two kinds of Hindu nationalism: moderate and strident. This is the shift that I have tried to document in this book through the example of the shifting JNU scenario. But, in my view, extreme positions are really unfortunate even in this changed terrain. Again, intermedial hermeneutics will show us a way forward.

Dharmic Nationalism, Not Merely Majoritarianism

A new India also needs a new politics. That is what the rise of Modi actually signifies. Divisive minoritarianism should not be replaced by aggressive majoritarianism and hyper-Hindutva. Both are accountable to the people and, if were are truly Sanatanis, to Dharma. It is dharmic and spiritual nationalism which is India's distinctive contribution to the world. It is also what Deen Dayal

Upadhyaya tried to propound in his idea of *Ekatm Manavvad* or Integral Humanism.[217]

Identity politics used to be ubiquitous. It permeated discussions of social, economic and political problems to the extent that no one was unable to approach, let alone propose solutions without first invoking identity questions, chiefly around caste, religion and gender. Similarly, economism and social justice narratives can also be excessive, if not abusive.

The media, intelligentsia, universities, students, even the legal system and political establishment—all seemed to invoke these as the starting and ending points of all political and reformative processes. In turn, such invocations often blocked the proper identification of the issues at stake. Problem formulation and solving remained, at best, superficial and, at worst, deepened crises.

Arguably, given the legacy of the colonial policies of *divide et impera*, identity politics pushed out most other ways of understanding and changing ourselves. What happened in India was also part of a worldwide trend, especially in the second half of the twentieth century.

In the West, identity politics had a very strong and vibrant upsurge with the rise of second-wave feminism, the civil rights movement and the gay, lesbian and aboriginal agitations for empowerment. Subsequently, identity politics was also one of the chief avenues of self-assertion of ethnic minorities, immigrants and diasporic communities. In India, we saw echoes of similar claims in the 1970's 'Dalit Panther' movement and in other struggles of disenfranchised groups for greater power within the system.

One key aspect of identity politics is to use those very aspects of a group's identity which are the source of its marginalization—

---

[217] See Ram Madhav's *The Hindutva Paradigm: Integral Humanism and Quest for a Non-Western Worldview* (Westland, 2021) for an excellent exposition.

race, colour, caste, ethnicity, religion, sexual preference and so on—to define the group, thereby, turning the source of victimhood to a demand for justice.

It is also interesting to observe that in societies such as China, we see no parallels to this rise of identity politics as a legitimate expression of political aspirations. The struggles of Tibetans or the Uighurs in China, for example, are regarded as illegal and illegitimate by the authorities.

No doubt, identity politics has been a powerful tool for the empowerment of the oppressed, but it has also resulted in social divisiveness and, in even more extreme cases, hatred and violence.

After all, jihadist terrorism may also be considered an extreme form of identity politics in which a small group of extremists, who consider themselves the chosen warriors of God, unleash calamitous aggression and bloodshed, often on innocent civilians, because they believe themselves to be fighting for a just cause.

The other fallout of identity politics, at least in India, is a politics based on caste, community, and some other special interest, which is usually expressed in opposition to some other groups perceived to be more privileged.

Thus, our public sphere is often characterized by a divisive contentiousness and a conflict mode, which creates new problems even as it tries to solve old ones. With the rise of identity politics, there is a premium on marginalization of some sort or the other. Everyone wishes to belong to or speak on behalf of some oppressed group or the other.

Jats in the North, Patels in Gujarat and Marathas in Maharashtra, powerful and privileged communities, now want the tag of being backward. This competitive backwardness, it seems, is actually the most effective method of going forward. Backwardness is no longer a handicap; it is a resource.

But has identity politics run its course the world over? In 'The Hubris of Culture and the Limits of Identity Politics' published in *Commonweal* a couple of years ago, noted Marxist literary critic

Terry Eagleton argued as much, saying that identity politics was culturist and superficial, while anti-colonialist struggles resulted in major changes.[218]

In India, such misgivings over identity politics are even more pronounced. Predicated upon a conflict instead of cooperative paradigm of problem-solving, identity politics fuelled caste and class hatred, minoritarian and divisive politics, thus privileging the margins and putting a premium on victim positions.

India's disenchantment with identity politics was best exemplified by its utter collapse in the recent UP elections. The politics of bijli, sadak, paani (electricity, roads, water), it would appear, defeated that of caste, religion and region. Pragmatist politics triumphed over identity politics.

All over India, one finds people increasingly suspicious and, at times, exasperated by what goes in the name of identity politics. Many, especially in the middle class, consider it a camouflage for unethical or dubious pursuits: unearned privileges and political chicanery. This is not to deny the existence of inequality or injustice, or for that matter, of difference, but pinning them on cultural and ideological difference is not convincing.

Culture and ideology, even religion, are, at most, skin deep. According to most spiritual traditions, they do not descend to the deepest reality of who or what we are. They have neither an ontological nor metaphysical foundation. In practical terms, it follows that human beings, Homo sapiens, are one culture, one race, one family even. All our differences—and we must recognize that these are many and significant—are yet not sufficient to make us non-separate from one another.

The structure of human experience, regardless of individuation determined by context is, therefore, quite similar. The struggle to

---

[218]Eagleton, Terry. 'The Hubris of Culture and the Limits of Identity Politics', *Commonweal*, 5 April 2016, https://www.commonwealmagazine.org/hubris-culture. Accessed on 10 December 2021.

right wrongs, redress injustice and assert one's identity will, of course, go on as they should.

However, to try to root these fights in essential alterity is as unconvincing as it is questionable.

Does the victory of Hindutva signify a decisive shift from identity to dharma-based politics in India? It is too early to be sure, but the true test would be sarvodaya, commonwealth—the good of all; not just of one group, community, region, caste, class, religion or gender.

If, as a first step, the forces of unity have won over those of divisiveness, at least for the Hindus, who are about 80 per cent of the population, this is a welcome step in the right direction.

Why JNU Still Matters

At the heart of the JNU emergency was a watershed rethinking of nationalism. Were the Left-wing agitators in JNU, who used the university as a platform to launch an attack not just against the Indian state, but also against the Modi sarkar, anti-national?

Or were they merely exercising their constitutional rights to freedom of expression and dissent? Was the reaction of the establishment an assault on the autonomy of universities and the attempt to clamp down on independent thinking? Was JNU a den of parasites and hypocrites or the site of heroic and inspiring resistance against an authoritarian state and the forces of intolerance?

Five years after February 2016, no one is in doubt about what the answers to such questions are. The JNU anti-national, anti-administration, anti-establishment lobby has found itself on the wrong side of history. No matter what the faults and flaws of the JNU administration or the government, their protesters have not acquired legitimacy in the rest of the country.

While truth is more complex, resisting simplistic black-and-white binaries, it is clear that the reform of JNU is a foregone conclusion. As I have argued throughout this book, I only hope that this so-called reform is not really a destruction in disguise. If that happened, it would be sad, lamentable and regrettable.

JNU is still an academic and ideological powerhouse, a PhD factory almost. Its products populate the teaching faculties of many of India's best universities and colleges. A transformed JNU would mean a huge fillip to dharmic nationalism, the multiplier effect of which would be incalculable.

We need trained professionals, not just amateurs in fields such as history, sociology, political science, international relations, language and literature studies and so on. One such trained academic can really sustain the alternate narrative and ecosystem that we have tried to nurture in the last decade or so.

I think the key is in the last words of my unknown interrogator who confronted me in JNU during the so-called anniversary of the tukde tukde rally. 'No more, Sir, no more,' he had lamented.

Left-sectarianism will no longer get a walkover in the public sphere in India. Likewise, no simplistic framing of the nationalism debate will work now. The thinking people of India have spoken up in huge numbers calling the bluff of those, Left, Right or Centre, who hide their own intolerance, hypocrisy and undemocratic practices behind noble-sounding ideals and slogans. JNU has contributed significantly to the righting of the discourse of nationalism in India.

Student politics in Indian universities used to be run by so-called radical groups, which, though a minority, rule the roost. 'No more, Sir, no more' also applies equally to them. Their time is over.

If one looks at their manifestos and the party journals, one senses how regressive, undemocratic, irrational and, in today's times, irrelevant they are. With the failure of the revolutionary ideology all over the world, these groups have a limited cache, which is in Indian universities, where young, impressionable and socially sensitive minds fall prey to them. They are captured, if not brainwashed, and mobilized against all forms of authority.

But now, even the misplaced idealism of such romantic revolutionaries lies exposed as a mask of ugly opportunism. Their slogan, which they used in their strike at JNU, was 'social justice'. It, however, was only an excuse to target the Modi sarkar, the UGC and the JNU administration.

The Left and ultra-Left then tried to use the OBCs as their shields, as they earlier used SCs and Muslims. But even that came a cropper. Now they have nowhere to hide, nowhere to run. Their time is up.

By exposing and discrediting them against their own contrary moves and intentions, JNU has made an invaluable contribution to the new national awakening and reconstruction of India. I feel privileged to have played a part, however small, in this revolution.

EPILOGUE

As this book drew to a close, JNU and, indeed, the whole country was locked down in a nationwide curfew. Prime Minister Narendra Modi, in his speech on 24 March 2020, asked all Indians to stay indoors for three weeks. In a historic broadcast, he said:

> From midnight tonight onwards, the entire country, please listen carefully, the entire country, shall go under complete lockdown. In order to protect the country, and each of its citizens, from midnight tonight, a full ban is being imposed on people from stepping out of their homes.
>
> All the states in the country, all the Union Territories, each district, each municipality, each village, each locality is being put under lockdown.
>
> This is like a curfew only.
>
> This will be a few levels more than Janata-Curfew, and also stricter.
>
> This is a necessary step in the decisive fight against Corona Pandemic.[219]

I wrote an op-ed, calling it 'PM Modi's Surgical Strike against the Coronavirus.' It was published in *ThePrint* on 25 March 2020.

In retrospect, no one could have properly predicted that it was not the first wave of the pandemic which would be devastating.

---

[219] PMO, 'Text of PM's Address to the Nation on Vital Aspects Relating to the Menace of COVID-19', Press Information Bureau, Government of India, 24 March 2020, https://pib.gov.in/PressReleseDetail.aspx?PRID=1607995. Accessed on 11 January 2022.

The second wave, which struck a year later, affected many of us, in one way or another. We lost members of our families or friends. We ourselves or those we knew closely were infected. India lost half-a-million lives to the tiny virus, most of them during the second wave. Those of us who survived have a lot to be grateful for.

It was in this second wave that the publication of this book was also blocked. Incongruous though this may seem, the reasons were extra-pandemic. The story of that attack and how the book survived must be recounted another time. For they do not directly form part of this book's contents.

But during this entire time, JNU's gates were also shut. No one was allowed to go in or out. Even campus residents were discouraged from stepping out of their homes. The second wave brought COVID-19 deaths to the JNU campus too.

Students were sent home, classes suspended.

For a change, the campus went quiet not because of political unrest or student protests but because of a global pandemic. Of course, this was an enforced, not desirable peace. The peace of the grave or the cremation ground almost—with the threat of a highly contagious disease driving out most of the students and confining their teachers at home under a virtual house arrest.

Ironically, the Left always endorsed and espoused what has been called JNU's 'anti-hygiene politics'.[220] It made for an open, but somewhat dirty campus. But with the novel coronavirus pandemic, it is hygiene—clean hands and face masks—that sees our best defence. And, of course, vaccination.

This pandemic may also serve as an opportunity to be JNU's inflexion point, 'cleansing' it, so to speak, of excessive Leftist and Right-wing politics.

Winter 2020 onwards, classes have been virtual, that is

---

[220]'It was very significant that the politics of JNU developed along anti-hygienic lines'. Batabyal, Rakesh. *JNU: The Making of a University*, HarperCollins, 2015.

conducted without contact hours, classes or lectures. The new students were also admitted, for the first time, in contactless objective-style examinations, conduced online.

Studies, when resumed, are entirely in the virtual mode.

Even as I write this, the 2020 batch continues to pursue their MA degree from home. They have not yet arrived on campus.

These students, quite expectedly, are definitely less politically motivated than their predecessors. At least so far.

Students may be allowed back, as reports suggest, in January 2022. As for campus politics, it is likely to take a back seat, at least for a while.

Perhaps the COVID-19 pandemic will do what the administration couldn't: reboot JNU comprehensively.

Will post-COVID-19 JNU be entirely different from its tainted and embattled past? Yes and no. There's a great opportunity here, provided we grab it. To start anew, to revive the system as it were. But we may fail to make good and things may slide back into confrontation or chaos.

There is life after the contagion—as there must be—and as we are now seeing, then, all those who care and are responsible, will have, once again, to ask how to fix JNU.

Would it be too much to dream of a clean and spruced up campus, with decent-looking, fee-paying students regularly going to classes? As in most respectable universities in other parts of the world?

What would it take to make that happen? It will happen by cleansing the campus of too much 'dirty' politics, for one; restoring academics and excellence as our top priority; bringing back accountability both to the teaching and non-teaching parts of the university.

If we have to affect a turnaround in JNU, we must start seriously planning to make all of the above probable in the coming months. Not just the university administration, but the Ministry of Education, needs to start taking the right steps right now.

Rather than waiting for another crisis to overtake the university.

The first admissions to JNU for the MPhil/PhD programmes took place in 1971. MA courses began two years later, in 1973. But the university took a while to become fully functional, moving to its present 1,000-acre campus only in 1979.

These 50 years, or more properly the four decades from 1980 to 2020, constitute most of the active life of the university. Of these 40 years, I myself have been a JNU professor for 21 years, or over half this period. Today, I find myself to be one of the senior-most of JNU professors. Those who became professors before me have mostly retired. Some have even passed away.

Of course, those who joined as students, then became assistant professors, gradually moving up to full professorship, are not only younger, but have a long way to go. When our careers have been coextensive with much of the university's growth, why shouldn't we also wish and work for its transformation in the years to come?

Throughout its nearly 50 years of active existence, JNU has been a hotbed of political activities. But its last five years, 2016–2021, which this book covers, have been the most cataclysmic. I have tried to show how both its character and identity are poised to change radically.

In that sense, this book telescopes the five decades of JNU into just over five years. It also compresses the 20 years of my life as professor of English at JNU into these 60-odd months.

As far as I am concerned, there is no other place that I have spent more years of my life, either professionally or personally. When I joined in 1999, I never imagined that I would stay so long, let alone possibly retire from JNU when I turn 65.

I have no doubt in my mind that JNU should not be demonized, destroyed or turned into a horribly restricted, regimented or brain-dead institution. It should not become a mediocre, soul-killing, single ideology habitation—dull, flat and uninteresting.

Instead, it should be reformed, supported and led to greater heights of academic excellence and freedom. Its culture of discussion, debate, even dissent, should be protected and nurtured.

A simple blueprint for what needs to be done may be summarized as follows:

1. Reduce campus politics, especially that which is directed by and affiliated with political parties.
2. Do not merely substitute the Left with the Right, but try to facilitate a comprehensive reform, which will include a better administration, cleaner campus and better amenities.
3. Shift from student politics to student governance, possibly along the lines of IITs or evolve a totally new model exclusively for JNU.
4. Ensure that all admissions and appointments are purely based on competence and suitability, complying, of course, with the government's statutory provisions. Ideology should be kept aside, while competence given priority.
5. Increase and rationalize the fees without turning JNU into an elite institution that is unaffordable to ordinary or economically disadvantaged students. A differential fee structure, with professional courses in engineering and management, attracting higher fees is desirable. Arrange to give guaranteed student loans to those who cannot afford the higher fees. Integrate JNU admissions with other central universities on the model of the joint entrance exam (JEE) of IITs, with the provison that each university so covered has some leeway in admissions, say, 15 per cent out of the 100 per cent of the marks.
6. Build upwards, not just sideways, with private support and funds if necessary, so that all students have hostel accommodation, but at a fair price, not free.
7. Ensure that students do not stay on indefinitely, nor accommodate too many guests and hangers-on. JNU is for JNUites, not a free for all.

8. Review and rationalize faculty positions centre and school wise. Some centres may no longer need as many positions as have been sanctioned, while others may need more. Demand and marketability need to be taken into account.
9. Avoid overambitious expansion with impractical plans such as the currently mooted medical college and hospital. Along with the Sciences and new faculties such as Engineering and Management, strengthen Humanities and Social Sciences too.
10. Monetize the land and other resources of the university so as to make it self-sustaining. Create a Research and Incubation park, on the lines of some of the IITs, to attract revenue and industry presence on campus.

These steps will not only reform JNU but also protect its autonomy in the future.

Saving and transforming JNU will require tact, determination and visionary leadership. It would also need support from the government as well as joint efforts of the faculty, staff and students. A tall order, perhaps, but not impossible.

As an optimist, I shall always hope for the better rather than settling for the worst.

INDEX

9/11, 5
2019 Lok Sabha elections, 2

Ahmed, Najeeb, 170, 171, 173, 174, 175, 180, 182
Akhil Bharatiya Vidyarthi Parishad (ABVP), 36, 37, 43, 56, 173, 174, 176, 205, 232, 239, 240
Ali, Agha Shahid, 46
Alliance Française, 15
All India Coordination Committee of Communist Revolutionaries (AICCCR), 36
All India Students' Association (AISA), 36, 109, 173, 204
All India Students' Federation (AISF), 37, 173
anekantavada, 11
anti-establishment, 55, 132, 212, 234, 266
anti-intellectualism, 4
anti-national, 1, 67, 68, 86, 114, 156, 200, 202, 213, 226, 230, 248, 266
Archer, William, 41
Arendt, Hannah, 146
azadi rallies, 1

Babri Masjid, 10, 62
Bakshi, G.D., Major General, 200
Balakrishna, Sandeep, 45

Banaji, Jairus, 37, 60, 66, 108
Banerjee, Abhijit, 37, 108, 219, 220, 222, 223
Bharatiya Janata Party (BJP), 6, 14, 16, 43, 56, 97, 109, 142, 174, 205, 214, 220, 232, 245, 261, 262
Bharatiyata, 9
Bhat, Maqbool, xiii, 46, 51, 54, 58, 114, 122, 137
Bhattacharya, Anirban, 43, 44, 59, 141, 157, 158, 222
Bhushan, Shanti, 53
Bhyrappa, S.L., 45

Centre for Linguistics and English (CLE), 21
Centre-Right, 3
Chinese Communist Party (CCP), 72
Chomsky, Noam, 68
Citizenship (Amendment) Act, 181, 237
Communist Party of India (CPI), 2, 36, 37, 60, 98, 103, 104, 105, 117, 173, 220
Communist Party of India-Marxist (CPI[M]), 36
Communist Party of India (Marxist-Leninist) Liberation (CPIML), 36
Congress, 2, 12, 18, 37, 43, 60, 93, 99, 103, 104, 237, 244, 258, 259

conservative nationalism, 4
Constitution, 99, 100, 124, 148, 149
Covid-19, 12, 238, 247, 270, 271

Dabholkar, Narendra Achyut, 48
Datta, Asis, 34
Datta, Rajat, 120, 121, 143
Dawkins, Richard, 13
Delhi University, 26, 38, 157, 173, 232, 236
Democratic Students' Federation (DSF), 37, 204
Department of Humanities and Social Sciences (HSS), 21, 27, 28
diatopical hermeneutics, 69, 70, 71

European Union, 17

Fernandes, Naresh, 127
festival of letters, 45

Gambhir, Gautam, 200
Gandhi, Indira, 37, 103, 219, 246
Gandhi, M.K., xiv, 74, 92
Gandhi, Rahul, 60, 244
Geelani, S.A.R., 53
Ghose, Sagarika, 13
Ghosh, Aishe, 217
Gill, H.S., 22
Golwalkar, M.S., 11, 102
Gonsalves, Colin, 53
Guru, Afzal, xiii, 38, 43, 46, 47, 48, 49, 50, 51, 52, 54, 58, 98, 100, 114, 117, 118, 122, 123, 125, 132, 137, 141
Guru, Shaukat Hussain, 53

Harris, Lee, 5
hyper-nationalism, 19, 78, 84, 261

Illiberal Liberalism, 5, 6
Indian Institute of Advanced Study (IIAS), xvii, 216
Indian Institute of Management (IIM), 152, 154, 162, 248, 249, 256, 258
Indian Institute of Technology (IIT), 152, 154, 162, 248, 249, 253, 256, 258, 273, 274
intermedial hermeneutics, xii, xiii, 15, 69, 262
Islamophobia, 8

Jain, Sreenivasan, 13
Jaipur Literature Festival (JLF) 2019, 12
Jaishankar, S., 37, 108, 221
Jaish-e-Mohammed (JeM), 52
Jamia Millia (Jamia), 173, 180, 181, 182, 232, 236, 238, 239
Jammu and Kashmir Liberation Front, 137
Jawaharlal Nehru University (JNU), xi, xii, xiii, xiv, xv, xvi, xvii, 1, 2, 4, 9, 13, 16, 19, 21–30, 32–44, 46–52, 55–62, 64–68, 71–74, 88, 96, 97, 100, 101, 104, 105, 107–112, 114–133, 135, 137, 139–144, 146, 147, 151–157, 161, 162, 167, 169–178, 180, 182–194, 196–218, 220–230, 232–245, 255, 262, 266–274
JNU Court, 33
JNU Students Union (JNUSU), xiv, xvii, 1, 2, 36, 37, 43, 52, 61, 63, 101, 108, 117, 124, 130, 172–176, 191, 204, 205, 209, 217, 219, 220, 227, 240
JNU Teachers' Association (JNUTA), 1, 44, 49, 57, 60–64,

114, 116–118, 120, 121, 124, 125, 127, 129, 130, 132, 176, 205, 209, 227
JNU Teachers' Federation (JNUTF), 117

Kalam, A.P.J. Abdul, 53
Kalburgi, Malleshappa Madivalappa, 48
Kanwal, Rahul, 220, 223
Kargil Vijay Diwas, 199
Karlekar, Hiranmay, 33
Kashmiri Pandits, 55, 97
Kashmiri separatists, 6, 54, 72, 97, 152, 196
Khalid, Umar, 43, 44, 47, 59, 108, 137, 141, 222, 237
Khurshid, Salman, 13
Kidwai, Ayesha, 60, 62, 126, 127, 128, 135, 137, 140, 142, 143, 205
Kumar, Kanhaiya, xiv, 2, 37, 43, 49, 52, 60, 103, 114, 117, 130, 131, 172, 190, 220, 222, 228, 244
Kumar, M. Jagadesh, 56, 171

Lady Shri Ram College, 26
Lankesh, Gauri, 48
Left-Liberal (LeLi), 3
liberalism, xiii, 4, 5, 6, 7, 8, 9, 11, 13, 14, 16, 48, 158, 216
love jihad, 6, 237

Mahatma Gandhi National Rural Employment Guarantee Act (MGNREGA), 99
Malhotra, Rajiv, 200, 201
Mansingh, Sonal, 13
Maoist Democratic Students Union (DSU), 43, 59, 108
Marxism, 38, 67, 109, 111, 165

Mehta, Pratap Bhanu, 9, 253, 254
Mhatre, Ravindra, 54
minoritarian coalition, 4
Mishra, Sudhir, 37
Modi, Narendra, 2, 16, 50, 56, 134, 214, 260, 269
Mukherjee, Meenakshi, 22, 26
Mukherjee, Pranab, 54
Mukherjee, Shyama Prasad, 11
Muthukrishnan, J. (Rajni), 183, 184, 185, 186

Nafees, Fatima, 172
Naidu, M. Venkaiah, 50, 229
NaMo nationalism, 18, 20
national, xi, xiii, xiv, 1, 2, 3, 4, 6, 13, 15, 17, 19, 43, 50, 53, 66, 67, 68, 79, 81, 82, 84–87, 96, 105, 113, 114, 118, 129, 140, 156, 163, 171, 176, 183, 187, 188, 189, 196, 200, 202, 213, 214, 219, 226, 230, 232, 233, 243, 244, 246, 248, 249, 250, 256, 260, 261, 266, 268
National Educational Policy, 187, 250
National Democratic Alliance (NDA), 56
nationalism, xi, xiii, xiv, 4, 9, 11, 16, 17, 18, 19, 20, 57, 60, 61, 62, 63, 64, 66, 72, 73, 74, 75, 76, 77, 78, 79, 80, 81, 83, 84, 86, 87, 88, 93, 101, 113, 127, 153, 189, 193, 222, 227, 245, 246, 261, 262, 266, 267
National Register of Citizens, 237
National Students' Union of India (NSUI), 37
Naxalite movement, 36
Nazism, 67
Nigam, Aditya, 67, 158

open letters, xiv, 2, 50, 115, 117,

145, 157, 161, 167, 169
Osmania University, 25
Other Backward Class (OBC), 24, 140, 252, 268

Pansare, Govind, 48
Phillips, Robin, 5
Pillai, Manu, 15
Pokhriyal, Ramesh, 229
Popper, Karl, 42
Pradhan, Dharmendra, 199
Prevention of Terrorism Act (PoTA), 53
Puri, Hardeep Singh, 13

Rahman, A.R., 163
Ram Mandir, 10
Rashtriya Swayamsevak Sangh (RSS), 6, 7, 9, 12, 36, 48, 97, 102, 120, 126, 166, 237
Roy, Arundhati, 55

Sahitya Akademi, 45, 51, 52, 57, 114, 121, 124, 125, 135, 155
Sampath, Vikram, 13
Sanyal, Kanu, 36
satyagraha, 48, 71, 90, 91, 92, 100, 194
Savarkar, V.D., 11, 74, 89
Selection Committee, 23, 34
Sharma, Mihir, 13
Shinde, Sushil Kumar, 54
Shiv Sena, 237
Shukla, Maitreyee, 143, 160, 162
Sibal, Kapil, 13
Singh, V.K., 199
Sitharaman, Nirmala, 37, 108, 220, 221

Soviet Union, 8, 13, 104, 105, 106
Sri Aurobindo, 15, 17, 32, 41, 206
St Stephen's College, 26
Students' Federation of India (SFI), 36, 37, 66, 108, 173, 204
Sujith, P.V., 48
Supreme Court, 37, 53, 62, 98, 257

Tagore, Rabindranath, xiv, 74, 77, 86
Teach-in, xiv, 1, 60, 63, 65
The Pondy Lit Fest (PLF), 14
totalitarianism, 5, 6
Tripathi, D.P., 37
Trump, Donald, 13, 17
tukde tukde, 1, 38, 42, 43, 88, 170, 190, 195, 196, 224, 233, 242, 244, 267

United Progressive Alliance (UPA), 18, 258
University Grants Commission (UGC), 192, 210, 212, 268
University of Hyderabad, 25, 26, 30, 140, 150, 183, 201, 236, 243
Upadhyaya, Deen Dayal, 11, 262
Urban Naxals, 66, 144

Vemula, Rohith, 88, 140, 141, 142, 150, 165, 183, 185, 244

Yeats, W.B., 35

Yechury, Sitaram, 37, 60

Zakir Husain College, 53